MAKING IT LEGAL

A Law Primer
for Authors, Artists
and Craftspeople

by Martha Blue

Northland Publishing

Mountain under heaven:
In what is small,
perseverance furthers.

THE I CHING

I dedicate this revised and expanded book to Marlene McGof-
fin, a beautiful person, a fine sister,
and a truly creative artist; and Roy
Ward, an exceptional person and
first-class law partner.

Legal Advice? Not On Your Life.

This book does not contain legal advice. It is designed to provide accurate information with regard to the subjects covered as of September 1, 1988. It is sold with the
understanding that neither the author nor the publisher is engaged in rendering
legal, accounting, or other professional services. If you have a legal problem, we urge
you to see an attorney, or, for a tax problem, an accountant.

SECOND EDITION
ISBN 0-87358-470-8
Library of Congress
Catalog Card Number 88-60921
Composed and Printed in the
United States of America
Designed and illustrated by David Jenney

Contents

See last page for an important tax information update.

ACKNOWLEDGMENTS

Without the enthusiasm, interest, and support of a large number of wonderful craft-makers, artists, and writers, this book would never have happened, and certainly this revised and expanded edition would never have come to life.

I am grateful for the work that Marion Davidson, my co-author on the first edition of this book, shared with me, and am sorry that she could not participate in the expansion and revision.

I would like to give special thanks to Oliver W. Johnson for his encouragement and patience while I revised and expanded this work.

In making this revised edition come true, I would also like to thank Daryl Contryman, CPA; Martha Shidler; Jeri Tisdale; Susan McDonald; Bruce Andresen; all my artist/author clients; and my students at Northern Arizona University who have taken Law for the Creative Person.

INTRODUCTION

In the beginning, I was a weaver as well as a lawyer, and many friends were potters, illustrators, poets, sculptors, photographers, printmakers, jewelers, et cetera. They seemed to know so little of the basic legal information relevant to their work. I gave them books and pamphlets—too hard to read, they said. In response, I set out with my then-co-author, Marion Davidson, to put together a book that would help our friends answer some of their questions.

In an attempt to inform them in a way that would hold their attention as well as impart useful, basic knowledge, we presented much of the legal information in charts, forms, cartoons, memos, and last but not least, the allegories of Alice the Craftmaiden, wending her way toward law and order. When particularly relevant, we also listed major laws and cases at the end of some chapters, and included a "further readings" list.

In revising and expanding this edition of *Making It Legal,* I decided to keep the allegories of Alice since, even though she is outrageous at times, they give the reader a chance to see the application of law to a particular fact situation. That is what a lawyer does for a client. Second, they make the book more readable. While some of the writers in the book's original audience did not like the allegories, I found that the artists did, and since Alice is an artist, she deserves to be retained.

Writing about the law for a lay audience is like walking a tightrope. On one side are lawyers complaining about the lack of citations and the oversimplification of this case or that missing exception. On the other side are the lay people complaining that the text is too technical or too hard to understand.

Any law starts in two ways—by the writing and passing of legislation through legislative bodies, or from the common law, which began in England centuries ago and was a potpourri of local regulations and common practice. It is a principle of common law that cases that are alike should be decided the same way. Thus, precedents—earlier written reports of cases—guide courts in deciding new cases. Courts in both Canada and the United States follow and hark back to the structure of English law and courts. The Canadians, like the Americans, have courts of a federal nature, although ours form a more completely separate system. It is the fact that the laws of those two countries have a common source as well as the fact that the two countries are active trading partners that encouraged me to add some highlights from Canadian law to this revised and expanded text. A *caveat.* It will not benefit you to look up Canadian law in the index and read just those sections. You need to read, for instance, about contracts or copyright *generally* before you can grasp the principles discussed under Canadian law, which is why I have not made Canadian law a separate chapter.

I omitted from this expansion and revision the listing at the end of each chapter of citations to major laws and cases, since those cases, I found, were not used at all by the average reader. Also omitted is the section previously entitled "Further Readings," as so many of the books were not in print. Instead, I opted to include in the text and footnotes resource books and pamphlets relative to the particular subject matter.

This revised edition eliminates references to state-specific laws, since state legislatures continually expand and contract the body of law on a given subject. Too, while certain states have passed laws such as those that eliminate the requirement for filing a financing statement to protect work on consignment, each varies somewhat and you need to find out the wrinkles in the laws of the states where you do business.

This book does not contain all the answers; it does not contain legal advice for specific legal problems that may arise over the course of your particular creative career. It does, however, present an overview of the legal information that concerns craftmakers, visual artists, and writers. It will alert you to laws that you perhaps did not know existed and outline the requirements of laws to which you closed your eyes and crossed your fingers.

Because every legal problem is different and because laws change, this book cannot be relied upon to solve your legal ills. Sample forms are included as guides and should be tailored to meet the needs of your particular situation. Remember, the forms are samples only and should be used as guidelines only. For your individual problems, it is generally better to use forms prepared or approved by your attorney for your jurisdiction and your situation. Although federal laws and regulations govern operations in the fifty states and Puerto Rico, many of the state laws discussed vary substantially from state to state; again, remember that federal and state laws constantly change. The discussion is not meant to be exhaustive but rather, to impart an overall view. So see this book as a preventative, informational reference tool. It is not a substitute for a qualified lawyer, an accountant, or your own common sense.

CHAPTER ONE

Legal Steps in Surfacing Your Business

CHOICE OF LEGAL STATUS

SOLE PROPRIETOR
PARTNERSHIP
INCORPORATION
CANADIAN BUSINESS ORGANIZATIONS

FEDERAL STATE, AND LOCAL REQUIREMENTS

DOING YOUR OWN DETECTIVE WORK
ZONING, BUILDING, HEALTH, AND FIRE CODES
CERTIFICATE OF DOING BUSINESS UNDER A FICTITIOUS NAME
STATE SALES TAX NUMBER
FEDERAL EMPLOYER IDENTIFICATION NUMBER
BUSINESS LICENSE
EMPLOYEES

MISCELLANEOUS CONSIDERATIONS IN SURFACING

STUDIO RENTAL AGREEMENTS
INSURANCE

LEGAL ADVICE? NOT ON YOUR LIFE.

Alice's Allegory #1 or the Pitfalls of a Craftmaiden

Alice the Craftmaiden sat behind her table of pots at the local arts and crafts fair, warming herself in the delightful spring rays, dreaming of the summer to come.

Her mellow state was shattered by the growling of Max the State Tax Collector.

"Where is your state sales tax number?" barked Max, with the proper authoritarian sneer.

Alice smiled her sweetest I-am-totally-confused, save-me smile, hoping that Max would vanish as the Cheshire cat once did.

He did not.

INTRODUCTION

A DIRTY BUSINESS

How do you deal with the requirements of the business system? Many artists, craftmakers, and writers choose their work to avoid contact with the *business* world. In fact, even the word, *business,* is distasteful to many in artistic professions. What's in a word— *business*—anyway? It's none of your *business.* Cut out the monkey *business.* Let's get down to *business.* That's show *business.* Is it really a dirty *business?*

Just because you don't agree with the greedy-tycoon method of doing business doesn't mean that you have to sabotage your operation by ignoring the laws that govern businesses. It is not copping out to comply with the simple legal rules governing small businesses—it may be survival. I hope this chapter lessens unpleasant feelings concerning business by presenting information about the requirements for starting a business. Through an understanding of these basic concepts, business requirements become manageable, and most important, you achieve peace of mind.

This chapter is called "Legal Steps in Surfacing Your Business" because in my opinion, most artists, craftmakers, and writers don't actually decide to start a business and then go through the required steps. Getting into business is an organic process. By understanding the requirements of operating a business, the decision of "going legit" or "surfacing" your business can be timed—not too early and not too late. Avoid the pitfalls of the craftmaiden and climb through the looking glass to join me in a tour along the legal steps involved in surfacing a small business. This chapter discusses *legal* considerations in surfacing a business. Capital, labor, markets, and materials should also be considered before starting out.*

STEPS TO SURFACING YOUR BUSINESS

Some legal steps to surfacing your business are:
- choice and implementation of one of the three basic business forms—sole proprietorship, partnership, or corporation
- meeting federal, state, and local requirements
- considerations of studio rental agreements and liability insurance for your business

Remember, each individual situation is different. So are the laws of each state. I will provide you with the general legal requirements for setting up a small business. Once you know these, you can obtain the specifics from local sources in your state as well as from the federal offices of the Internal Revenue Service and the Small Business Administration; your state's corporation commission, tax department, unemployment and workers' compensation departments; and your city or county treasurer's office, zoning department, building, fire, and health departments. If you decide after reading this chapter that you need a lawyer's assistance in starting your business, read Chapter 8, "Obtaining Legal Assistance."

---

*For additional reading, see Bernard Kamoroff, *Small Time Operator: How to Start Your Own Small Business, Keep Your Books, Pay Your Taxes, and Stay Out of Trouble,* Bell Springs Publishing, Layton, CA, rev. ed. 1987, $10.95. An excellent book on starting your own business.

Alice's Allegory #2 or The Liability of Unlimited Liability

Having regained her decorum after the Big Max Attack, Alice sat thinking of her new life. How free and beautiful it was—so simple, no bosses, no time clocks—so close to nirvana.

Suddenly, Crafty Crank the Elderly Customer tripped over a large umbrella stand that Alice left in front of her display at the arts and crafts fair to scare away other representatives of the law. Crafty Crank the Elderly Customer lay on the floor squeaking and rapidly swelling in the area of her ancient ankle.

As if this was not enough and before Alice consulted her astrologer, Handsome Harry attached her savings account which enjoined Alice's inheritance from her Aunt Theresa, who died of smog asphyxiation.

Alice said, "I should go back to being a social worker. It's hassle-free, and at least I can pay my rent."

Sole proprietorships abound in the United States. This business form is the simplest, cheapest, and easiest to begin, manage, and end. Quite simply, a sole proprietor owns and runs his or her own business. **SOLE PROPRIETOR**

Since the law does not require the preparation and filing of articles of incorporation or a partnership agreement for a sole proprietorship, this choice initially saves time and money. A sole proprietor manages a business with a free rein—without partners or a board of directors—and sells it at any time. Business profits which swell the owner's regular income are reported on Schedule C of the individual's 1040 federal income tax return. **FORMATION** **MANAGEMENT** **SALE** **TAX**

The major drawback of a sole proprietorship is the owner's personal liability for business debts. This means a court judgment against the owner or the business swallows the sole proprietor's business and non-business property as well. **UNLIMITED LIABILITY**

Keep in mind two important legal rules. First, with minor exceptions, no one can force you to give up any of your belongings, wages, et cetera, except through court proceeding which includes your right to notice, to answer the complaint, and to a trial and final judgment.* Second, even after a final judgment against you, some of your belongings and wages are exempt. Exemptions vary from state to state. Generally, your home, car, tools of trade, and some personal belongings cannot be seized to satisfy a court judgment.** **EXEMPTIONS FROM EXECUTION LEGAL LIMITATIONS**

The purchase of business liability insurance cuts down the sole proprietor's problem of unlimited personal liability. This insurance protects the sole proprietor from any claims arising from a business-related injury to another person, but only to the policy's maximum. However, the sole proprietor still is personally liable for any business debts or loans, because liability insurance does not cover such transactions. **INSURANCE**

Alice's P. S.

For future liability problems Alice bought a year's worth of business insurance from Peter's Protection Group. She says that it is worth every one of the one hundred fifty dollars because not only will Peter pay off the injured and the maimed but also Peter's company pays Irving the Insurance Lawyer for defending cases such as Crafty Crank the Elderly Customer v. Alice the Craftmaiden.

P. P. S. Debtor's prisons were outlawed many years ago.

---

*Also, when considering the problem of unlimited liability, take into account any property that you own with others and, if married and living in a community-property state, any community property. The rules concerning the availability of community and joint assets for satisfaction of a court judgment obtained against an individual vary greatly. If there are common assets that could be affected, see a lawyer for more information about your state's laws.
**To get a homestead exemption, you must file documents at the county courthouse.

PARTNERSHIP

Memorandum of Law
TO: Wood Shaver File
FROM: MB
RE: Liability for Individual and Partnership Debts

FACTS

Client Wood Shaver agreed with Smith Skiptown to rent studio space, share costs, materials, equipment, and overhead, and to produce a line of wooden bookends, each person to receive half the profits. After the studio had been rented and outfitted for the two woodworkers, materials purchased, and business cards printed, Smith Skiptown disappeared without a trace. A few months later, Carl the Car Dealer appeared at Wood Shaver's door demanding that he pay Smith's overdue car payments.

QUESTION

Who pays for:
1. The studio rent and other debts contracted by Wood Shaver and Skiptown to start the bookend production?
2. The overdue car payments?

THEORY

A partnership agreement can be either oral or written. Also, a partnership can be implied from the behavior of any one of the partners toward a third party (creditors, etc.). From the particular facts of this case it seems clear that Wood Shaver and Smith Skiptown entered into a partnership.

In this state, both the assets of the partnership and the assets of the individual partners can be taken to pay the partnership debts. Also, the individual indebtedness of each partner can be satisfied from that partner's share of the partnership assets.

SOLUTION

1. Wood Shaver is personally liable for all the debts contracted by Skiptown and him for the bookend venture. Of course, all the partnership assets are liable for these business debts.
2. Skiptown's share of the assets of the bookend venture are available to Carl for Skiptown's car payments.
3. Wood Shaver can sue Skiptown if he ever locates him.
4. Advise Wood Shaver of the importance of choosing the right partner so that he will not be burned again.
5. Offer creditors reduced settlement amount. See if they will accept Wood Shaver's work as part of compromise settlement.

CHOOSING A PARTNER

If you are going into business with a friend or group of friends, a partnership may be the business form for you. Like marriage, partnership is a very intimate relationship. Disagreements between partners account for the large number of partnership terminations, so your choice of a partner is a *very* important one. Don't choose a fox for a partner if you are a little red hen, because in a partnership, any one of the partners can bind the entire partnership in most matters, including purchase and sale of land, contracts, leases, and so on. This is true even if the partner acts without the approval or knowledge of the partnership.

DEFINITION

A partnership occurs whenever two or more people own a business together and the business is not incorporated. A partnership is best created by the signing of a partnership agreement so that the partnership terms are clear.

PARTNERSHIP AGREEMENT

A partnership agreement states the objective of the parties, that is, that it is an association of two or more persons for the purpose of conducting a certain business as co-owners for profit, with the profits and losses shared. Also a partnership agreement spells out each partner's share of the profits, losses, capital, assets, and management; explains how partners leave and how others become partners; and provides ways to resolve disagreements and value assests. A sample form for a simple partnership follows.

A partnership can be formed, too, by an oral agreement or can be found to exist by a court through an examination of the behavior of the parties to the alleged partnership (implied partnership). It is better to enter into a thorough written partnership agreement. If there is no written agreement or if an oral or written partnership agreement is silent, ambiguous, or confusing on the point in question, then state partnership law spells out that term. For example, a court assumes that the partners intended to share the profits equally if there is no agreement containing a different method of allocating each partner's share. States impose few restrictions on doing business as a partnership.*

This agreement is made between _____ of _____ , _____ , _____ of _____ _____ , and _____ of _____ , _____ intending to be legally bound and to form a partnership and do business as _____ which shall be located principally in _____ , _____ and other locations that the parties may agree upon.

    1. PURPOSE: The purpose of this partnership is to engage in a _____ business and such other businesses as may be agreed upon by the partners.

    2. DURATION OF THE PARTNERSHIP: This partnership shall begin on _____ , _____ and will continue until terminated by agreement of the partners or by the retirement, death or insanity of any one of the partners.

    3. CAPITAL CONTRIBUTION: The original capital of the partnership shall consist of the amount of _____ cash, goods or services contributed by each partner in the following fashion:

Name	Contribution	Percentage

This capital and any future capital contribution cannot be withdrawn except by the unanimous agreement of all the partners or upon dissolution.

    4. PROFITS AND LOSSES: The net profits and losses shall be apportioned to each individual partner in proportion to his/her percentage of the capital contribution and paid as the partners see fit.

    5. FISCAL YEAR AND ACCOUNTING METHOD: The fiscal year shall be the calendar year and the accounting method for income tax purposes shall be the _____ method.

    6. DUTIES AND AUTHORITY OF PARTNERS: Each partner shall apply all of his experience, training and ability to his/her partnership tasks. No partner shall enter into a business that in some way competes with the partnership except with the unanimous agreement of the other partners. No partner shall buy any goods or articles or enter into any contract exceeding the value of _____ dollars ($_____ , without the prior consent in writing of the other partners. Each partner shall pay his/her separate debts on time and shall indemnify and repay the partnership for any liability of the partnership for his separate debts.

    7. DECISION MAKING AND ARBITRATION: Partnership decisions shall be made by majority vote except for any decision that is contrary to this agreement which shall require the consent of each partner. In the event of a disagreement as to the rights or liabilities of any partner, the difference shall be determined by _____ , acting as arbitrator.

    8. RECORD KEEPING: In addition to the normal business books, the partnership shall maintain records of all contributions, withdrawals and profit shares for each partner. These books shall be available for inspection by any partner.

    9. INVOLUNTARY DISSOLUTION: Any partner can leave the partnership after giving _____ days notice to the other partners. Retirement, death or insanity of any of the partners shall result in an immediate dissolution of the partnership. Upon dissolution, an accounting shall be made of the capital shares of each partner, the profits received by each partner and the net profit or loss of the partnership from the date of the previous accounting.

*Nolo Press (950 Parker St., Berkeley, CA 94710) publishes numerous reference books which may be of assistance to the creative entrepreneur, including *The Partnership Book* by Dennis Clifford and Ralph Warner, and *Legal Care for Your Software* by Donald Rener.

If one partner retires, dies or becomes insane, the other partners may continue the partnership with themselves or with others that they might choose but they shall pay the retiring partner or his/her representative the value of his/her interest in the partnership. The value of the existing partner's interest is, as of the date of dissolution:

    1. partner's share of capital

    2. partner's share of profit or loss

10. DISSOLUTION BY AGREEMENT: Upon the agreement of the partners to dissolve, the assets of the partnership shall be liquidated and the proceeds shall be paid in the following order:

    a. creditors of the partnership

    b. profits *owed* to the partners

    c. repayment of the capital investment to each partner.

    d. payment of proportionate share of any remaining profits.

11. BOILERPLATE: This agreement is the entire agreement made between the partners and can be modified by agreement of the parties placed in writing. The laws of the state of _____ governs this agreement.

_____ Partner (Provide a signature line and notary for each partner.)	Subscribed and sworn to before me this _____ day of _____ , 19 _____ . _____ Notary Public My Commission Expires: _____

TAX   Each partner pays tax on partnership profits individually in proportion to his or her share of the partnership profits. The partnership itself does not pay tax. The tax rate is the same as that for the individual, and the income is reported on an individual 1040 tax return. A partnership return (see Figure 1.1) has to be filed with the U. S. Internal Revenue Service for information purposes only. A partnership

DISSOLUTION   automatically dissolves upon the death, insanity, withdrawal, or bankruptcy of any partner *unless* the partnership agreement specifically provides for continuation after such an event.

UNLIMITED LIABILITY   As with a sole proprietorship, the major drawback of this form of business is the unlimited liability of each general partner for *any* partnership debt and the liability of the partnership for the personal debts of a partner up to the amount of the partner's share. This means that the personal and business property of each partner is available to satisfy a court judgment arising from a partnership debt and that the partnership assets can be taken to satisfy a partner's individual debt up to the amount of that partner's share.

LIMITED PARTNER   Sometimes partners escape the problem of unlimited liability by becoming a limited partner. Limited partners do not participate in the management of the business. They simply provide economic backing and receive a proportionate share of the partnership profits. Limited partners are basically passive investors. Personal assets of limited partners are not liable for partnership debts.

In order to create a limited partnership, very specific rules of formation *must* be followed, and unlike a general partnership agreement, the limited partnership agreement must be filed with a state or county office. Thus the services of a lawyer are required.

Memorandum

TO: Wood Shaver File

FROM: MB

RE: Drafting Limited Partnership Agreement between Wood Shaver and Rich Katt

Wood Shaver has located a new partner who will provide the economic backing for the bookend production. Check Limited Partnership Act and draft a limited partnership agreement showing Wood Shaver as the general partner and Rich Katt as the limited partner. Arrange a meeting with clients to work out details of allocation of profits, et cetera.

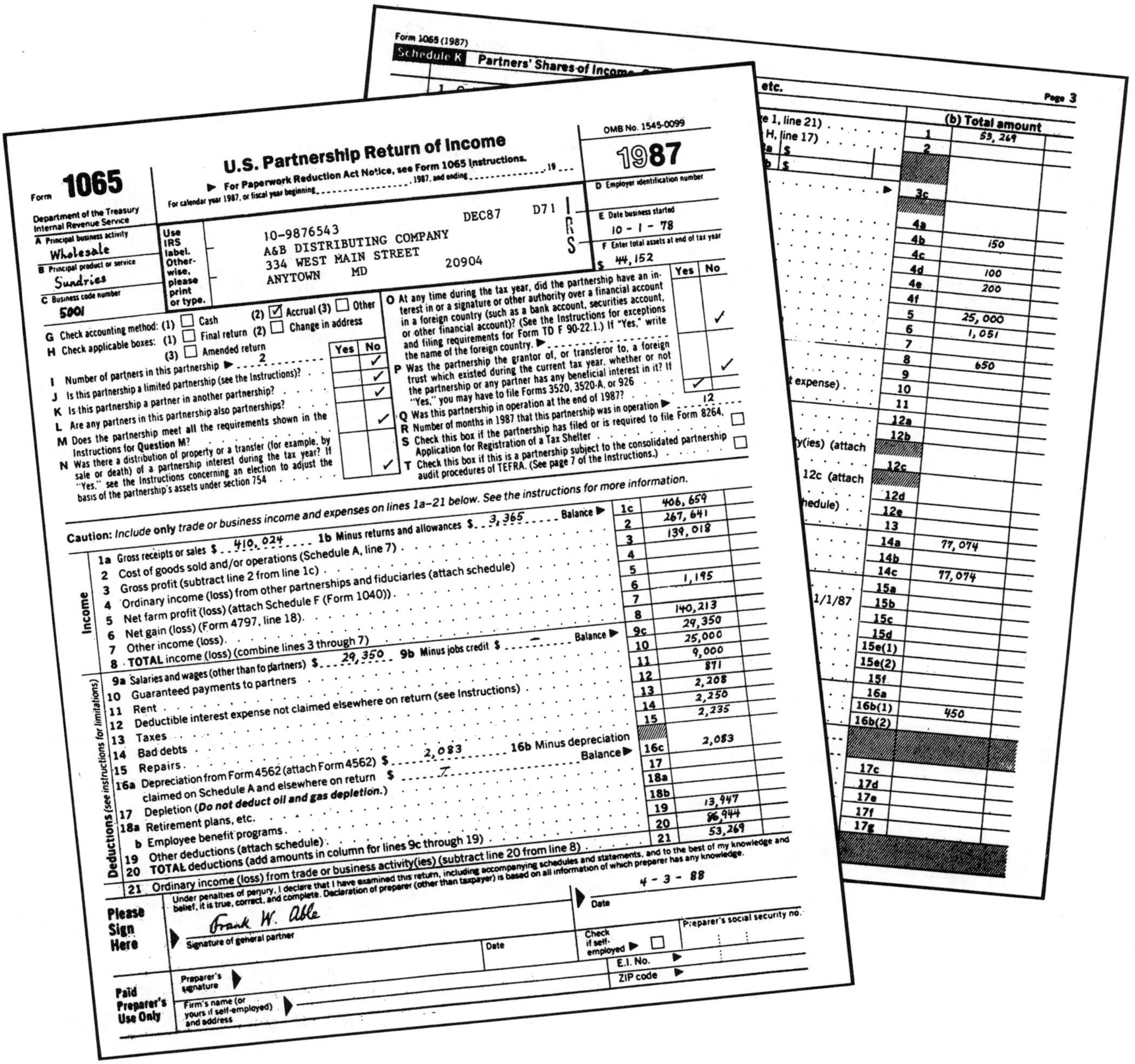

Figure 1.1— United States Partnership Return of Income Statement

The corporation is by far the most complicated of the three basic business forms. Should your business flourish, then you should consider the option of incorporation for the tax advantages as well as for the benefits of limited liability and the increased ability to attract investors.* A good accountant will know the point at which it is advantageous tax-wise for a business to incorporate.

INCORPORATION

*For an excellent discussion of the advantages of incorporation, see Judith H. McQuown, *Inc., Yourself*, Macmillan, New York, 1977, presently out of print. Out-of-print references may be available at your local library.

TAX ADVANTAGES

Maria had an adjusted gross income of $40,000 after deducting her business expenses last year from her booming stitchery business. As a sole proprietor, she would pay income tax in the amount of $8,296 for 1987:

$39,990	Net Income
− 2,540	Standard Deduction, Single Person
− 1,900	Exemption
$35,550	Taxable Income
	$8,296 Tax

A corporation is an artificial being, invisible, intangible, and existing only in contemplation of the law.
—CHIEF JUSTICE JOHN MARSHALL

As a corporation, Maria could reduce her tax bill for the time being by $3,036:

$19,990	Retained Corporate Earning (profits kept by the corporation)
× 20%	Corporate Tax Rate
$2,998	Corporate Tax
$20,000	Net Income (salary)
− 2,540	Standard Deduction
− 1,900	Exemption
$15,560	Taxable Income
2,262	Personal Income Tax
$ 5,260	Total Tax

Remember, Maria will have to pay personal income tax on both the wages and dividends paid to her by the corporation. However, the corporation can delay such payments until a more opportune time by retaining earnings. Also, Maria must weigh her tax savings against the additional time and paperwork involved in maintaining a corporation.*

DEFINITION

The corporation is the Cheshire cat of Legal Land because it is elusive and hard to visualize. Sometimes when searching for a corporation, all you can find is its smile. The corporate concept is a legal fiction. It is created by the law to develop business through the protection of the owners from personal liability for corporate debts.

LIMITED LIABILITY

Legally, the corporation is like a separate person who can make contracts, incur debts, purchase property, sue and be sued. The individuals who make up the corporation are not personally liable for any of the corporate transactions even though their corporation may be totally bankrupt, *provided* the corporation operates within the law. Another advantage of the corporation is the variety of financing arrangements. In addition to contracting for loans,** a corporation sells shares to

AVAILABILITY OF FINANCING

TRANSFERABILITY OF SHARES

obtain additional capital. Investors in the corporation incur no personal liability for any corporate debt and can transfer their shares of corporate stock. When a corporation reaches a certain number of actual or potential shareholders, state and federal securities laws enter the picture. State laws (Blue Sky Laws) come into play at around ten shareholders and the federal law at approximately thirty-five. Even offering shares to more than a limited number of potential investors may subject a corporation to these laws.

---

*These tax calculations ignore Social Security taxes on wages and self-employment taxes on income from self-employment. Your tax advisor should calculate these for you.

**Most lending institutions will require the directors of small corporations to personally obligate themselves on a corporate loan.

Since the corporation is separate from its shareholders, the corporation continues despite the death or withdrawal of any of the shareholders or directors. The corporation pays tax on its net profits and is liable for any other tax or licensing fee that is required in order to exist and do business in the corporate location.

Among the disadvantages of the corporate form are the time and expense of incorporating. Attorney's fees for incorporation vary. Fees for filing articles of incorporation with the state are usually around sixty-five dollars. Each year, reports must be filed and fees paid to the state.

Since the services of an attorney are necessary for incorporation, I shall only briefly cover the requirements for incorporation. In some states, the initial step of incorporation is the selection and reservation of a corporate name. Then articles of incorporation are drafted and submitted to the state corporation commission. The articles contain the details of the business of the corporation including its name, purpose, location, duration, names and addresses of the initial board of directors, name and address of a designated agent for legal purposes, and information concerning the shares to be issued. Some states such as Arizona require the publication of these articles in a local newspaper for a period of time.* Also, a few states require that a percentage of the value of the capital stock be deposited in a bank before the state issues the certificate of incorporation. These steps must be carefully followed, otherwise courts deny the special protection of limited liability for corporations not set up and managed according to the law.

Just as starting a corporation is complicated, so is shutting it down. An attorney will be required for this process. Dissolution requires the filing of a statement of intent to dissolve. Thereafter, steps to liquidate are taken and creditors are notified.

Various restrictions on doing business exist within the home state of the corporation as well as outside that state. Many of the activites of the corporation are governed by state law—shareholders' and directors' meetings, management of stock, et cetera. If a corporation wishes to do business in another state, a certificate of doing business must be filed with the state official in every foreign state where the corporation does business.

CONTINUITY

COST OF FILING INCORPORATION

RESERVATION OF CORPORATE NAME

ARTICLES OF INCORPORATION

PUBLICATION

INITIAL CAPITALIZATION

DISSOLUTION

RESTRICTIONS ON DOING BUSINESS

WHAT FORM OF BUSINESS ORGANIZATION?

SOLE PROPRIETORSHIP

ADVANTAGES	*DISADVANTAGES*
Ease of formation	Unlimited personal liability
Low start-up costs	Lack of continuity
Least regulation	Difficult to raise money or get grants
Owner control	Tax disadvantage for high profits
All profits to owner	

PARTNERSHIP

ADVANTAGES	*DISADVANTAGES*
Ease of formation	Unlimited personal liability and liability for partners' debts
Low start-up costs	Lack of continuity
Broader management base	Divided authority—lack of extensive control
Shared responsibility and losses	Difficult to raise additional capital or get grants
Limited outside regulation	Hard to find suitable partners
No direct tax on business	Possibility of personal difficulties
Satisfaction and benefits of working with someone	Tax disadvantages for high profits

*Publication of the articles in my local newspaper now runs over two hundred dollars.

CORPORATIONS	*ADVANTAGES*	*DISADVANTAGES*
	Limited liability	Closely regulated
	Possible tax advantages	Most expensive form to organize
	Continuous existence	Charter restrictions
	Legal entity	Extensive record keeping necessary
	Ownership transferable	Double taxation

VARIATIONS ON A CORPORATE THEME

Corporations are varietal. The law makes a distinction between the small closely held corporation and the large, public corporation. The small corporation is less strictly regulated. Some of the types of corporations that would interest artists and craftmakers are the Subchapter S corporation, the not-for-profit corporation, and the cooperative.

SUBCHAPTER S CORPORATION

The Subchapter S corporation—a hybrid business form created by the federal tax laws—is treated as a partnership for tax purposes with all the net profits allocated to individual shareholders and then taxed at the individual tax rate. For all other purposes the Subchapter S corporation is treated as a corporation, including the right to limited liability. The requirements for the formation of the special Subchapter S corporation are the same as for any corporation, but the IRS must be notified by the corporation within the first month of its existence of the intent to be taxed as a Subchapter S corporation.

NOT-FOR-PROFIT STATUS

If you are engaged in a not-for-profit operation that is set up for charitable, educational, or other worthy purposes, such as a museum or an art school, you should look into obtaining special "not-for-profit" status from the Internal Revenue Service. A large portion of grants to the arts are available only to not-for-profit organizations which have been granted tax-exempt status by the IRS. An unincorporated association as well as a corporation can achieve the not-for-profit status. Once a corporation has been granted this status the corporation is not liable for sales or income tax, although the not-for-profit corporation must file an informational federal tax return.*

COOPERATIVES

A cooperative is a special kind of business form usually set up under the state cooperative law. The cooperative is in the business of providing at-cost services or goods to its members. Control of the cooperative is by its entire membership. I know a successful marketing cooperative that simply rents a small store and sells the crafts of its members. Each member works at the store a required number of hours each week.

CANADIAN LAW—BUSINESS FORMS & ORGANIZATION

While there are sole proprietorships,** partnerships, and limited partnerships, under Canadian law the concept of an artificial entity created by law is more often referred to as a "limited company" rather than a corporation. Limited liability of shareholders developed after two English debacles. One, the "South Sea Bubble," was a 1719 scheme for whale fishing and slave trade in the West Indies that failed and ruined its investors; the other was the 1878 City of Glasgow Bank failure, in which shareholders purportedly paid the creditors 27½ times the par value of their bank stock. Company or corporation law exists at the federal and provincial levels; the former is for nationwide companies, while the latter varies from province to province. Some of the information required parallels that necessary in the United States.

There are also non-trading companies whose purposes are social, religious, or sporting in nature, and cooperatives incorporated under the Cooperative Associations Act.

*California Lawyers for the Arts (CLA), Fort Mason Center, Building C, San Francisco, CA 94123, handles Nolo Press's publication, *The Non-Profit Corporation Handbook* by Anthony Mancuso, $24.95.

**If the sole proprietorship uses a name other than that of the owner, then it must be registered at the local registry office.

Over a decade ago, Canada adopted the Foreign Investment Act, which makes the Canadian government a party to all agreements by which foreign interests acquire control of a Canadian business enterprise or establish new ones. An overview of this act is described in the American Bar Association's booklet, *Current Legal Aspects of Doing Business in Canada.* A small-business exception, dependent on gross assets of not more than $250,000 and sales of not more than $3,000,000, was in effect when the act was adopted.

Alice's Allegory #3 or To Incorporate or Not to Incorporate

Since we last saw Alice, Romero entered Alice's life with hearts and flowers and a small inheritance.

Once a lousy outlaw, now Alice is trying to straighten up her business act, and so when Romero suggested a little business venture of hand-glazing clay pots and distributing them to florists and nurseries on a mass basis, Alice immediately launched a full and complete inquiry into all the possible legal pitfalls, traps, Blue Sky Laws, and Green River ordinances.

To incorporate or not to incorporate, that was the question. Romero's inheritance was high on the list of problems, because without his inheritance, Romero would be poor like everyone else. The limited liability of the corporate form looked like the answer.

But the articles of incorporation, the lawyer's fee, the bylaws, the filing requirements, the corporate tax returns, the annual reports, and the annual meetings, all to protect Romero's inheritance? There must be a better way.

One day, the Fairy Godmother appeared to Alice in a dream and said, "Business insurance, my dear." Alice then realized that she, by extending her liability insurance coverage, could protect Romero's inheritance from all claims arising from damage or injury caused by the business.

"Hurrah," said Alice as she rushed out to find Romero who was sitting under a rainbow. Right then and there, Alice and Romero formed a partnership appropriately called the Rainbow Company. This agreement later reduced to writing, included a term requiring Alice and Romero to both agree to any expenditures involving more than $100.

In this section, I discuss the general federal, state, and local requirements for starting a business, regardless of the legal structure of the business.* Because each location is different, the requirements for setting up a business vary, as will the names of the licenses and taxes. However, the general requirements of obtaining a state sales tax identification number, at least one business license, and complying with health, fire, building, and zoning regulations are pretty much the same wherever the business is located.

Because each state and locality has its own requirements for starting a business, you must research the exact requirements of starting a business in your location. Step one in your detective work is to locate the agency or office in your area equivalent to each of the agencies described in this section and to find out the exact requirements of each of these agencies. This research is not easy. If you have a friend who has already found out what to do, you are *very* lucky.**

*For Native American artists living and working on a reservation, the state and county requirements usually do not apply. Tribal and federal regulations would apply.

**An eight-page guide to initiating an Arizona business is available from the Small Business Administration, 2005 N. Central Ave., 5th Floor, Phoenix, AZ 85004. Check your state's SBA office for a comparable guide.

Dear Chatty Lawyer Syndicated Column:

HELP. I tried to find out whether my new gallery, called Manuel's Friends, is required to file a certificate of doing business under a fictitious name. I called the local chamber of commerce. They had no information but referred me to an industrial counseling service. No information either and another referral— Small Business Administration. By that time, it was 4:20 in the afternoon and I was informed that all the counselors had gone home for the day and that I should call in the morning. I doggedly pursued the directions and called back the Small Business Administration the next morning and was told that all the counselors were in a meeting and to call an organization of retired business men who volunteered their time to assist new businesses. . . . Do I need to file a certificate of doing business under a fictitious name?

Manuel

TWO TIPS FOR DEALING
WITH BUREAUCRATS

Manuel called the wrong offices. He did not call the office that would *benefit* from providing him with the correct answer. In his case, that office was the county clerk's office, because they required a filing fee for a certificate of doing business under a fictitious name. So, rule one is to contact the agency which *benefits* from providing the correct information. Don't call the city mayor's office to find out about getting a state sales tax certificate, call the state tax department. They will have the information because they want your tax payments.

BUREAUCRAT'S RULE

Rule two is to ask as specific a question as possible, using as much of the local lingo that you can pick up. It is hard for some bureaucratic types to comprehend the fact that an "occupational license" is the same as a "business permit." Remember, the average bureaucrat's rule is "Conserve Energy—Don't Think." If after using these techniques, you still get the royal runaround, consult someone in a similar business in your location.

Don't forget to untangle the various tax, licensing, and zoning requirements so that you know which are city or county, which are state, and which are federal. Write down all the requirements. Use the following checklist as a guide.

CHECKLIST—ALL BUSINESSES (adapt to your location)

_____ Determine business organization.
_____ Check city zoning office or county zoning office for restrictions on use of your location for a business.
_____ Check building, health, and fire codes for requirements for special equipment or construction.
_____ If required, file a certificate of doing business under a fictitious name.
_____ Apply for a state sales tax number at the state revenue department.
_____ Apply for state, city, or county business license(s).
_____ Register tradename/mark with state

WITH EMPLOYEES
_____ File application for Federal Employer's Identification Number.
_____ Obtain necessary forms and information from the Internal Revenue Service for federal withholding, Social Security, and unemployment taxes.
_____ Obtain necessary information and forms from the state tax department for withholding.
_____ Obtain necessary information and forms for state unemployment tax.
_____ Obtain information and forms for workers' compensation.

ZONING, BUILDING, HEALTH,
AND FIRES CODES

Make sure that you can legally work at the location you have selected. Usually, artists' studios are legal in residential zones. However, most zoning laws do not allow businesses with direct sales or employees to be located in a residential area, although occasional "visitors" to a studio are tolerated, provided the neighbors do not object.

In most locations, zoning-office approval is required for the address stated on an application for a business license before the license is granted, so check with the zoning office before you apply for a city license. For zoning information, contact the city or county government offices, depending upon where your business is located.

ZONING LAWS

If you discover that the proposed location for your business is in violation of the zoning laws, you may be able to get a variance. A variance is an exception to the zoning laws. Depending on the complexity and size of the locality, the process of obtaining a variance ususally entails some cost and time, and requires notice to the neighbors and a hearing.

VARIANCE

If your business requires special equipment or construction, like a kiln, rewiring, or new plumbing, you had better check with the city or county building inspector to make sure that any work will comply with the building-code requirements as well as health and fire regulations. A potter I knew ran a new gas pipe to her kiln only to discover when the inspector arrived that the pipe was six inches too low and had to be raised before she could get the gas hooked up.

BUILDING CODES

If you plan to do business under a name other than your own, you may be required to file a certificate of doing business under a fictitious name. Most states require filing at the county clerk's office where you do business. Some require publication of the certificate in a local newspaper. Others require license renewal every few years. You pay a minimal filing fee. This document enables a member of the public to locate the person(s) behind the fictitious business name. Incorporated businesses do not have to file these certificates because the state corporation commission has all the information necessary to locate the principals of any corporation located in the state. Contact your county clerk's office or the state corporation commission about this requirement.

CERTIFICATE OF DOING BUSINESS UNDER A FICTITIOUS NAME

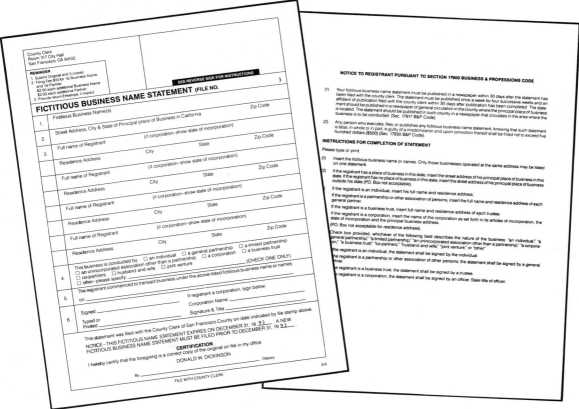

Figure 1.2 California Fictitious Business Name Statement

STATE SALES TAX NUMBER

Alice's Allegory #4 or Getting It Together

After the Big Max attack, Alice was so frightened that she even got the VW's muffler fixed so that she wouldn't be stopped and thrown in jail for failure to have a state sales tax number. (Little did she know that the fear was just a figment of her imagination.)

One full moon day, Alice decided to get it together and do the tax-number thing. She and Romero got into their VW and drove down to the Bureau of Revenue's office.

Since the Bureau of Revenue was on the eleventh floor, Alice was a bit light-headed when she arrived, so she had to look twice to make sure that she saw a handsome young man behind the desk asking if she needed help. Feeling reassured, Alice told the revenue officer that she wanted to register for a state tax number. "Just fill out this form and you will receive your Registration Certificate in the mail." "That's all there is to it?" stammered Alice. The handsome young man nodded his head.

Most states that levy sales tax require a state tax number from anyone in business. The tax or resale number is used on the form you will complete when paying state sales tax collected on sales made within your state and when you purchase materials for use in your business.*

Sometimes states require a cash deposit. The deposit is credited against the state sales tax due. The amount of deposit required in some states is so large that many artists and craftmakers cannot afford a tax number and therefore do not make any direct sales.** Theoretically, the deposit amount is based upon the estimated sales tax liability for the business.

SALES TAX EXEMPTION ON MATERIALS

When you purchase materials (silver, wood, wool, clay, etc.) you do not have to pay sales tax on these materials once you have a sales tax number. The reason for this exemption from sales tax is to avoid double taxation—for example once when the clay is purchased from the distributor for a hand-thrown vase, and again when the clay is sold to the customer in finished form. This sales tax exemption also applies to the cost of services purchased for use in the final product in some states. Contact your state's revenue office for information concerning state sales tax as well as state income tax.

CANADIAN LAW— RETAIL SALES ACT

Many of the provinces' retail sales acts are substantially the same but administrative positions vary, such as those relating to the taxation of computer software.

In Ontario, the provincial legislature passed a Small Business Development Corporations Act which gives various incentives to small businesses.

FEDERAL EMPLOYER IDENTIFICATION NUMBER

A federal identification number is required for all corporations and partnerships and for any business with an employee. This section also considers requirements for businesses with employees.

BUSINESS LICENSE

You will need at least one business license. If your business is located within city limits, call the city for more information. If the business is located in a county, then call the county clerk's office.

PEDDLER'S LICENSE

If you make street sales or otherwise use public property, you might need a special peddler, vendor, or huckster's license or permit in addition to your regular business license. Because street sales cut into more established businesses' clientele, some cities regulate street sales. Street sellers have successfully challenged restrictive regulations in some cities.

*See figure 1.3 for a sample application form.

**If you sell your work through a gallery or other outlet, they will collect the sales tax for you.

For some peculiar reason, many states require that photographers obtain special licenses. Some of these have been found invalid by the courts. For information on these and other state license requirements, contact the state consumer protection office.

STATE LICENSE

Taxation & Revenue	STATE OF NEW MEXICO			148
RP-31	TAXATION AND REVENUE DEPARTMENT			
Mar., 1987	APPLICATION FOR REGISTRATION			

FOR OFFICE USE ONLY

Batch Control Number	Identification Number	Date Issued	SIC Number	☐ Six Month Filer
	-00-	mo / day / yr		☐ Quarterly Filer

PLEASE TYPE OR PRINT IN BLACK INK - Please read instructions on reverse side.

Telephone Area Code ( )

1. Business Name | City | State | Zip Code

Mailing Address

2. Principal Business Location (Street, City & State, Zip Code)

3. Date business activity started or is anticipated to start in New Mexico
mo / day / year

4. Type of Ownership (Check One):
01 ☐ Proprietorship/Sole Owner
02 ☐ Partner/Joint Venture
03 ☐ Corporation
04 ☐ Cooperative Association
05 ☐ Sub-Chapter S Corporation
06 ☐ Federal Agency
07 ☐ State Agency
08 ☐ Munic. or County
09 ☐ Fiduciary
10 ☐ Indian Tribe or Pueblo
11 ☐ Other (Specify)
12 ☐ Exempt
13 ☐ Non-Nexus (PL 86-272)

5. Federal ID Number (if any)

6. Principal office in NM located:
Municipality/County Code

7. Date began paying wages in New Mexico
mo / day / year

8. Method of accounting:
C ☐ Cash   A ☐ Accrual
O ☐ Other (Specify)

10. Liquor License No.

9. Primary type of business in New Mexico (Check One):
01 ☐ Agriculture
02 ☐ Mining
03 ☐ Contract Const.
04 ☐ Manufacturing
05 ☐ Trans. Comm. Utility
06 ☐ Wholesale
07 ☐ Retail
08 ☐ Finance, Ins. & Real Estate
09 ☐ Service
10 ☐ Government

11. Description of primary goods or services sold in New Mexico:

12. Former owner's business name and address: (if any)

Former owner's CRS ID No.

If ownership identical, do you wish to use the same CRS ID number for all business locations?
☐ YES   ☐ NO

13. Are you currently operating any other business in New Mexico?
☐ YES   ☐ NO
If yes, give CRS ID number   CRS ID No.

14. Have you operated a business in New Mexico in the past?
☐ YES   ☐ NO
If yes, give business name and CRS ID number   Name _____ CRS ID No.

GASOLINE SALES REGISTRATION:
15. Will business sell gasoline? ☐ YES ☐ NO   If yes, check type of business.
1 ☐ Retail   2 ☐ Wholesale   3 ☐ Distributor

CIGARETTES OR TOBACCO SALES REGISTRATION:
16. Will business sell cigarettes? ☐ YES ☐ NO
17. Will business sell tobacco products? ☐ YES ☐ NO
If yes, check type of business.
1 ☐ Retail   2 ☐ Wholesale   3 ☐ Distributor
4 ☐ Manufacturer   5 ☐ Vending Machine
Type(s) of resource

SEVERANCE TAX AND RESOURCES EXCISE TAX REGISTRATION:
18. Will the business be engaged in severing natural resources? ☐ YES ☐ NO
19. Will the business be engaged in processing natural resources? ☐ YES ☐ NO

20. If proprietorship, list owner; if partnership, list partners; if assoc/joint venture, list members; if corporation, list officers and majority stockholders.
Name and Title | Home Address/City/State/Zip code | Social Security Number or Federal ID Number

21. Location of records (street, city & state, zip code)

Under penalty of perjury, I swear or affirm that the information reported on this form and any attached supplements is true and correct as to every material matter.
DATE: _____ TITLE: _____
SIGNATURE: _____
PRINT NAME: _____

Application must be complete or processing will be delayed
Please return **both** copies to the TAXATION AND REVENUE DEPARTMENT, OFFICE LOCATIONS ON REVERSE SIDE.

Figure 1.3 Sample application for state sales tax number

EMPLOYEES

INDEPENDENT CONTRACTOR

Hiring an employee raises your red-tape quotient by 1,000 percent. One way to avoid this is to use independent contractors rather than employees, if possible. Normally, you pay an independent contractor by the job or piece and not by the hour. An independent operator who is responsible for providing any equipment required by the job generally has control over the project and performs a specialized service.

Wood Shaver needed his bookends sanded and oiled, so he contracted with a cabinetmaker in town to do this work. Before Wood Shaver made the decision to take on Leander the Sander as an independent contractor, he thought long and hard because he did not want Uncle Sam breathing down his neck for back withholding, Social Security, and unemployment taxes for Leander. Wood Shaver was so concerned with this problem that he obtained a memorandum from his extended family lawyer on the question of setting up and maintaining an independent contractor relationship with Leander the Sander.

Memorandum

TO: Wood Shaver
FROM: MB
RE: Independent Contractor: Yes or No

THE IMPORTANCE OF BEING EARNEST ABOUT THE SUBJECT

I am glad that you have requested this memorandum on the question of independent contractors. It is an important subject, because should a court or the government decide that your independent contractor is an employee, the consequences may be serious—for example, liability for the damage caused by an employee while on the job as well as payment of back federal and state payroll and withholding taxes.

WHAT IS AN INDEPENDENT CONTRACTOR?

There is no set answer to the question of what is an independent contractor. Each situation is different. There are many tests that can be applied to the relationship between you and your worker to see if he or she is an independent contractor. The following list of principles should be helpful in establishing an independent-contractor relationship between yourself and Leander the Sander:

1. Independent Contractors set their own hours. You just agree on the completion date.
2. Independent Contractors should keep a regular set of business books and be in business for themselves with a realistic opportunity for profit or loss.
3. Independent Contractors have the power to choose their own workers.
4. Independent Contractors should provide their own equipment and tools.
5. Independent Contractors are paid by the piece or by the job, not by the hour.
6. Independent Contractors usually work at their own place of business.
7. Independent Contractors should maintain all required business licenses, permits, et cetera, and pay all other job-related expenses.
8. Independent Contractors should not be covered by your liability and health insurance, nor any bonus, vacation, sick-pay program, or training programs that you may have.
9. Independent Contractors should not be fired if they perform according to your agreement with them.
10. Independent Contractors should perform the entire job, including cleaning up without supervision.
11. Since Independent Contractors are in business for themselves, they provide their services not only to your company but to the general public as well.

DOCUMENT THE INDEPENDENT CONTRACTOR STATUS

It is best to write down your agreement with Leander the Sander covering as many of the points listed above as are relevant to your contract. You certainly do not have to include every item on the list—a court looks at the overall situation to determine if independent contractor status exists. Also, clip any of Leander's promotional literature or advertising to the contract. Take a picture of Leander's van showing the business name and address. Attach that to the contract.

Finally, get used to calling Leander the Sander Leander the Independent Contractor, for that is who he is.

BUSINESS TAX OBLIGATIONS

Kind of Tax

FEDERAL TAXES

Employee Income Tax
and Social Security Tax

Owner-Manager's and/or
corporations' income tax

Unemployment Tax

STATE TAXES

Unemployment Taxes

Income Taxes

Sales Taxes

Franchise Tax

LOCAL TAXES

Sales Tax

Real Estate Tax

Personal Property Tax

Licenses (retail,
vending machine, etc.)

Figure 1.4 Business tax obligations (Adopted From "Steps in Meeting Your Tax Obligation," Small Business Administration Small Marketers Aids No. 142, no longer in print.)

FEDERAL EMPLOYER'S IDENTIFICATION NUMBER

WITHHOLDING

FEDERAL SOCIAL SECURITY TAX

FEDERAL UNEMPLOYMENT TAX

Before you hire anyone, remember that the secret to success in the area of employee requirements is to understand the federal and state regulations regarding employees. An accountant would be of great assistance here. On the federal level, all employers must have a federal employer's identification number, which is obtained by filing an application with the Internal Revenue Service. You will be required to withhold federal income taxes from the wages of all your employees unless your employees file Form W-4, Exemption from Withholding. An employee who includes false information on a Form W-4 is subject to a $500 penalty. You will also have to pay Social Security taxes. Finally, you will have to pay federal unemployment tax. You will get credit for any state unemployment tax paid in this federal tax assessment.

Since each of the above taxes require setting up of special records, filing returns, and making payments, a business about to hire employees should obtain the assistance of the local office of the Internal Revenue Service. Publication 15 of the Internal Revenue Service, *Employer's Tax Guide,* discusses withholding, Social Security, and unemployment taxes. *Your Business Tax Kit,* also available from the Internal Revenue Service, contains most of the forms that are required by an employer to file and pay these taxes. If you have any questions, the taxpayer's service of the Internal Revenue Service will provide assistance. Other federal laws governing employees are the Minimum Wage Law (Fair Labor Standards Act) and the Civil Rights Act as amended (be especially aware of equal-employment-opportunity provisions).

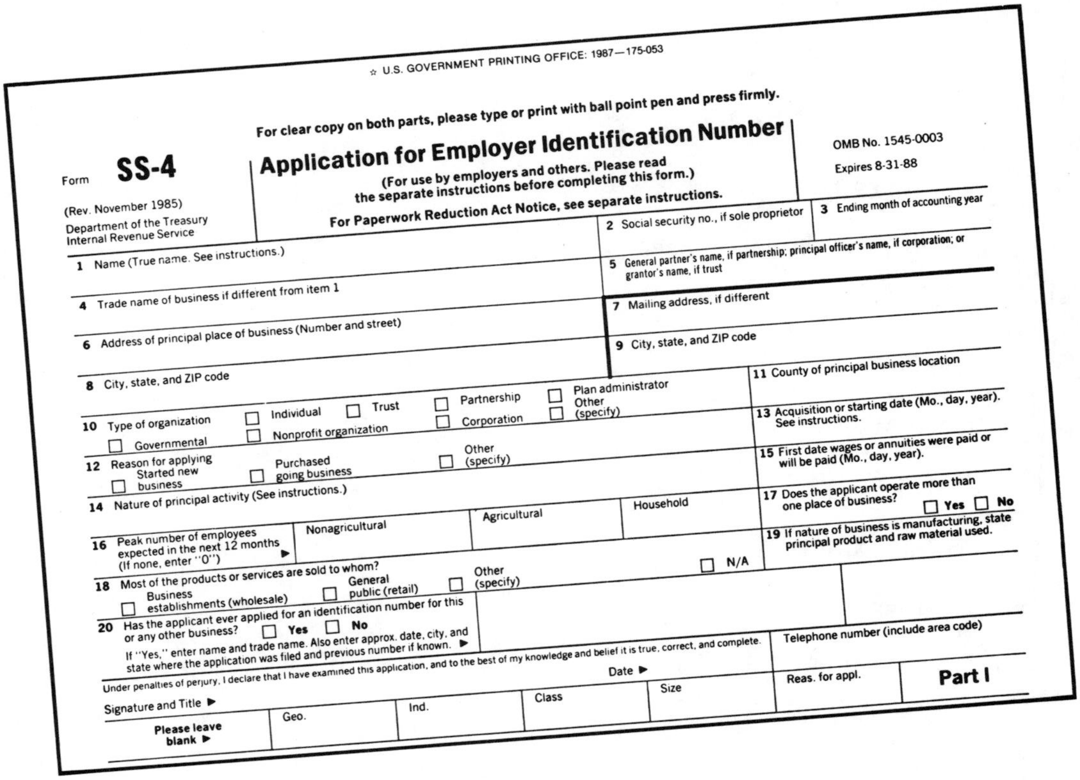

☆ U.S. GOVERNMENT PRINTING OFFICE: 1987—175-053

Form **SS-4**
(Rev. November 1985)
Department of the Treasury
Internal Revenue Service

For clear copy on both parts, please type or print with ball point pen and press firmly.

Application for Employer Identification Number
(For use by employers and others. Please read the separate instructions before completing this form.)
For Paperwork Reduction Act Notice, see separate instructions.

OMB No. 1545-0003
Expires 8-31-88

1 Name (True name. See instructions.)
2 Social security no., if sole proprietor
3 Ending month of accounting year
4 Trade name of business if different from item 1
5 General partner's name, if partnership; principal officer's name, if corporation; or grantor's name, if trust
6 Address of principal place of business (Number and street)
7 Mailing address, if different
8 City, state, and ZIP code
9 City, state, and ZIP code
10 Type of organization ☐ Governmental ☐ Individual ☐ Nonprofit organization ☐ Trust ☐ Partnership ☐ Corporation ☐ Plan administrator ☐ Other (specify)
11 County of principal business location
12 Reason for applying ☐ Started new business ☐ Purchased going business ☐ Other (specify)
13 Acquisition or starting date (Mo., day, year). See instructions.
14 Nature of principal activity (See instructions.)
15 First date wages or annuities were paid or will be paid (Mo., day, year).
16 Peak number of employees expected in the next 12 months (If none, enter "0") ▶ Nonagricultural | Agricultural | Household
17 Does the applicant operate more than one place of business? ☐ Yes ☐ No
18 Most of the products or services are sold to whom? ☐ Business establishments (wholesale) ☐ General public (retail) ☐ Other (specify) ☐ N/A
19 If nature of business is manufacturing, state principal product and raw material used.
20 Has the applicant ever applied for an identification number for this or any other business? ☐ Yes ☐ No
If "Yes," enter name and trade name. Also enter approx. date, city, and state where the application was filed and previous number if known. ▶
Under penalties of perjury, I declare that I have examined this application, and to the best of my knowledge and belief it is true, correct, and complete.
Telephone number (include area code)
Signature and Title ▶ Date ▶
Please leave blank ▶ Geo. | Ind. | Class | Size | Reas. for appl. | **Part I**

Figure 1.5: Application for Employer Identification Number

CANADIAN LAW

Canadian law generally distinguishes among independent contractors, employees, and agents.

STATE WITHHOLDING TAX

The state tax scheme for employees somewhat parallels the federal system. Withholding of state income tax is required by most states. A few cities, such as New York City, have withholding requirements. To obtain the necessary forms and information concerning state withholding tax, call the state tax department.

In most states, the law requires that employers pay an unemployment tax. Each state has its own rule on when an employer must provide unemployment compensation coverage. This requirement usually is based on the number of employees and employee hours per year for the business. A special state agency normally handles questions about unemployment insurance.

STATE UNEMPLOYMENT TAX

Also required by state law is some form of workers' compensation insurance to cover any employee injury on the job. States vary in the manner in which workers' compensation is provided. The state office administering this program should be contacted for further information.

STATE WORKERS' COMPENSATION

MISCELLANEOUS CONSIDER-ATIONS IN SURFACING

STUDIO RENTAL AGREEMENTS

Any lease agreement should be checked for the following provisions: amount of rent, term of the lease, renewal provisions, right of the tenant to sublet, and any restrictions on the tenant's use of the property imposed by the lease, including the tenant's right to hang out a sign or make alterations.

GENERAL LEASE PROVISIONS

In addition to the above considerations, the artist and craftmaker should especially check the lease agreement for a clause concerning fixtures. If you pay for the installation of special rooms, cabinets, shelving, windows, or other valuable fixtures that cannot be removed when you leave, the lease agreement should contain both a provision concerning the tenant's ownership of these improvements and a procedure for the tenant's selling of these improvements at the end of the rental period, if possible. Without this agreement, any improvements which are permanently attached to the walls, floors, and ceiling of the rented premises become the property of the landlord and cannot be removed or sold without the landlord's permission.

FIXTURES

Prior to signing a lease, check the local zoning ordinances, building codes, health, and fire laws. It would be an expensive mistake to sign a lease and find a notice of zoning violation nailed on your door the next week. If there is not enough time to check with these agencies, the lease should contain a clause allowing you to break the lease if you cannot use the rented space for the intended purpose because of city zoning, fire, health, or building-code restrictions.*

FIRE, HEALTH, ZONING, AND BUILDING CODES

Business insurance (a catchall term for a variety of insurance) is an important consideration. For most artists and craftmakers, a major loss early in their business life would spell the end to their business. For some craftmakers, like jewelers, the cost of most business insurance is prohibitive. For other artists and craftmakers, however, insurance is many times both desirable and reasonably priced.

INSURANCE

The first step is to find a good insurance broker. If possible, get estimates from several brokers. Your broker should understand your particular business and personal needs so that he or she can develop an insurance package tailored to suit your particular situation, and generally assist in all insurance matters. Also, look for insurance from a mutual insurance company which pays profits back to the owner/customers in the form of reduced premiums. Make sure that your broker sells a variety of insurance so that the package can include coverage from several companies.

COMPARISON SHOP

INSURANCE BROKER

If you look long enough, you could find insurance to protect you from most types of losses. The major types of insurance coverage are for fire, theft, extended coverage (vandalism, malicious mischief, damage caused by aircraft or vehicles, etc.), premise, and auto liability. Many times, the policy only pays the fair market value of the item destroyed, not the replacement value. So if you want to get enough money from your insurance company to replace the loom that blew away when the explosion rocked your town, consider paying a little extra for a rider to the policy that contracts to pay you the *replacement* value of lost items. Make sure you know what types of coverage you are getting for your money.

TYPES OF COVERAGE

---

*If you are buying business property, be sure to condition the final sale on the approval of the premises for the intended purpose by the proper authorities.

As discussed in Chapter 2, "Legal Restrictions on Content and Materials," crafts-people should add product liability coverage. Product liability coverage insures you against any loss caused by your sale of a defective item. Suits for personal injuries caused by defective products are costly. Sometimes the nature of your product makes this insurance cost prohibitive, or simply unavailable.

Other types of insurance available to businesses include business interruption and unpaid accounts receivable. Your broker should know about employee benefit insurance—health, life, and disability; workers' compensation; and unemployment compensation.

Since purchase of an insurance "package" often reduces rates for coverage, all your insurance needs should be examined when purchasing business insurance to ensure the greatest coverage at the lowest price.

Members of the American Craft Council, 40 West 53rd St., New York, NY 10019, are eligible for health, life, and studio insurance coverage (ACC Insurance Administrator, Suite 200, 3535 University Blvd. West, Kensington, MD 20895-9987). The Foundation for the Community of Artists (280 Broadway, Suite 412, New York, NY 10007) has health and life insurance programs available to their members, as well as a credit union.

Dear Gentle Reader:

Between the craftmaiden and the corporate executive lies vast possibilities of business forms, sizes, styles, and requirements. As with everything else in life, most businesses fall somewhere in the great gray middle between the two extremes.

My advice to you is to place a premium on keeping your business simple, manageable, and comprehensible. Simplicity means a sole proprietorship, no employees, a minimal bookkeeping system, and working out of your home.

As you become comfortable with the requirements of a business of this size and stature, all too soon your simple business will burgeon and you will take on more requirements and responsibilities.

Remember the old Chinese proverb: A journey of a thousand miles begins with a single step.

From,
Chatty Lawyer
Syndicated Column

CHAPTER TWO

Legal Restriction on Content and Materials

RESTRICTIONS ON CONTENT

RESTRICTIONS ON MATERIALS

LEGAL ADVICE? NOT ON YOUR LIFE.

In this chapter you will bump into an odd assortment of topics—rules of negligence, lawsuits for invasion of privacy, the Wool Products Labeling Act of 1939, obscenity decisions, the Consumer Product Safety Commission, the Migratory Bird Treaty Act, and other legal fandanglry—all relating to legal restrictions on the content and materials used in art, crafts, and writing. The information in this chapter cannot possibly cover every legal restriction—the laws are too many, and who knows what might show up on the wall of an art museum. This chapter divides the major areas of restrictions into two categories: limitations on content (obscenity, flag laws, invasion of privacy, and defamation), and limitations on materials that make up the work (textile labeling and flammable fabrics acts, laws governing use of bones, feathers, and other parts of wildlife and plants, the rules of negligence and product liability, laws regulating the stamping of gold and silver, and some pertinent consumer protection statutes).

This chapter's subject area bulges with controversy—obscenity, feather laws, flag burnings, libel, and so on. The speeches and solutions concerning the big picture and the long balance I leave to the politicians and philosopher kings.

Not every "erotic" work is legally obscene. This section carpenters a yardstick to measure works that could be "obscene."

A variety of laws regulate the sale, display, and transportation of "obscene" materials in the United States. Many obscenity busts occur on the state or local level. For instance, Larry Flynt of *Hustler* magazine was prosecuted under a state law. While some states prohibit obscene materials from being either publicly displayed or sold to minors, others prohibit only the sale of such materials to minors. Many cities enforce their own anti-obscenity laws, some of which prohibit *any* commercial dealings in pornography. If you are curious about the anti-obscenity laws that govern your area, ask a lawyer or the local chapter of the American Civil Liberties Union.

Because obscenity laws carve out an exception to our right of free expression, the United States Supreme Court has ruled these laws must be clear and specific in their language. An old New York State laws which prohibited the showing of "sacrilegious" films was deemed too vague a yardstick with which to restrict free expression.

The Supreme Court currently defines obscenity as material that expresses sexual conduct in a patently offensive way and, taken as a whole, appeals to the prurient interest in sex (applying contemporary community standards) and does not have a serious literary, artistic, political, or scientific value. In order to legally send the distributor to jail, the material must be truly "obscene." The film *Carnal Knowledge* was held *not* obscene under the above test. Where borderline "obscene" materials

are sold to minors, publicly displayed so that minors and members of the public cannot avoid them, or peddled with an emphasis on the prurient aspects of the work (like *Eros* magazine), the Supreme Court dealt more harshly with the distributor and

used a looser interpretation of obscene. Ralph Ginsburg discovered this as he was sentenced to five years for publication and sale of *Eros*.

Across the country, states have adopted so-called Minor's Access Laws (general distribution and display of obscene material to minors). "Kiddie porn" laws are designed to discourage child abuse and generally prohibit the distribution of books and other materials depicting sexual performance by children even if the materials themselves may not be proven obscene. Publishers, booksellers, and authors agree that these laws have had a chilling effect on the right of free speech.

The "kiddie porn" laws signed by President Reagan in 1984 make it a crime to ship books depicting minor children in a sexual manner through the mail or via interstate commerce. When a publisher cancelled three books which had language that was objectionable, particularly the word "goddam," according to *Publishers Weekly* magazine,* both the Authors League of America and the American Society of Journalists and Authors protested the action.

Possession of "obscene" material in the privacy of your home is your business, but transporting it across a state line or national border even for personal use is forbidden by federal law. It is a crime to send "obscene" material through the U. S. mail, punishable by jail. An entry in the 1976 New York Film Festival titled *In the Realm of the Senses* was held up by U. S. Customs and did not appear in the film festival. It later was released. IN THE PRIVACY OF YOUR HOME

FEDERAL ANTI-OBSCENITY LAWS

Since only local, state, and federal governments and their representatives are prohibited from violating the citizens' First Amendment right to free expression, a privately sponsored art show can legally refuse to hang any works showing bare skin, et cetera. On the other hand, Straitown City Museum probably cannot legally refuse to hang a so-called obscene work until *after* a hearing determines that the work violates the local anti-obscenity law. No agency of government can legally prohibit a showing prior to such a hearing. To do otherwise would violate the artist's First Amendment rights. The Supreme Court ruled that a theater leased by the City of Chattanooga violated free-speech rights by flatly refusing its use for the production of the musical *Hair* because of the play's allegedly "obscene" content. For those adventuresome souls who still find themselves running afoul of the authorities for violating the obscenity laws, the National Coalition Against Censorship in New York City or your local branch of the American Civil Liberties Union may provide assistance. NATIONAL COALITION AGAINST CENSORSHIP

CANADIAN LAW—OBSCENITY

Canadian Courts tend to a contemporary judgment of morality. This view is illustrated by a United States case quoted by the Canadian court in which a Federal Court Judge, in the *United States of America v. One Book Called "Ulysses"* refused to determine *Ulysses* obscene. In the judge's opinion, "The words which are characterized as dirty are old Anglo-Saxon words known to almost all men. . .and are such words as would be naturally and habitually used, I believe, by the type of nature whose life, physical and mental, Joyce is seeking to describe. In respect of the recurrent emergence of the theme of sex in the minds of his characters, it must always be remembered that his locale was rural and his season, Spring."

In 1961 in England and in 1962 in Canada, D. H. Lawrence's *Lady Chatterly's Lover* was held to be not obscene. The Canadian decision rested on the definition of obscenity in the Canadian Criminal Code. When the Ontario Court of Appeal held that *Fanny Hill: Memoirs of a Woman of Pleasure* was not obscene, it looked at the book as a whole to assess the purpose of the author, that is, did he demonstrate a serious literary purpose or a base purpose.

The content of protest art is ruled by several principles. First, the constitutional right of freedom of speech governs works of visual expression as well as the spoken and written word, and physical behavior. So important is the right of this freedom that the courts have ruled that the laws restricting the right to freedom of expression—obscenity, flag desecration, and so forth—must be very clear and specifically describe the prohibited activity. Usually, the courts require a hearing before a judge *prior* to seizure by the police, because a governmental body is not to restrain speech or expression without a judicial hearing. **FLAGS AND PROTEST ART**
*Congress shall make no law. . .abridging freedom of speech. . .*FIRST AMENDMENT TO THE CONSTITUTION

LAWS RESTRICTING FREE SPEECH MUST BE CLEAR AND SPECIFIC
HEARING PRIOR TO SEIZURE

Most of the cases in the area of protest art involve the use of flags, often in times of political controversy. Many states have two kinds of laws that apply to the use of flags—desecration statutes and misuse statutes. The desecration statutes prohibit behavior that would expose the flag to contempt. Misuse statutes sound like: "No FLAG LAWS

*Publishers Weekly comes out 51 times per year; a subscription is $91 annually and is ordered from Box 1979, Marion, OH 93305-1979. It bills itself as "the international news magazine of book publishing," and its many departments and columns keep the reader abreast of the news of the publishing world. Each issue includes, among many other things, an interview with an author and a rights column that reports book advance figures as well as rights and movie sales figures.

person shall...affix...to any flag...any inscription, design, symbol, name, advertisement...." The New Hampshire Supreme Court voided the flag misuse law quoted above because its broad language restricted important freedoms of speech and expression. Courts often find flag desecration and misuse laws to be in conflict with the First Amendment to the Constitution.

TEST FOR PROTECTION

The Supreme Court constructed a two-part test to determine if the free-speech guarantees of the Constitution protect a flag creation. First, the Court determines if the flag-related conduct is within the protection of the First Amendment, that is, whether the work was intended to convey a particular and comprehensible message. If the Court finds this to be so, then it looks to see if there is some state interest so important that the constitutional right of free expression can be restricted. Under this criteria, the free-expression rights of a sixties draft-card burner lost out to overriding governmental interest.

A WORD TO THE WISE...

If you use a flag motif in your work, check to see your state's flag use laws. Then remember, the clearer your message, the more likely it is that a court will rule that your work is protected from the application of the flag laws by the First Amendment right of free speech. The conviction of an owner of a gallery displaying flag sculptures to express anti–Vietnam War sentiment was reversed after a seven-year court battle. But convictions of persons using a flag motif in advertising generally have been upheld by the courts. You also should remember that the written or spoken word is better protected than a purely visual work, so mix your media.

INVASION OF PRIVACY

Alice's Allegory #5 or Lessons from City Park

With all the messages from the human potential movement (hpm) bombarding his peaceful hillside home, Romero realized that he had to humanize his art. Porcelain portrait hangings would do it—from each plaque a shining human face, full of expression and love!

Romero gathered up Alice, his trusty camera, and chugged off one windy day in search of portraits. City Park at lunch time seemed a good place to begin.

Sitting on the bench surrounded by pigeons was a luscious portrait complete with horn-rimmed glasses and a three-piece, gray suit. Just before Romero snapped the shot, the portrait spoke: "Tsk, Tsk, my friend, you might be invading my privacy, so please do not proceed. Do let me introduce myself, Cautious Caldwell attorney-at-law, at your service."

Romero knew that he had finally found the lawer of his dreams and stuck Cautious Caldwell's card in his hatband.

DEFINITION

Invasion of privacy is what Ron Galella did to Jackie Kennedy Onassis when he poked his camera lens too closely into her life. State law spells out the areas protected from invasion by private parties. Most living persons have a right to privacy, which is basically the right (with many qualifications) to be let alone. If invasion of privacy could be

CHECK IT OUT

a problem in your work, see Chapter 8, "Obtaining Legal Assistance," for information on getting good legal advice concerning the privacy rules of your state.

APPLICATION

A state privacy law usually prohibits commercial exploitation of the name or portrait of a living person without consent. Often it does not apply to the commercial use of photographs of animals, buildings, and so forth, although other restrictions (copyrights, ownership rights) could prohibit the commercial use of these.

What about your sneak street shot of that gorgeous tuba player in last year's Independence Day Parade? Don't sell it to a tuba company for their next big advertising campaign. Without a release (written permission) you might get sued for invasion of the tuba player's privacy. But the local gazette could print the photograph of the tuba player alongside an article on the Independence Day festivities with no problem because the photograph was part of a news story.

FREE SPEECH AND FREE PRESS: EXCEPTION TO PRIVACY LAWS

Many of the cases in this area focus on whether the use of the plaintiff's name, et cetera, is for commercial and trade purposes or for news purposes. A fine line divides the public's right to know and the individual's right to privacy. A participant in a St. Patrick's Day Parade lost his invasion-of-privacy case against *New York* magazine. The court ruled that printing the marcher's photograph on the front of the magazine to illustrate an article called "The Last of the Irish Immigrants" was published "in connection with the presentation of a matter of legitimate public interest to readers" and therefore denied recovery for invasion of privacy. Since anyone thrust willingly or unwillingly into the public eye is considered temporarily a "public figure," he or she, as such, is fair game for comment. A "public figure" will have a hard time winning an invasion-of-privacy suit unless a clear commercial purpose can be demonstrated.

COMMERCIAL PURPOSES

You should give a dollar and obtain a release from any subject of a portrait or photograph you may use for advertising or other commercial purposes. Figure 2.1 contains a sample release form you can tailor to your specific needs. When you photograph identifiable human subjects, get a release. You never know what you might do with the photograph or drawing. You do not need a release to publish or distribute a photograph of someone involved in a truly newsworthy event, but because of the great gray area between the clearly newsworthy and the clearly commercial, when in doubt, get a release. Our law firm recovered damages for a client who was photographed but from whom no written release was obtained. The photographer-painter then rendered a painting from the man's photo, and prints as well, a clear invasion of privacy.

RELEASE

RELEASE

For the sum of $1.00 [or more], receipt of which is hereby acknowledged, I hereby grant to _____ _____, and
(photographer)

to anyone whom he or she may appoint or assign, the right to make any use of the photographs taken of me on _____ at
(date)

_____.
(location)

I do/do not waive the right to inspect the finished photograph.

_____
(signature)

_____
(address)

_____
(date)

Figure 2.1 Photographic Sample Release Form

DEFAMATION*

SLANDER

LIBEL
CANADIAN LAW—DEFAMATION

MORE ABOUT U.S.
DEFAMATION LAWS

Defamation laws are as old as Moses and are designed to protect a person's reputation (including artistic reputation) from the taint of falsehood. Under defamation laws, private citizens can sue to recover money damages for the harm caused by any oral or written misrepresentation of their name, personality, or behavior. So don't depict your worst enemy with an unnatural or obscene deformity. When the defamatory statement is oral, it is called *slander*; when it is written it is called *libel*.

The definition of defamation runs about the same in both countries, as a defamatory statement is one that lowers a person in the estimation of others.

The defamatory material can be a drawing, photograph, et cetera, as well as the printed or spoken word. A business organization can be defamed as well as an individual. California's libel law, enacted in 1872, looks like this:

> Libel, what. Libel is a false and unprivileged publication by writing, printing, picture, effigy, or other fixed representation to the eye, which exposes any person to hatred, contempt, ridicule, or obloquy, or which causes him to be shunned or avoided, or which has a tendency to injure him in his occupation.

The person making a defamatory statement is liable to the defamed person. So is anyone else who participates in its distribution—publisher, newspaper editor, gallery owner.

In order to win a defamation suit, the defamed person must prove that the defamatory statement was *communicated* to others; that the statement clearly *identified* the plaintiff (the person bring the suit); that the plaintiff suffered *injury* because of the statement; and most important, that the maker of the statement was somehow at *fault* with regard to the statement. Because each state has its own definition of defamation, these requirements will vary.

But publishers, editors, and authors may be sued for libel in any state in which their material is circulated and may be forced to travel to another state to defend libel charges. The two Supreme Court cases responsible for this rule involved *Hustler* magazine and the *National Enquirer* tabloid.

COMMUNICATION

IDENTIFICATION

INJURY

FAULT

PUBLIC FIGURES

A notorious falsehood whispered to a friendly tree would not be defamation, nor would a statement calling the mystery man a thief and a philanderer. You can defame a person without using his or her name—"All the kids from Juniper Grove are swindlers." The requirement of showing *injury* is slightly complicated by the fact that if the defamer *knew* that the statement was false or at least entertained serious doubts as to its truth; then, no actual injury has to be shown in order to win a defamation case.

It is the requirement of proving fault in a defamation suit that has made headlines for the last few years. In order to strengthen the constitutional right of free speech, the Supreme Court has adopted two standards of fault—one which applies to public officals and figures and another which governs private persons. A public figure must prove that the defaming statement was made either with knowledge of its falsity or with reckless disregard for the truth. Barry Goldwater recovered $50,000 from *Fact* magazine and $25,000 from its editor, who ran a story portraying Goldwater as a latent homosexual, a "cruel" practical joker, a paranoid, and so on. But a deputy sheriff who had been falsely accused of bribery lost his defamation suit for lack of proof that the defamer acted with reckless disregard for the truth. Erma Bombeck complained in her January 1988 column about an unauthorized biography written about her by a man whom she doesn't know and has never met. She said that "once you enter the Public Domain, [she means that once she became a public figure] you'll be misquoted [and] misunderstood by all those things you've supposedly said and done."

---

*At various times, there are national organizations or lobbies concerned with defamation. Good examples are the National Coalition Against Censorship and the Libel Defense Resource Center.

Private persons only have to show that the defamer acted negligently in failing to check the truthfulness of the statement. So a lawyer accused of framing a Chicago policeman and of being a "communist fronter" by the John Birch Society magazine won his libel case. Because he was not a public figure, he only had to prove that the magazine was negligent in not checking out the statements made about him. Mrs. Firestone, a Palm Beach socialite, also recovered a $100,000 libel judgment from Time, Inc., for defamatory remarks concerning her divorce. The Supreme Court refused to throw out the judgment, saying that Mrs. Firestone's divorce case was not of sufficient *legitimate* public interest to apply the test for public figures. In a recent Supreme Court case, the Court ruled that the trial judge must apply the "clear and convincing evidence" standard to the public-figure-libel Plaintiff's documenting proof, and thereby required a lesser standard than preponderance of the evidence. The Author's Guild (Winter 1987 issue) reported that this could increase the use of summary judgments to shorten and resolve libel litigation because the legal fees to prepare and make a summary judgment are $45,000 as compared to $400,000 to prepare a case for trial.

Usually truth is a defense to a lawsuit for libel. However, the truth is sometimes hard to prove, especially in the controversial areas in which libel suits usually occur. Retraction of the libelous statement is not a defense to libel but can serve to reduce the amount of damages recovered.

Fiction writers are not immune from libel actions. As fact becomes stranger than fiction, and fiction writers become "faction" (fact plus fiction equals faction) writers, this area raises a whole list of new questions concerning libel which have not yet been considered by the courts.

Research factual material very carefully. Any potentially defamatory statements should be confirmed and verified and the notes of this research retained. In fiction, carefully disguise beyond recognition any real-life persons used as a model for a character. Obtain a release if possible.

These tips may help you avoid defamation and invasion of privacy charges.

1. Check your facts carefully.
2. Avoid accusations of dishonesty or inability about an individual's profession if you can't prove them.
3. Avoid remarks of unchastity, a criminal act or crime, physical or mental disease, if you can't prove them.
4. Avoid associating an individual with a cause or group that's generally held in disrepute, if you can't prove them.
5. Change not only the name of the subject but make sure the person cannot be recognized.

Not only may you be skidding into liability if you write untruths that injure a person's reputation for business, competence, chastity and sexual preferences, health, honesty, and so forth, but going a step further, your words could be truthful and invade the privacy of an individual who is not a public figure.

This right to be left alone centers around the publication of embarrassing or disagreeable facts—ordinarily offensive—about a private person whose activities are not matters of public interest. If the unpleasant facts are well known, then they aren't private.

I know fiction authors whose publishers demanded that they change not only the name, physical characteristics, and residence but also gender of minor characters to avoid problems.

In the chapter "Especially for Writers," I touch on this area again from the point of view of a legal manuscript review.

In 1982, the Charter of Rights and Freedoms was annexed to the Canadian Constitution. Until then, Canada was cast as a consumer's society, with accommodation, compromise, and concern for the general welfare the focal points rather than

PRIVATE PERSONS

TRUTH IS A DEFENSE

RETRACTION

TIPS ON DEFAMATION AND INVASIONS OF PRIVACY

CANADIAN LAW—PRIVACY

American individualism and its liberties. The charter will affect the laws on defamation, but that extent is beyond the scope of this book.

In an old privacy case in Quebec (1879), the court said that the doctor who published the nature of his patient's malady in his lawsuit for unpaid fees violated confidences. Another spin-off of the privacy tort in Canada is the commercial appropriation of a likeness, best illustrated by a photograph of a police constable mopping his brow on traffic duty; the photo later appeared in an ad for a foot bath captioned, "Phew! I am going to get my feet into a...foot bath." Many of the provinces have passed privacy legislation.

RESTRICTIONS ON MATERIALS

INTRODUCTION

To discuss every material that is somehow regulated by state or federal law and that an artist or craftmaker might use in his or her work would take more pages than this book has available. This section covers only the major federal laws governing materials ordinarily used by artists and craftmakers and the rules of product liability and negligence. Because health hazards to artist and craftmakers arising from materials used in their work are also beyond the scope of this book, we do not discuss this important area. For more information, contact the Center for Safety in the Arts (CSA), 5 Beckman Street, New York, New York 10030; CSA is a national clearinghouse for research and education on hazards in the visual arts, performing arts, educational facilities, and museums. CSA publishes a newsletter, offers nearly 20 publications, and over 70 data sheets. The hazard of toxic chemicals in many arts-and-crafts materials is acute, according to CSA.

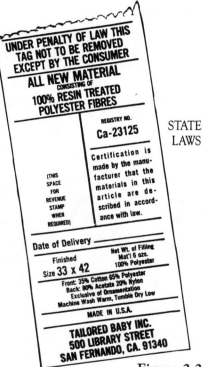

STATE LAWS

Because there is so much variation in the state laws in the area and because the major areas are covered by the federal laws, state laws concerning the use of certain materials are not discussed here. Those craftmakers selling stuffed things—quilts, pillows, and so forth—should get information on their state's "bedding laws"—the law that requires those threatening tags that are attached to most pillows and comforters indicating the fiber content of the filling. Your state consumer protection office should be able to give you information on your state's legal requirements. A special state license may also be required under these laws. Figure 2.2 has a sample of a bedding law label.

Figure 2.2
Sample of bedding label

In this section there will be many references to the laws covering sales of products that have crossed state lines. This is because, under the commerce clause of the Constitution, the federal government is allowed to regulate commerce between states (interstate commerce) but not within a state (intrastate commerce). As the power of the federal government grows, the necessary contact with another state may be very slim. Ollie's Barbecue, a family-owned restaurant in Birmingham, Alabama, discovered this when the Supreme Court ruled that the federal anti-discrimination-in-public-accommodations laws applied to their restaurant, through the commerce clause.

NEGLIGENCE AND PRODUCT LIABILITY

Alice's Allegory #6 or The Mexican Connection

Alice and Romero spiffed up Viola the VW, bought some Mexican auto insurance, and headed off for a few lost weeks on the coast of Mexico. The pineapples and the papayas were delicious and the sun was warm and wonderful. Alice, in her new tan, was checking out the *marcado* in town when she came across clay glazes for sale. Since Romero was the Spanish-speaker of the group, Alice dragged him away from his third fruit-juice treat of the day to negotiate the sale of the glazes.

No way could Romero remember the world for *lead* in Spanish. So Alice bought a small jar full of glaze to bring home and have tested before she purchased enough glaze to do a whole line entitled Lost Mexico Reverie.

Although there is no law on the books which says "No one shall sell ceramics with poisonous glazes for home use," a potter could be successfully sued for selling a clay platter with a glaze which caused the purchaser to become ill after eating food served on it. Consumer suits continue to grow for defective products or service, and these suits can affect artists and craftmakers as well as doctors, car manufacturers, and airlines. For instance, a customer, after his flameware skillet exploded, sued the potter. You could be liable if your macrame plant hanger collapses on a silly customer who hung it full of a passionflower vine over his bed. Who wants a plaster wall hanging to come crashing down on top of a good patron's prize Lhasa Apso? Especially hazardous areas where great care must be taken to protect the consumer from injury are neon and kinetic sculptures and children's items. But all craftmakers and artists should be concerned about injuries to their customers arising from the sale of a defective product.

YOU COULD BE LIABLE

The legal doctrine of product liability tips the scales in favor of consumer victory. It is the theory of many that this concern for consumer injury grows from a mass-production economy which unavoidably produces defective products, and that manufacturers and retailers are better equipped to bear the loss caused by defective products than injured Charlie Consumer.

WHY CONSUMER VICTORY?

The legal rule amounts to: defective product plus injury arising from customary or foreseen use equals maker or seller pays. It is no defense that the customer should have known to cover the transformer box to your Flash Jordan neon sculpture—you are liable for the frizzled ball of fur that used to be a kitten.

RULE OF PRODUCT LIABILITY

In Canada, defective products also raise the question of tort liability. If you recommend a product that is later found to be defective, you may be liable for the tort of misrepresentation in Canada. Thus, where a person gives advice or information in circumstances where a reasonable man would know that his skill and judgment is being relied upon, that person accepts the legal duty to exercise such care as the circumstances require. If there is no contract, then the failure to exercise that care means that there could be negligence. If the contract excludes a cause of action for that negligence, it may be effective to exclude liability for negligence. The Supreme Court of Canada recognized the tort of product liability in *Rivtow Marine Ltd. v. Washington Iron Works*, S.C.R. 1189 (1974), and held that the manufacturer has a duty to warn of latent product defects.

CANADIAN LAW—
PRODUCT LIABILITY

Several steps can be taken to guard against customer injury and consequent liability of the seller. First, exercise some quality control—make sure you are not selling items with defects that could harm a customer, such as chipped goblet rims, fragile-handled mugs, and so on. Second, "idiot-proof" your work—figure out all the possible mishaps that could be caused by your work and guard against them by changing the design, perhaps adding a guard rail, a heavier gauge hook, et cetera. If you cannot design away the potential harm, then warn the public of this harm. Include instructions on use of your work to avoid the possible harm. Also, write the name and address of each customer on your carbon copy of the sales receipt, so you have that information in the event of a recall. The Audi is not the only item recalled these days. Take any consumer complaint quite seriously and do not delay in beginning settlement negotiations, if called for. Finally, look into the possibility of purchasing product liability insurance coverage for your business, if it is available.

AN OUNCE OF PREVENTION

WARNINGS

Writers need to be wary of editorial-products-liability claims for damage caused by publication of erroneous material or material with a foreseeable degree of risk. Attention focused on this potential exposure by the over $1 million jury verdict in the *Rand McNally* "exploding chemistry experiment litigation and the lawsuit against NBC for a rape allegedly caused by the television program, "Born Innocent."

FIBERS, FUR, AND TEXTILES

If you are selling fiber or fur products like wool hangings, tie-dyed scarves, handwoven pillows, batik shirts, quilts, fur jackets, wool hats, and so on, the federal laws governing the labeling of textiles concern you. Although individual artists and craftmakers seldom are prosecuted for violation of these laws, some of your works could well be covered by the labeling requirements contained in these laws.

At first reading, these labeling requirements look like a lot of trouble. But federal requirements aside, many in the fiber field routinely do inform their customers concerning the fiber content as an integral part of the creation and sale of handmade fiberwork. In addition to notifying your customers of exactly what they are getting, the fiber-content information also helps with the care of the textile.

The major federal laws and regulations in the textile area are the Wool Products Labeling Act of 1939, the Fur Products Labeling Act, the Textile Fiber Products Identification Act, the Flammable Fabrics Act, and the Care Labeling of Textile Wearing Apparel. There is also a Trade Practice Rule on shrinkage of woven cotton yard goods. These laws pretty much cover most people who sell textile, wool, and fur creations and require that these products be labeled with certain information. This section will amplify who and what is covered by these laws and the labeling requirements for each law.

WOOL PRODUCTS LABELING ACT OF 1939

The Wool Products Labeling Act (WPLA) of 1939 was the first of the textile labeling acts passed and covers any wool product sold in the United States, except wool rugs and upholstery fabric. Wool rugs are covered by the Textile Fiber Product Identification Act. The purpose of the law is to protect the unsuspecting consumer and processor from buying wool goods that are supplemented with undisclosed nonwool fibers or used wool.

COVERAGE

If you are selling wool products, you probably are covered by the requirements of WPLA of 1939. Technically, the wool product must cross a state line in the course of its sale or distribution for the federal law to apply. If you sell a shawl woven from the wool of your own sheep to a well-known gallery that sells it to a tourist from out of state, the WPLA would apply, and you are required to label the shawl.

LABELING REQUIREMENTS

A label for a handwoven wool jacket might look like this (William places his copyright notice on the same label).

The law requires the name of the maker or seller, the percentages of new wool, "reprocessed" wool (wool which was made into a product and then respun or woven into new fibers), and "reused" wool (wool which was respun or woven after use by the consumer). The law also requires that any other fibers that constitute 5 percent or more of the fibers present in the product be disclosed on the label. Nonwool fibers present in individual portions of less than 5 percent must be disclosed together as "other fibers."

ORNAMENTATION

There is no need to disclose the fiber content of any ornamentation, if it is 5 percent or less of the entire product, provided that you state on the label that the fiber-content information is "exclusive of ornamentation."

Disclose the fiber content of lining, padding, stiffening, trimming, and facing that:
- contains wool
- is included for warmth
- is customarily disclosed
- or if wool product *is not* wearing apparel

Interlinings *must* be labeled separately, as William Weaver did on his handwoven-jacket label. A quiltmaker using miscellaneous wool and other cloth scraps can state: "Made of miscellaneous cloth scraps, composed chiefly of cotton, minimum of 40 percent reused wool," on the quilt label. The percentage of any nonfibrous filling material must also be disclosed. In addition to the above information, the country where the wool products are processed or manufactured must be indicated on the label, that is, "Made in USA of imported fabric," "Woven in USA from imported yarn," and so forth.

The WPLA of 1939 requires that records substantiating the information on the label be kept for at least three years. These records must show the date and item(s) involved in any purchase or sale, the fiber contents of the item sold, and the source of the raw materials in the sold item, including source, quantity, fiber content, and the date of purchase of these materials.

A simple way to do this is to use the job work cards reproduced and discussed in Chapter 5, "Federal Income Tax." This card should show among other things the percentage by weight of each fiber contained in each piece of work and the date of sale, if any. Additionally, a fiber card with a snip of the fiber, fiber name, description, source, and receipt date (or attached receipt) would give you a cross-reference between raw materials used and final products sold.

If you are concerned that the label of some wool you are buying is incorrect, you should have the seller write on your invoice, "We guarantee that the wool indicated on this receipt is not misbranded under the Wool Products Labeling Act." This guarantee would protect you if it later turned out that the wool was indeed misbranded.

Since the law is geared for large commercial manufacturers of wool items, their lables usually comply with the law. So if you have any questions about how to label a piece, check your local department store for labels on similar products.

Unlike the Wool Products Labeling Act of 1939, the Fur Products Labeling Act (FPLA) requires disclosures on invoices and advertising as well as on a label attached to most fur wearing apparel sold in this country. The exceptions to coverage by the FPLA are even more complicated than those of the WPLA of 1939, so it would seem simplest to label all wearing apparel containing fur.

The following information must appear on the fur product label and on any invoice or advertising:

- name of animal that produced the fur
- name of maker
- if the fur is used, using the words "second-hand used fur"
- if the fur is colored or bleached in any way
- if the product contains waste furs (ears and throat) or paws, tail, or belly fur
- if imported, the country of origin
- number assigned to each item*

The label is required to be no smaller than Fredricka's label (1¾ by 2¾ inches) and can contain hand printing but no handwriting. The print on the label must be at least twelve-point type—the size of pica typewriter type.

As with the WPLA of 1939, the Fur Products Labeling Act has extensive record-keeping requirements, which include retaining any documents regarding the purchase or sale of the furs. Essentially, you must maintain all records necessary to prove the information disclosed on the label for three years and also keep the purchase and sale documents and the number you are required to give each finished fur piece. See the above discussion on record-keeping for the Wool Products Labeling Act for more information. You also have to keep a record showing that any processing (bleaching, dyeing, pointing, etc.) of the fur was done according to the regulations concerning the processing of furs.

The Textile Fiber Products Identification Act (otherwise known as TFPIA) generally applies to those folks who are selling or advertising household creations made of nonwool fibers, but also includes wool rugs.** The textile products covered by this labeling law include clothes, bedding, pillows, curtains, quilts, tablecloths and napkins, rugs, towels—generally, articles normally used at home. Wall hangings, hats, handbags, and luggage are not covered.

*Not required to appear on invoice or advertising.

**Handwoven Navajo rugs, which are labeled with a certificate of genuineness of the Indian Arts and Crafts Board of the U.S. Department of Interior, are exempt from the disclosure requirements of the Act.

RECORDS REQUIRED

SELLER'S GUARANTEE

FUR PRODUCTS LABELING ACT

LABELING REQUIREMENTS

RECORDS REQUIRED

TEXTILE FIBER PRODUCTS IDENTIFICATION ACT

COVERAGE

LABELING REQUIREMENTS

This laws requires first that the label contain the name of the maker or processor of a textile. William Weaver is fine for the label on his handwoven bedspread. The labels must state the names of each fiber contained in the work in a quantity of 5 percent or more and the percentage of each such fiber.

BEDSPREAD
Handwoven by William Weaver
50% Linen, 22% Cotton
10% Thai Silk, 8% Other Fibers
(Exclusive of Decoration)

"Other fibers" is used to designate other fibers present in the material in individual quantities of less than 5 percent. William Weaver used 4 percent acrylic and 4 percent acetate in his bedspread and disclosed these fibers under "8 percent other fibers." You need not disclose the fiber content of decorative trim if you state on your label "exclusive of decoration" and the trim does not exceed 15 percent of the product's fiber content. Those selling quilts and anyone else selling warmies with interlinings, fillings, or padding included for warmth should label these separately. The stuffing contents may require a label under the state bedding law or the federal down product guide. The TFPIA requires that *reused* stuffing be labeled.

RECORDS

Under the TFPIA, records must be kept concerning the fiber content of a textile product for at least three years from the date of manufacture. For information on the specific content of the required records see the discussion of record keeping under the Wool Products Labeling Act earlier in the chapter. If you substitute your own tag for the one on the shirt you bought to tie-dye, then you need to keep the information concerning the old tag and where you purchased the shirt as well as all the other required information.

PENALTIES

Enforcement of the Wool Products Labeling Act, the Fur Products Labeling Act, and the Textile Fiber Products Identification Act is in the hands of the Federal Trade Commission, which can seize the mislabeled or unlabeled wool, fur, and textile products, obtain cease and desist orders, and finally prosecute offenders for willful violation of the law. The maximum penalty is $5,000. Free pamphlets on these labeling acts are available from the FTC, Washington, D.C. 20580.

FLAMMABLE FABRICS ACT

The Flammable Fabrics Act basically prohibits the sale across a state line, or the in-state sale of materials obtained from out of state, of any product which fails to conform to the federal flammability standards. The law applies to clothing, children's sleepwear, rugs, mattresses, and mattress pads.

FLAMMABILITY STANDARDS

The concern of the legislators who passed this law was for special fabrics that were highly flammable, like synthetic fabrics that melt when heated, cotton and rayon which burn faster than wool, and fuzzy fabrics that go up in a flash. The standard for clothing prohibits the interstate sale of any highly flammable wearing apparel. The standard for the remaining items covered by the law—children's sleepwear, fiber rugs, mattresses, and mattress pads—is higher. These products must be "flame retardant," which usually requires either using a natural fiber that does not burn readily or chemically treating the fabric. For more information on the individual standards set forth by the Flammable Fabrics Act, see the Code of Federal Regulations, Volume 16, Subchapter D, Flammable Fabrics Act Regulations.*

The U.S. Consumer Product Safety Commission in Washington, D.C., oversees the enforcement of the law and will provide interested parties with additional infor-

---

*Many large retailers will require a guarantee concerning the fabrics covered by the act. This guarantee certifies that the fabric has been tested and conforms to the standards of the act. Textile laboratories routinely provide these testing services.

textile clothing:
requires that a piece of "oven dried" fabric, which is placed in a holder at a 45° angle and is exposed to a flame for one second, not ignite and spread flame up the length of the fabric in less than 3.5 seconds for smooth fabrics or 4.0 seconds for napped.

vinyl plastic:
requires that sample when placed in a holder at a 45° angle, not burn at a rate exceeding 1.2 inches per second.

rugs & carpets:*
requires that a sample exposed to a matchlike agent dropped on the carpet not char more than 3 inches in any direction.

children's sleepwear:
requires that when five samples are suspended vertically in a cabinet and exposed to a small gas flame along its bottom edge for 3 seconds that the average char length be no more than 7 inches; that no single sample can have a char length of more than 10 inches and no single sample can have flaming material on the bottom of the cabinet 10 seconds after the ignition source is removed.

VERTICAL TEST CABINET FOR CHILDREN'S SLEEPWEAR

* Small rugs (no greater than six feet on a side and a square footage of 24 feet or less) do not have to meet the flammability standard if labeled with: **Flammable (Fails US Department of Commerce Standard FF —2-70): Should Not be Used Near Sources of Ignition.**

Figure 2.3
Federal Flammability Standards

mation concerning the Flammable Fabrics Act. At the time of this writing, the Consumer Product Safety Commission has a toll-free number (800/638-2772) for information requests and reports of hazardous products.

Anyone selling items of clothing or piece goods should check into the Care Labeling of Textile Wearing Apparel regulations. This rule governs anyone selling items of clothing across state lines and simply requires that information about the care and maintenance of the article of clothing be "permanently affixed" to the garment.

CARE LABELING OF TEXTILE WEARING APPAREL

If feathers and bones are in your line of business, this section is for you. Both state and federal laws affect this area. As discussed earlier in this chapter, the federal laws cover goods that travel in *interstate* commerce. Wildlife that migrate across state lines are also covered by federal laws. State laws (which sometimes include more species than the federal laws) govern transactions regarding nonmigratory species that occur within the state. Your state fish and game office should have information available on state laws and regulations in this area.

The federal laws that restrict the sale or possession of items containing parts of protected wildlife and plants can be divided into two groups. The first totally prohibits the killing, use, or sale of items containing parts of the protected species (the Migratory Bird Treaty Act and the Bald and Golden Eagle Protection Act). The second group of laws prohibits the killing, use, or sale of items containing parts of the protected species unless obtained according to specific regulations issued pursuant to these laws (the Endangered Species Act and the Marine Mammal Protection Act).*

This area is presently full of controversy. Only the facts concerning the requirements of the current laws are presented here. I take no position on the question of

FEATHERS, BONES, AND CLAWS: RESTRICTIONS ON THE TAKING AND USE OF PROTECTED WILDLIFE AND PLANTS

*Endangered and threatened plants can be taken but not sold or transported in interstate commerce. Don't forget to check the state law regarding protected plants.

whether the government should regulate this area or whether the current laws are enlightened or properly and fairly enforced.

In 1987, the *Navajo Times* newspaper reported that federal and New Mexico Fish and Wildlife officers arrested persons in the area for selling illegal feathers; "illegal feathers" are defined as those of the bald eagle, the golden eagle, the redtail hawk, the owl, the woodpecker, and the scissor-tailed flycatcher. Simultaneously with these arrests were others of people in Wisconsin, Idaho, Texas, and Utah. The officers, using the authority of court-issued search warrants, entered the homes and businesses of a number of individuals and found and confiscated kachina dolls, peyote fans, and loose feathers. It is interesting to note that those arrests were for selling, not possessing, the feathers.

The most stringent of the wildlife protection laws are the Migratory Bird Treaty Act and the Bald and Golden Eagle Protection Act. These laws essentially prohibit any taking or sale of *any* part of *any* bird protected by the two laws.* It does not matter if you found the eagle feather beside the powwow grounds or that the red-tailed hawk's claws came from a bird that had been electrocuted by the power lines behind your house, or that the feather fan had been in the family for at least twenty years. You *cannot sell* protected feathers, period! These two laws simply outlaw *any* sale of any feather or other part of a protected bird by *any* person.

However, Native Americans can possess and exchange protected feathers if the feathers are used in religious and cultural activities. Feathers for these religious objects can be obtained by Native Americans from wild migratory game birds which are legally taken during open season and additionally from the U.S. Fish and Wildlife's eagle depository in Pocatello, Idaho.

The law does not cover feral pigeons, starlings, English sparrows, domestic fowl (chickens, turkeys, ducks, geese, and guinea fowl), and resident game birds (pheasant, grouse, quail, and wild turkeys). However, most states do have laws concerning their resident birds and these laws should be checked. Migratory game birds—ducks, geese, et cetera—are covered by the law but can be legally hunted pursuant to local regulations and their parts sold, but only for use in down products and fishing flies.

The penalties for violation of these laws are a maximum fine of $2,000 and/or maximum time of two years for violation of the Migratory Bird Treaty Act and $5,000 maximum fine and/or one year of prison time for violation of the Bald and Golden Eagle Protection Act. A current list of the protected birds can be obtained from the U.S. Department of the Interior's Fish and Wildlife Service.

The Endangered Species Act and the Marine Mammal Protection Act essentially prohibit the interstate sale or transport of any items made of protected animal parts which were not obtained according to the regulations as well as any selling of the protected wildlife which is not according to the law. The complete list of protected wildlife and plants can be obtained from the U.S. Department of Interior's Fish and Wildlife Office. It is illegal to sell a wallet made from an alligator skin not taken according to the very long rules concerning the killing of the American alligator. Further, according to a ruling of the U.S. Supreme Court, it is illegal to construct a dam which will wipe out a protected snail-darter fish population. A wall hanging using the skull of a gray wolf (a protected species) would be illegal to sell. The zoology department of the local college or university may be helpful in identifying any parts of unknown wildlife that may be on the endangered species list. Alaskan Native Americans are exempt from the coverage of these two laws, providing that their taking of the protected species is for subsistence reasons.

The teeth, bones, and ivory of the protected marine mammal (polar bear, manatee, dugong, walrus, and sea otter) can be collected for personal use if the proper authorities are contacted, and can even be sold if the agent contacted gives her or his approval.

Certain antique articles are exempted from coverage by the act. The penalties for violation of these laws are a maximum fine of $20,000 and/or one year in jail.

*Taking of these birds is allowed by special permit obtained for scientific, educational, or public purposes.

There is no requirement that Raymondo the Jeweler stamp his jewelry with a karat or sterling stamp. But if he decides to stamp his jewelry with information concerning the content of gold or silver, then he must follow the rules of the Falsely Stamped Gold and Silver Act.

Essentially, this law prohibits the sale in interstate commerce* of any silver or gold item which is marked as containing a higher grade of silver or gold than the item actually contains. The law then defines "sterling" as silver which contains at least 925 parts per thousand of pure silver and "coin" as silver which contains at least 900 parts per thousand. The item can legally deviate from this standard by not more than 4 parts per thousand when considering the piece without the solder, and 10 parts per thousand when considering the piece with the solder.

For a gold piece, the allowable deviation from the number of karats stamped on the piece is one-half of a karat excluding the solder and one karat when considering the solder. Gold flatware and watch cases can only deviate 3 parts per thousand not including solder. The allowable variation in gold objects is 3 parts per thousand without solder and 7 parts per thousand with solder included.

Another rule that Raymondo must consider when deciding whether to stamp his jewelry is the requirement that any item stamped with a karat, sterling, or coin stamp must also be stamped with a trademark registered with the federal trademark office.**

Gold- and silver-plated items, if stamped at all, must clearly indicate the item as "plate." Further, the words *sterling* and *coin* cannot be used on plated items. The penalty for a violation of the Falsely Stamped Gold and Silver Act is a maximum of three months in jail and/or $500.

The Consumer Product Safety Commission has as its primary goal the reduction of injuries associated with consumer products. The Commission is attentive to consumer problems and at the date of this writing is available by telephone at 800/638-2772 except for Maryland residents, who must call 800/492-8363. CPSC oversees the administration of five laws:

- Consumer Product Safety Act
- Federal Hazardous Substances Act
- Flammable Fabrics Act
- Poison Prevention Packaging Act of 1976
- Refrigerator Safety Act

Besides the Flammable Fabrics Act, which was discussed earlier in the section on fibers, fur, and textiles, of most concern to the craftmaker and artist are the first two laws.

The Consumer Product Safety Act prohibits the marketing of a product which creates a substantial risk of injury to the public or which violates one of the Commission's standards. The act operates on the basis of consumer complaints as well as self-policing and reporting by the sellers, who usually agree to repair, replace, or refund the money paid for the defective product.

Another law implemented by the Consumer Product Safety Commission is the Federal Hazardous Substances Act. This law deals with any consumer product which is toxic, flammable, corrosive, irritating, pressurized, et cetera. Under the authority of this law, the CPSC has issued regulations governing many areas, including children's rattles, electric toys, cribs, high chairs, walkers, nursery furniture, playground equipment, bunk beds, electrical equipment, lead paints, and so forth. If you are working in any of these areas, call the Consumer Product Safety Commission and request that they send you the fact sheet on the product that you are interested in.

GOLD, SILVER, TOYS, CHILDREN'S FURNITURE, CURRENCY, STAMPS, ET CETERA
STERLING SILVER

COIN SILVER

ALLOWABLE VARIATION

GOLD

ALLOWABLE VARIATION

GOLD AND SILVER PLATE

PENALTY

CONSUMER PRODUCT SAFETY COMMISSION

CONSUMER PRODUCT SAFETY ACT

FEDERAL HAZARDOUS SUBSTANCES ACT

---

*See the discussion of the requirement of interstate commerce in the introductory paragraphs to this section on the Restrictions on Materials.
**See the discussion of obtaining trademark in Chapter 3, "Copying."

LABEL FOR PROTECTION

According to a staff member of the CPSC, 95 percent of the injuries that occur in this area could be avoided by proper education and labeling. Simple use instructions like "COOL IT before plunging in water" or "WARNING: Keep away from children and other small people" will save you from problems and legal entanglements and your customer from unnecessary injury.

REPRODUCTION OF U.S. STAMPS, COINS, OR CURRENCY

There is no longer an absolute prohibition on the reproduction of U.S. postage stamps, coins, or currency. Reproductions of these items can be printed in black and white (except for postage stamps, which can appear in color) if the copy is less than three-fourths of the actual size of the stamp, coin, or currency. The reproductions cannot be used for advertising purposes, and the plates for the prints must be destroyed after use. Finally, the law allowing the limited reproduction of these items requires that the reprints appear in a bound publication, not in individual prints.

FEDERAL TRADE COMMISSION TRADE PRACTICE RULES

The Federal Trade Commission has issued federal trade practice rules governing a number of businesses, some of which are in the craft area. These rules generally prohibit fraudulent and unfair business practices. Others set specific standards, such as the rules on shrinkage of woven cotton yard goods. The list below shows the Federal Trade Commission Practice Rules which pertain to crafts and are available from the Federal Trade Commission, Washington, D.C. 20580.

LIST OF FEDERAL TRADE COMMISSION TRADE-PRACTICE RULES THAT REGULATE CERTAIN ARTS AND CRAFTS BUSINESSES

- Jewelry
- Shrinkage of Woven Cotton Yard Goods
- Millinery
- Feather and Down
- Upholstery and Drapery Fabric
- Branding of Content of Leather Belts
- Ladies' Handbags
- Mirror
- Portrait, Photographic
- Household Furniture

CHAPTER THREE

Copying

LEGAL ADVICE? NOT ON YOUR LIFE.

BACKGROUND

This chapter treats copyright, patents, design patents, trademarks, trade secrets, unfair competition, fakes, and forgeries. The overall concepts are how to protect your work from copying and how to control the use of your work.

DEFINITIONS

Definitions of these topics overview what is ahead.

A *patent* protects inventions, and sometimes designs, as well as hybrid plant varieties. The government grants patents. *Design patents* are available for original ornamental designs for articles of manufacture, such as jewelry, furniture, fabrics, vehicles, and industrial equipment.

A *trademark* is a protected symbol or mark used to identify and distinguish goods.

Copyright provides protection and a remedy if others copy your original work—literary, artistic, musical, et cetera.

A *trade secret* is any formula, pattern, device, or compilation of information which is used in one's business and is kept secret, giving you an advantage over your competitors.

Unfair competition covers fraudulent conduct, such as palming off or sale of goods as those of another.

A *fake* or *forgery* is a misrepresentation—a work that purports to be something other than what it is.

A *trade name* is a name, word, or phrase used as a means to identify one's business.

COPYRIGHT

More artists and craftpersons, now than before, use the copyright notice on their work to retain control over their work as well as to retain a future financial interest in it. Robert Indiana's uncopyrighted serigraph *Love* illustrates the lack of control and loss of potential profits for uncopyrighted works. His design was freely used by others in jewelry, cards, posters, stamps, a box cover, and other commercial products. The *Love* design is reproduced without Mr. Indiana's permission because the design lacked a copyright notice and accordingly passed into the public domain for anyone to use freely.

My message for you is to copyright and not to copy wrong, to watch agreements and sales receipts so you do not give away copyrights unless you intend to, and to remember that even a copyrighted work can be used in certain situations without permission.

LIMITATIONS TO THIS CHAPTER

This chapter explains general copyright legalities and practice but does not deal with all the nuances, ambiguities, and vagaries of copyright law for a particular situation. If you are a writer, read this and read Chapter 7, "Especially for Writers." Be patient as you read this chapter, for each concept depends on others. I suggest rereading this chapter several times.

In case of infringement or copyright questions or troubles, always consult a knowledgeable lawyer. Be sure to write to the Copyright Office for a packet of free information on the federal copyright law and for registration forms. (See figure 3.1.)

HISTORY

Copying is an old practice. St. Benedict's rules included copying as a virtuous activity. There is an old story of St. Columbo who copied Abbot Finnian's Psalter, whereupon the Abbot demanded the copy and was refused. The problem was referred to the Irish King Diarmid in his palace at Tara, A.D. 567, who in settling the disputed property rights, ruled in favor of the Abbot, saying, "To every cow her calf," and accordingly to every book its copy. The first recorded instance of copyright occurred in Venice in 1469. John of Spira received an exclusive five-year right to print the Epistles of Cicero and Pliny.

"TO EVERY COW HER CALF"

PRINTING PRESS

The printing press advanced the art of copying, thus scribes vigorously opposed it. In 1476, Caxton established a press in Westminister, England. Mass confusion followed regarding the products of the new device, as well as proclamations, decrees, and laws relating to copying. By the mid-sixteenth century, the leading printers in London formed the Stationer's Company, and the Catholic Queen Mary in 1556 gave them a monopoly on printing to control the spread of Protestantism. Thus, the English history of copyright is intertwined with literary censorship. After 274 years of confusion, Parliament adopted in 1710 the first copyright statute and called it "An Act for the Encouragement of Learning."

FIRST COPYRIGHT STATUTE, 1710

Summarized, the Statute of Anne provides:

> Whereas printers. . .have of late frequently taken the liberty of printing. . . books. . .without the consent of the authors. . .to their very great detriment and too often to the ruin of them and their families. . .the author of a book shall have the term of fourteen years. . . .[E]very such offender. . .shall forfeit one penny for every sheet which shall be found in his. . .custody. . . .

Most copyright legislation modeled itself after this act.

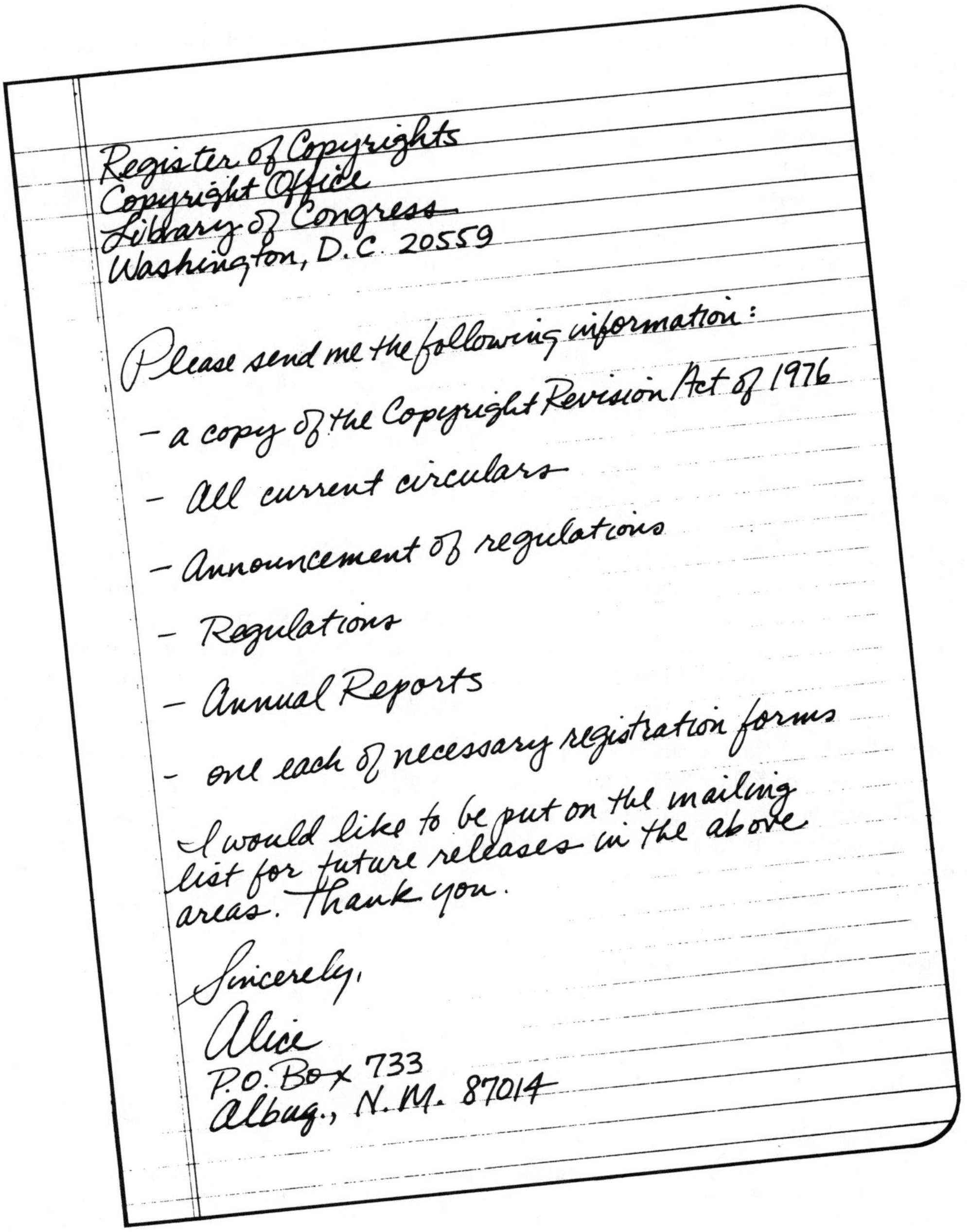

Register of Copyrights
Copyright Office
Library of Congress
Washington, D.C. 20559

Please send me the following information:

- a copy of the Copyright Revision Act of 1976
- All current circulars
- Announcement of regulations
- Regulations
- Annual Reports
- one each of necessary registration forms

I would like to be put on the mailing list for future releases in the above areas. Thank you.

Sincerely,
Alice
P.O. Box 733
Albuq., N.M. 87014

Figure 3.1 Sample request letter for copyright information

The American Colonists adopted state copyright laws and then a United States Constitutional provision, which gave Congress the authority to enact national copyright (and patent) laws. Article 1, section 8, clause 8, provides: "The Congress shall have the power...to promote the Progress of Science and useful Arts, by securing for limited Times to Authors and Inventors the exclusive Right to their respective Writings and Discoveries."

The first federal copyright act of 1790 was amended at fairly regular intervals until the Copyright Act of 1909, which remained the basic law (referred to as the old law) until January 1, 1978, the effective date of the new law. The new law, formally called the Copyright Revision Act, I refer to as the new law.

The old law, rooted in the old English legal principles on literary property, failed to keep pace with modern technology and new communication techniques—communication satellites, cable television, computers, video tape, records, photocopying machines, etc.

This chart illustrates the evolution of the subject matter under our federal copyright law:

- 1790:   maps, charts, and books
- added 1802:   historical or other print or prints
- added 1831:   musical compositions
- added 1865:   photographs and photograph negatives (because Mathew Brady's photos of the Civil War were attaining fame)
- added 1870:   paintings, drawings, chromos, statuettes, statuary, models or designs of fine art
- rewritten 1909:   a major consolidation of the above statutes. All the above plus composite and encyclopedic work, directories, gazetteers, periodicals, newspapers, lectures, sermons, addresses, dramatic or *dramatico-musical* compositions, works of art, reproductions of works of art, drawings or plastic works of a scientific or technical character, and pictorial illustrations
- added 1912:   motion pictures
- added 1971:   sound recordings
- changed 1976:   Copyright Revision Act. Original fixed work which can be perceived including: literary works, musical works (including accompanying words), dramatic works (including accompanying music), pantomime and choreographic works, pictorial, graphic, and sculptural works, motion picture, and other audiovisual works and sound recordings.

Generally, the old law covers works "published"* before 1978 and the new law covers works either created or "published" after January 1, 1978.

The new law came about because there was confusion between what was known as common law copyright in the state, and federal copyright law. American copyright practice was out of step with that of the rest of the Western world. Congress wanted one copyright system that would keep pace with the new technology, modernize and standardize protection, and preempt the state from legislating in this area, so it passed the Copyright Revision Act.**

Publication is a technical term discussed later in this chapter.

**The revision resulting in the new law started in 1955 with numerous studies, drafts, and negotiations. The Register of Copyrights, speaking on the new law, commented that "practically everything in the bill is the product of at least one compromise, and many provisions have evolved from a long series of compromises reflecting constantly changing technology, commercial and financial interests, political and social conditions, judicial and administrative development, and—not least by any means—individual personalities...."

Copyright is a remedy given by the law to the "authors" of literary, dramatic, musical, artistic, and other intellectual works when the author's copyrighted work is copied. *Author* is a technical term which refers to the creator of intellectual property, whether it be a writer, musician, artist, or craftperson. The author can also be a purchaser, heir, or other who acquires the creator's rights. The essence of copyright is the right of the author to protect and control the reproduction of his or her created work.

Under the old law, there was dual protection. The first was called "common law copyright." It existed from the moment of creation and continued to "publication." This protected any work, such as old letters or unpublished manuscripts, from unauthorized copying before publication or disclosure. Once the work was made public without a copyright notice on it under the old law, it then passed into the public domain and could be freely copied by anyone.

COMMON LAW COPYRIGHT

Memorandum of Law

DATE: December 1, 1979
FROM: MB
RE: Batiks of M.G.

Client wants to know if batiks that she exhibited in 1975 without any copyright notice at several art festivals in metropolitan shopping-center malls can now be copyrighted if she has not sold them. Answer: No.

Under the facts of this case, client's situation would be covered by the old law.

Under *Letters Edged in Black Press, Inc. v. Public Building Commission of Chicago*, 320 F. Supp. 1303 (N.D.Ill. 1970), the answer is no. In that case, Picasso designed a monumental sculpture for the plaza of the Chicago Civic Center. After Picasso donated the design for the sculpture, the Commission began a publicity campaign to publicize the Chicago Picasso. This included press shows, distribution of photos to the public, and display of the model at the Tate Museum. Neither the model nor the photographs had the copyright notice attached.

Later the sculpture itself was dedicated with a copyright notice and registered with the copyright office. The court held that as a result of the publicity, the Chicago Picasso was in the public domain *prior* to the attachment of a copyright notice on the monumental sculpture and anyone could copy the work without paying the owner of the work.

If the work bore a copyright notice, the federal law gave the author a remedy if someone copied the work. The dual system of common law copyright protection before publication and federal law protection after publication has now been replaced by a single federal system for all fixed work, published or unpublished, which makes federal protection available from the moment of creation.

The ownership of the copyright initially belongs to the person who creates the work, except in the case of employees. Traditionally, the common law copyright passed with the sale of the creation, unless a written agreement provided that the author retained the copyright. The new law provides that the creator retains the copyright *unless* it is conveyed in a signed writing.

What if more than one person contributes to a single work? The creators are co-authors and co-owners if the work is indivisible. This is called a joint work. The court-made law provides that the co-owners shall have free use of jointly owned property, subject to the duty to account for profits. Since you can't infringe your own copyright, unresolved problems between co-owners of a copyright are handled by filing a lawsuit for an accounting.

In a divisible work, a series of separate weavings displayed together, as part of a single work, for example:

- each creator can obtain individual copyright for each part.
- one can obtain copyright in the name of all.
- one can obtain the copyright in trust for the rest.

"WORK FOR HIRE" RULE

An important exception to the general rule that the creator owns the copyright concerns works created by an employee for an employer. Then the employer is presumed to have the copyright for the employee's work.* Thus, the new law continues the general rule that "work for hire" belongs to the employer where the work is made by an employee within the scope of employment. The new law recognizes a long-standing trade practice that the copyright of certain works, created by employees outside the scope of their job or by independent contractors, belongs to the creator, *unless* the parties agree in writing that the piece shall be a work for hire and it's specially commissioned or ordered work falling into certain categories:

- work ordered or commissioned as a contribution to a collective work
- part of a motion picture or work for other audiovisual use
- translations
- supplementary works
- compilations
- instructional texts
- atlases

Under this rule, if a painter teaches drawing classes in the art department of POW University and also writes a how-to-draw book, the copyright in the book belongs to the painter, not the employer.

The work-for-hire issue raises its ugly head so much that I'll explain it from a different point of view. An employer, and sometimes a party commissioning a work, owns the copyright in it as if they created it. Thus, the artist could infringe the copyright on his/her own creations! Works for hire are born when an employee creates a copyrightable work during the term of employment, or when the work was commissioned/ordered, both parties agreed in writing that the piece was a work for hire, and it falls within the categories listed above.

Sometimes copyright cases treat free-lancers as employees if the other party exercises a certain amount of control and direction. Free-lancers beware.

At a 1982 hearing in the United States Senate, testimony attested to the take-it-or-leave-it attitude of mass-market publishing, where 65 percent of the 25 largest mass-market magazines are created as work for hire! New legislative proposals are continually introduced to reform this law.

Don't, then, agree in writing that any work is a work for hire, and refuse to sign anything that is similar in language. Or do as one free-lancer I represent did: charge two different rates, a higher rate for work-for-hire pieces because the other party's use rights increase.

Let's restate the new rule: When you sell a work with the proper copyright notice, you retain the right to copy it, as long as you have not transferred the copyright in writing and the work was not work for hire.

WHAT CAN BE COPYRIGHTED?

Under the new law, you can copyright any "original work of authorship fixed in any tangible medium of expression" which can be perceived and communicated directly or through any mechanical means or device. Any minimal expression of originality is okay so long as it's reduced to tangible form. There are seven broad categories of "original works of authorship" fixed in tangible form that can be copyrighted:

---

*See discussion in Chapter 1, "Legal Steps in Surfacing Your Business," concerning the distinction between employee and independent contractor status.

- literary works
- musical works (plus accompanying words)
- dramatic works (plus accompanying music)
- pantomimes and choreographic works
- pictorial, graphic, and sculptural works
- motion pictures, other audiovisual works
- sound recordings

The category of "pictorial, graphic, and sculptural works" includes "two-dimensional and three-dimensional works of fine, graphic, and applied art, photographs, prints and art reproductions, maps, globes, charts, technical drawings, diagrams and models." Three factors—fixed in a tangible form, creativity, and originality—are requirements for statutory copyright protection. Thus, an idea cannot be protected by copyright until it is fixed in final form.

FIXED IN A TANGIBLE FORM

The drawing by my daughter (made when she was four) has the necessary creativity and originality to be copyrighted. Creativity refers to the work's nature, and originality refers to the creation by the author using his or her own skill, labor, and judgment. For instance, such unoriginal objects as butterflies, cocker spaniels, and flowers made into original art creations have been held copyrightable, as well as the artistic arrangement of panels on gift wrap. On the other hand, an arrangement of plastic flowers and a scaled-down reproduction of an Uncle Sam bank that had passed into the public domain did not have the necessary creativity and originality to qualify for copyright protection. Where works of art are reproduced, the first work already has creativity so the reproduction only needs to be original to be copyrightable.

CREATIVITY AND ORIGINALITY

Tweety crying

INDEPENDENT CREATION

Creation of the same work by two persons independent of each other gives protection if others copy the copyrighted works, but does not protect the two creators from one another.

Alice's Allegory #7 or Independent Ideas

Alice designed a pipe, calling it strike-it-easy, in the shape of a coiled Rocky Mountain rattler, and put the copyright symbol, her name, and date on the head of the rattler, and sold it to a young man on his way to Nepal for four years. Alice attended an arts and crafts fair in Bisbee, Arizona, the next year and saw an identical piece with a copyrighted notice dated a year later by another artist named Bohoe. Bohoe stated he had never seen or heard of Alice's piece either through a Nepalese-bound young man or anyone else and he had the idea on his own.

Who has the copyright?
Both have a valid copyright, for each of the works was original and creative.

You can copyright artwork (having pictorial, graphic, or sculptured features) that is embodied in useful articles. The artwork must be separately identified from and exist independently of the article's utilitarian aspect, for example, designs painted on cups and bowls, a batiked bird on a scarf. The new law incorporates the old case of *Mazer v. Stein*, which was an infringement case involving applied works of art. There, copyrighted statuettes of male and female dancers were used as manufactured lamp bases. The copyright of the statuettes was upheld by the court even though they were used as an item of utility. If you copyright a drawing of prickly pear cactus bordered by Indian baskets on a handwoven rug, then you get protection from someone copying exactly *that* design but you cannot keep persons from making floor rugs or from using any variation of prickly pear cactus–Indian basket design.*

UTILITARIAN ART OR APPLIED WORKS OF ART

*See discussion in *The Law (In Plain English) For Craftspeople,* by Leonard D. DuBoff, Madrona Publishers, 1984, 91 to 95.

In one lawsuit, Albert Gilbert, a well-known wildlife artist, painted *Cardinals on Apple Blossoms* and National Wildlife Art Exchange acquired the copyright on the painting. The Franklin Mint Corporation commissioned Gilbert to paint four wildlife pictures, one of which was entitled *The Cardinal.* The appellate court held there was no infringement by the new painting because the new painting was a variation on a theme and there were distinguishing differences of line, color, body position, foliage, and general composition.

Alice's Allegory #8 or "Oh those Pig Hunters"

Alice one winter day glazed and painted a design on an enormous serving platter commissioned by the Wild Turkey and Pig Hunters of Hobin. The design was a complicated collage of turkeys and wild pigs from birth to old age in a wide variety of natural scenes. On the back she put the copyright notice, the date, and her full name. The sales receipt stated "Platter sold to Wild Turkey and Pig Hunters of Hobin on 1/2/78 for $250." A month later, Alice received a Seedy catalogue in the mail which she sent for because their advertisement in *Father Meed News* stated "Beautiful textiles depicting nature's wild bounties." To her dismay, she found yardage entitled "Wild Turkeys and Pigs of North America" at $30 per yard which exactly duplicated her platter design. She discovered on contacting the platter purchasers that they had photographed the platter and sold the photo-design to Seedy to raise money for Wild Turkey and Pig Hunters of Hobin, which was publishing a book tracing the origins and treatment of wild turkeys and pigs in North America.

Alice excitedly went to see her family lawyer, who in turn put Alice in touch with a copyright lawyer in the big city who said: "Well, my dear, you indeed have a case of copyright infringement, for when you transferred the platter, you did not transfer the copyright unless you did so in writing, and the receipt does not indicate a transfer. The first thing we need to do is register the work and deposit copies with the Copyright Office. If we register within three months of publication, then the court could award you attorneys' fees and statutory damages."

WHAT CANNOT BE COPYRIGHTED

A LEGAL RULE

Copyright protection does not extend "to any idea,* procedure, process, system, method of operation, concept, principle, or discovery...."

Also, copyright is not generally available for works by the United States government; for obscene, libelous, and immoral work on public policy grounds; for minimal work (names, slogans, titles, lettering, coloring); for blank forms; for business operations or procedures; and for ideas or procedures for doing, making, or building things. The exclusion of government works from copyright protection covers works produced by officers and employees as part of their duties, but it does not necessarily cover work prepared under a contract or grant.** So, if you contract to photograph the work of U.S. Indian Arts and Crafts Board, be sure you get the government to agree in writing that you have the copyrights, if there are any to be had. Various government agencies have differing policies about an individual's ability to copyright works prepared with the assistance of federal grant money. It is wise to have a statement of such policy at the outset. As a matter of practice, the Copyright Office registers "obscene" works, since it does not want to make decisions on what is obscene. But, if someone infringes your "obscene" work and you sue the infringer, then the

COPYRIGHT OF "OBSCENE" WORKS

---

*If you want to protect your idea, do not disclose it. If you do, then contract first. For example, you can offer to disclose your idea to a person or company provided they will not make use of the idea until a mutually agreeable price is reached.

**The United States government sometimes requires those who contract with it to copyright the work in the contractor's name and then assign the copyright to the government. So you need to check to see if the work has been copyrighted in that fashion.

alleged infringer can raise a defense that there is not a valid copyright because the work is obscene. In a recent case involving the movie *Behind the Green Door,* a court ruled that the movie was obscene; hence no valid copyright and no infringement!*

The term *publication* is a technical term in the world of copyright. Under the old law, "publication" occurred generally if the work was sold or distributed to the general public or displayed in a public place with no restrictions. Under the new law, the date of "publication" becomes less important, for it simply serves to establish time limits for registration. If a work is not registered within three months of "publication," and there is a subsequent lawsuit for infringement, the infringer would not be liable to reimburse the plaintiff's attorney's fees and to pay statutory damages.

In addition, the five-year period to cure the omission of the copyright notice is determined from the date of publication.

The new definition of publication is ambiguous. The new law states that "public performance or display of a work does not of itself constitute publication . . ." but "the offering to distribute copies . . . to a group of persons for the purposes of . . . public display, constitutes publication." Treat it as meaning *public distribution.* Distribution occurs when you sell, rent, lease, lend, or transfer the work or copies to people not restricted from disclosing the work's content to others.

PUBLICATION

Protect your work. Don't exhibit, display, or sell your work without properly affixing a copyright notice to it.

REQUIREMENTS OF COPYRIGHT NOTICE

A copyright notice must contain three things:

CONTENTS

- the copyright symbol © or the word "copyright" or the abbreviation, "copr."
- the year of first publication of the work
- the name of the copyright owner

If you want some international protection, then you use the copyright symbol "©," the name of the owner, and the year of first publication. For protection in the Western Hemisphere you must add the words "all rights reserved."

SYMBOL FOR INTERNATIONAL PROTECTION

© 1988 Martha Blue
All Rights Reserved

As stated above, the year of "publication" of your work is generally the year you present your work to the public for sale, rental or lease.** If this date is unclear to you, then simply put the year of completion of your work on the copyright notice. Even if an earlier year or the wrong name is put in the copyright notice, it is likely you will receive all the protections of the Copyright Act.

DATE OF NOTICE

Put your first and last name on the notice of copyright (Hortense Mendleschmidt). However, it is acceptable to put your professional name (Yellow Bird) or symbol (H M), if you are very well known by these appellations.

NAME

The copyright notice must be placed on the work so that it is not concealed from view upon reasonable inspection. The notice can be placed on the front, back, or base of a work as well as on the frame or mounting. For jewelry and other works too small to house all the information required by the copyright notice, a tag can be firmly attached to the piece with the required information. To protect the designs on yard goods or decorative papers, place the notice every so often on the selvage or in the design itself. If this is not possible, put the notice on a tag which must be attached both to the material and the spool. It is sufficient that the notice be placed on only one of two earrings or other paired items.

PLACEMENT OF NOTICE

*See the discussion of obscenity in Chapter 2, "Legal Restrictions on Content and Materials."
**In compilations, derivations, or works using previously published material, the year of the first publication of the compilation or derivation work is sufficient. The date may be omitted where art work is reproduced on greeting cards, postcards, stationery, jewelry, dolls, toys, or any useful articles.

REMOVAL OR DESTRUCTION OF NOTICE

If the copyright notice is removed or destroyed without your approval, never fear, copyright protection is still available. In a case involving yardage, the copyright notice had been printed on the selvage edge of patterned cloth. The selvage was cut off in making dresses and the yardage copied. The court said that the removal of the copyright notice did not matter and the copyright protection was not lost.

OMMISSION OF COPYRIGHT NOTICE CAN BE CURED

Under the new law, the omission of copyright notice from works publicly distributed by the owner does not invalidate the work's copyright if:

- the omission is from a small number of works
- the registration of work is made within five years of publication and a reasonable effort is made to add notices to copies distributed
- the omission of notice violated a specific written provision that the work distributed bear notice (as in a publishing contract, where there was a requirement for notice that was not fulfilled)
- the notice is removed, obliterated, or destroyed without the copyright owner's permission

Thus, the situation presented in the old Picasso case would not have disastrous outcome today, since as of January 1, 1978, the omitted copyright notice can be added later. Under the old law, if the copyright notice was omitted from the work, you could not go back and cure the omission.

It does not matter if the omission was partial, total, unintentional, or deliberate. What is a "small number" of works or "reasonable effort" to add notice to all copies is unclear. Don't make trouble for yourself; put the full notice on your work when it is completed.

You might, before letting your work out of your sight, attach by tag the following notice (affix the appropriate copyright notice in the proper place as well):

Copyright © 1988 Martha Blue.

An express condition of any authorization to use this work is that the copyright notice in Martha Blue's name appear on all publicly distributed copies of this work in the format indicated above.

REGISTRATION

REGISTER PRIOR TO FILING SUIT

Publication with the complete notice gives the owner a valid copyright in the work *without* registration and deposit of copies. But, if you pick up a *Cheap Prints Catalogue* and see an exact copy of your copyrighted painting, *The Ghost at Coalmine Canyon*, being offered for sale as a reproduction, you canot file a suit for infringement until you have a Certificate of Registration, and you may lose some of the benefits of the act.

The simplest way to register and at the same time get the most protection is to deposit two copies* of the work along with the application and fee with the Copyright Office within three months of publication. This procedure also meets the copy deposit required for the Library of Congress collection.

DEPOSIT FOR LIBRARY OF CONGRESS COMBINED WITH REGISTRATION

Under the old law, deposit of copies for the collection of the Library of Congress and for purposes of copyright registration were taken as the same thing. The deposit of copies for the Library of Congress, Section 407 of the new act, may be required where the work is published in the United States with a notice of copyright, even if the copyright owner does not seek to register the work with the Copyright Office. Under Section 408 the copyright owner may be subject to certain penalties for failure to deposit following written demand by the registrar of copyrights. Deposit for Library of Congress can be combined with registration. But you can use the deposit accompanying an application for registration with the Copyright Office (Section 408) to satisfy the Library of Congress deposit provisions (Section 407). You only have to register with the Copyright Office:

---

*See later discussion of the deposit requirements, including acceptable copies. Some categories of material are exempt from the deposit of copies requirement, and identifying material may be deposited instead.

- If you want to take advantage of the five-year savings clause, that is, you have omitted the copyright notice and after curing the omission you must register.
- if the Copyright Office demands it.
- as a prerequisite to an infringement suit.
- if you want statutory attorneys' fees and damages (file within three months of publication) awarded in an infringement suit.
- if you want presumptive proof that you have a copyright, and the facts stated in the application are true.

EFFECTIVE DATE OF REGISTRATION

The effective date of copyright registration is the day on which an acceptable application, deposit, and fee have all been received in the Copyright Office. A delay in the effective date of registration can have serious consequences—for example, loss of statutory damages and attorneys' fees if work is not registered within three months of publication.

The application form consists of a single sheet, with spaces to be completed on the front and back. Detachable instructions are part of the form. There is a continuation sheet to use where more space is necessary.

Most applications will be submitted on one of these forms:

TYPES OF FORMS

- Form TX: for published and unpublished nondramatic literary works
- Form PA: for published and unpublished works of the performing arts (musical and dramatic works, pantomimes and choreographic works, motion pictures and other audiovisual works)
- Form VA: for published and unpublished works of the visual arts (pictorial, graphic, and sculptured works)
- Form SR: for published and unpublished sound recordings
- Form RE: for claims to renew copyright in works copyrighted under the old law

Two other forms are provided for special situations:

- Form CA: for supplementary registration to correct or amplify information given in the Copyright Office record of an earlier
- Form GR/CP: an adjunct application to be used for registration of a group of contributions to periodicals

Write the Copyright Office, Library of Congress, Washington, D.C. 20559 for free copies of the forms. Information specialists will answer your questions from 8:00 a.m. to 7:00 p.m. (703/557-8700).

GROUP REGISTRATION

You can register "a group of related works" under a single registration. The legislative report on the new law included as examples a group of related jewelry designs, a group of photographs by one photographer, and a series of related greeting cards. Registration of a group of works under a single registration saves time, money, and paperwork.*

DEPOSIT REQUIREMENT

In general, the material to be deposited is one complete copy of an unpublished work and two complete copies of a published work. There are some exceptions. One copy of greeting cards, postcards, stationery, labels, ads, scientific drawings, and globes may be deposited. Since actual copies of certain two- and three-dimensional works such as jewelry, ceramics, sculptures, and so forth would be impractical, a substitute for an actual copy, called identifying material, is allowed.

If the work is published as a reproduction, you'll have to send two actual reproductions, or one, if an unpublished production. For works published in five copies or less or in limited, numbered editions, you may deposit one copy (outside the numbered series, but identical) or identifying reproductions. For unpublished pictorial and graphic works, you can also use identifying materials. Generally, for the artist and

---

*Check with the Copyright Office for a copy of their current regulations on registration for a group of related works and their deposit requirements, which change.

craftmaker, the substitute can be photographs, slides, or drawings. The photographs or transparencies (slides) should meet the following requirements:

- they should be in the actual colors of the pictorial or graphic work.
- they should be complete, that is, clearly show the work.*
- slides must be at least 35mm and mounted if 3 by 3 inches or less.
- photographs should be not less than 5 by 7 inches or more than 9 by 12 inches—preferably 8 by 10 inches.
- the title and one or more dimensions of the work should be indicated on one copy.
- the image must be life-size** or if less, must be large enough to show clearly the entire copyrightable content of the work.
- the position of the copyright notice must be shown on one copy.***

The above is an example of an alternate deposit instead of the work itself, and would be appropriate for an unpublished motion picture, for certain pictorial and graphic works of limited copies or editions, very valuable work, three-dimensional works, and oversize works, et cetera.

I suggest that you write the Copyright Office for their updated deposit regulation before you send in a registration.

You should send all of the registration materials—the application, deposit, and required fees—in one package with the proper postage.

If this process seems confusing to you, you are not alone. As a result of the 1976 revisions, new forms and new procedures became mandatory, and there were ensuing complications. The Copyright Office sent out a public notice which explained that less than 20 percent of all the applications the office received could be acted on without correspondence to correct errors or to get missing information, and the communications created an enormous backlog of work. The deposit requirements are always in a state of flux, so watch for changes. Finally, be patient. It takes two to three months to get a registration back from the Copyright Office, even when it is filled out properly.

TERM OF COPYRIGHT

Copyright protection under the new law lasts for:

LIFE PLUS 50 OR 75/100 TERMS

- a basic term of life of the author plus fifty years after death.
- fifty years from the death of last author of a joint work.
- the shorter of seventy-five years from publication or one hundred years from creation for works for hire or anonymous and pseudonymous works.
- life plus 50 or 75/100 terms for unpublished or uncopyrighted works in existence before 1978.†

EXTENSION OF TERM FOR SOME COPYRIGHTED WORKS UNDER THE OLD LAW

Under the old law the first term of copyright was twenty-eight years, renewable for an additional twenty-eight years. Now those old copyrighted works (pre-1950) which were renewed prior to 1978 will be protected for seventy-five years from the date of the original copyright; and works copyrighted between 1950 and 1977 are extended forty-seven years *if* a valid renewal registration is made by December 31 of the twenty-eighth year.

The heart of the new copyright law is the grant of certain exclusive rights to the copyright owner. The exclusive rights of an author are broadly stated:

EXCLUSIVE RIGHTS OF COPYRIGHT OWNER

- to reproduce the copyrighted work in copies or phonorecords
- to prepare derivative works††

---

*If a design on a cup is being copyrighted, for example, the design should be clear.
**Does not apply to slides.
***If the size or the position of the copyright notice makes it difficult to see the notice, then you should attach a drawing showing the exact appearance, notice content, its dimensions, and its specific position.

†All pre-January 1, 1978, created but unpublished works are guaranteed copyright protection, until December 31, 2002, and if published prior to that date, the term is extended to 2027.

††Writers traditionally assign these rights to publishers.

- to distribute to the public
- to perform publicly
- to display publicly certain works

For example, the creator of a batik entitled *Three Women of Africa* could sell the piece to Ms. A, assign reproductions rights to Terrible Towel Manufacturing Co., and keep the other exclusive rights for herself. The sale of any part of the copyright must be in writing and signed by the party making the transfer.

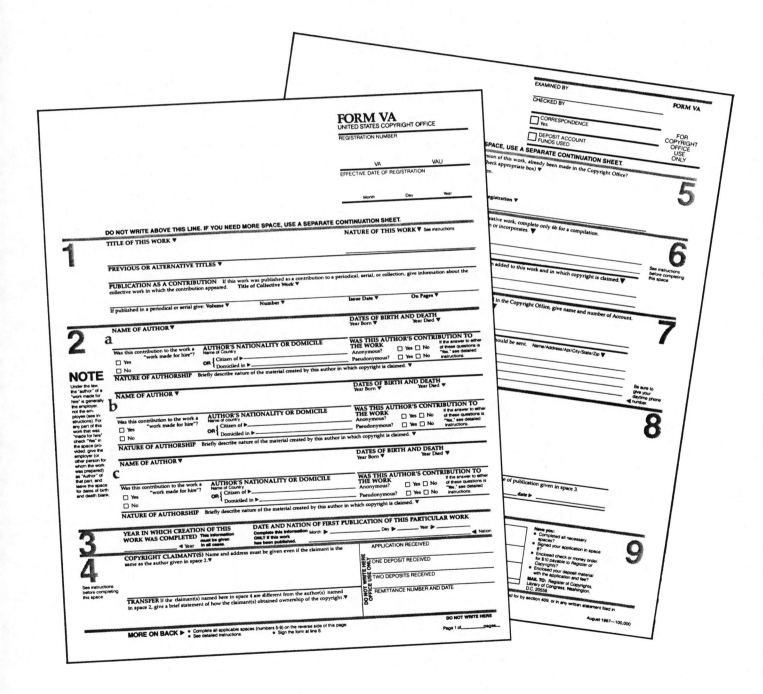

Figure 3.2 Visual Arts Copyright Registration Form

INFRINGEMENT

The new law provides that "anyone who violates any of the exclusive rights of the copyright owner. . .is an infringer of copyright." The copyright owner may file an infringement action in federal court against the infringer within three years from the date of the infringement.

EXAMPLES OF INFRINGEMENT

The following cases illustrate fact patterns of successful infringement actions: A copyrighted wall-covering design consisting of a grid of bamboo poles superimposed on three stripes was infringed upon by another wallpaper with similar design, medium, and colors, even though it had variations in size, spacing, and detail of the bamboo. A copyrighted rubber doll was protected against an infringer's doll. Even though the dolls were not identical in sculptural detail, it was still apparent that the infringer's doll was derived from the creator's.

INFRINGER MUST HAVE HAD ACCESS TO WORK

One thing the copyright owner must show in an infringement action is that the infringer somehow had access to the work, and, indeed, copied it. An independent creation of an identical work is not an infringement.

The major defense to infringement is the fair-use doctrine, which the courts developed under the old law and which was made an express part of the new law.

Fair use* allows others to use your copyrighted work without your permission. It is permissible to copy a small part of it for criticism and comment, scholarship, research, news reporting, and teaching (including multiple copies for classroom use). If you are unsure whether your proposed use is *fair,* or if you want to do a substantial amount of copying, then you should get permission from the copyright owner.** An overly simple permission form follows.

Dear _____ :
    I would like to use the following material in a book entitled _____ (TITLE) ____
that I am preparing to be published by _____ (PUBLISHER) _____ .
                            (DESCRIBE THE MATERIAL TO BE USED.)
    My book will be published in _____ (DATE) _____ at a list price of
_____ . It will be distributed _____ (TERRITORY) ____ .
    The material would be used in future revision and editions of the work. Should you not have sole control over these rights, would you let me know whom else I should contact.
    Unless you object, I will use the following credit line _____ .
_____ and copyright notice _____
    Thank you for your assistance. Enclosed for your convenience is a self-addressed, stamped envelope and copy of this letter for your files.
                            Sincerely yours,

                            _____
                            Writer
    I (we) grant the permission for use as requested above
and I (we) control those rights.
                            _____ (SIGNATURE) _____
    Date _____ _____ (PRINT NAME) _____

FAIR-USE DEFENSE

Courts consider these factors in each case to determine if the use is fair:

- purpose and character of use (whether of a commercial or noncommercial nature)
- nature of copyrighted work
- amount and substantiality of portion used in relation to the whole of the copyrighted work
- effect of use on potential market for value of copyrighted work

*For more information on fair use, see Chapter 7, "Especially for Writers."
**For a small fee, the reference division of the Copyright Office will search its own records to determine the ownership of a copyright. See Circular 22 for information.

A simple test for infringement is whether an ordinary observer, looking at the two works, would believe one is copied from the other. Thus, size does not matter, nor does a change in media, such as making a photograph of a painting. Altering trivial amounts of the original work is another ineffective technique. Forget the comment artists often make that all you have to do is change three parts of a work to beat the infringement rap! If a collage is made up of many copyrighted works, there could still be an infringement if any of the original works could be recognized.

If the use was not fair and there is infringement, then the court can:

- halt the infringer's activities
- in extreme cases impound and destroy copies, plates, et cetera of the infringer
- award damages
- award costs and attorneys' fees

Generally, there are three methods of measuring damages in a suit for copyright infringement:

- the copyright holder's out-of-pocket loss
- the infringer's profit
- damages provided by law (statutory damages)

Under statutory damages, the minimum award is $250 and the maximum award is $10,000 for each incident of infringement. If the infringement is willful, then the statutory damages can be increased to $50,000, but an *innocent* infringer could end up paying as little as $100 in statutory damages for each act of infringement.

Like a ferris wheel that rises from the ground to the sky, damages awarded in infringement cases vary from *low* ($250 to cartoonist whose cartoon was copied in political campaign literature and $3,000 plus $10,000 in attorney's fees awarded for infringing the copyright in dolls) to *high* ($50,000 statutory damages plus $19,000 attorney's fees against a defendant who persisted in infringing copyrighted fabric designs, and $430,000 against *Hustler* magazine based on the deliberate use of photographs).

In a recent lawsuit against the University of Virginia, the recovery of statutory damages and attorney's fees was barred for infringement of photographs that occurred before the copyright was registered. The continued use of photographs after registration did not re-establish the right to recover statutory damages and attorney's fees.

Although filing for a copyright is relatively simple, an action for infringement is complicated, so see a lawyer.

Alice's Allegory #9 or Coping with Copyright

After consulting with her lawyer Alice put the copyright notice on all her work, but only registered the scenarios on her production pieces, for example, her superficial forest of hearts and rainbows. For each scenario she sent photographs along with the fee and application within three months of completion. She hand-lettered a plaque for her studio wall:

Alice's copyright sign

CANADIAN COPYRIGHT ACT	In 1832, the Legislature of Lower Canada enacted the first copyright legislation in Canada. Various acts and amendments continued until the Copyright Act of 1921, which became effective January 1, 1924. This 1921 act was more favorable to authors than the pre-existing law and created copyright in Canada in every original literary, dramatic, musical and artistic work if the author met certain nationality or residence requirements. Thus, under the Canadian Copyright Act, the author is the first owner of the copyright in the work. Canada adheres to the Berne Convention; therefore, Canadian authors, artists, and composers have full copyright protection in countries following the Berne Convention, which requires no marking other than that that is required in the country the protection is sought. Furthermore, United States citizens are also entitled to full protection of the Canadian Copyright Act without any formalities, by action by the Canadian government. While copyright markings are
COPYRIGHT MARKINGS	not required in Canada, under the Universal Copyright Convention (which extends rights to some foreign countries), copyright markings *are* required in order to protect published works. (Canada is a signatory to the Universal Copyright Convention [UCC].) The marking required in the U.S. and under the UCC is ©, name of owner, and year of first publication. Under Canadian law, copyright protection lasts the life of the author plus 50 years. Fair dealing or fair use under Canadian copyright law is considered to be the use made of a copyrighted work, without such use infringing the copyright.
CANADA REQUIRES ORIGINALITY	The Canadian act's requirement of originality means that the product must originate from the author in the sense that it is the result of a degree of skill, industry, or experience employed by the author and that is not copied from another or not in the public domain. Copyright in Canada, as in the United States, has nothing to do with the merits of the work.
OWNERSHIP OF COPYRIGHT	Ownership of copyright is not affected by physical transfer of the subject. Also, the right to publish, to produce, or to reproduce a work is vested in the owner of the copyright, and the act provides that the author of the work shall be the first owner of the copyright. The author is generally the person who actually writes, draws, or composes the work. Works of joint authorship are produced by collaboration of two or more authors, in which the contribution of one is not distinct from the contribution of the others. Where ghost writers are used (cases in which a well-known person gives material for a story or article to a writer, who then actually composes the work), the copyright is not in the person's experiences, but only in the literary form or expression which clothes those experiences, and therefore copyright belongs to the writer. An older case involving a well-known jockey, Steve Donahue, illustrates this concept. Donahue related his experiences to a journalist, who thus wrote about these experiences, sometimes in the form of dialogue, and published the stories in the newspaper. The copyright was held to be the journalist's who wrote and published the material.
AUTHOR OF PHOTOS UNDER CANADIAN LAW	In the case of photographs, under the present act, the person who owns the original negative from which the photograph is derived at the time the negative is made is the author. However, if the photograph or portrait was ordered and paid for by a person for valuable consideration pursuant to that order, then it belongs to the person who ordered it. In ordinary situations, the customer goes in to sit for a photograph, orders copies, and pays for them, and therefore the customer owns the negative. However, if the photographer photographs celebrities, then the celebrity might be photographed at the request of the photographer and there may be no payment, as the photographer would own the negatives as well as the reproduction rights.
STATUS OF EMPLOYEE AS AUTHOR	The fact of employment has a definite effect on the first ownership of copyright. Where a work is made when the author is in the employment of a person or company under a contract of service or apprenticeship and is accomplished during the course of the employment, the employer, in the absence of an agreement, is the first owner of the copyright. The contract must be a contract *of* service and not a contract *for* services. Some of the factors considered by the Canadian courts in making

this determination are the existence of direct control by the employer, the degree of independence on the part of the person who rendered services, the place where the services were rendered, and so forth. The term "absence of agreement to the contrary" presents problems, as inferences of intention have been drawn and implications made. There have been some Canadian cases in which a person was employed to execute work as an independent contractor, but the work has been held to be the property of the person who paid for the work. It is best to provide in writing that the copyright belongs to the creator.

Neither the Universal Copyright Convention nor the Berne Convention require registration, therefore Canadian copyright is considered a proprietary right that arises from authorship alone; it is sometimes called an "automatic" copyright. Registration in Canada becomes important since in a copyright infringement action the only remedy against a defendant who says he didn't know a copyright existed and that there were no reasonable grounds to suspect copyright was in the work is an injunction to stop the offender's use of the work. A certificate of registration of copyright from the Copyright Office, which can supply appropriate forms for registration, is *prima facie* evidence of ownership—this means that it can be rebutted by other evidence.

The act further provides that "copyright in a work shall be deemed to be infringed by any person who, without the consent of the owner of the copyright, does anything the sole right to do which is by this Act is conferred on the owner of the copyright." This includes, under Canadian Law, the right to produce, reproduce, perform, or publish any translation of the work; to convert a dramatic work into a novel or other non-dramatic work; to convert a work into a dramatic work by way of performance in public or otherwise; to make any record or do other things by means of which the work may be mechanically performed or delivered; to present the work cinematographically; or to communicate such work by radio communication, among other things. Copying—which includes copying of the whole work or parts of it—is the essential element. Copying parts of it means a *substantial* part, and refers to quality as well as quantity. The purpose for which the work is taken will affect the question of infringement. It is equally as important as the issue of competition, but the absence of competition is not a defense.

Fair use of works published earlier is allowed. For instance, in an infringement of copyright case involving a compilation of biographical sketches of Canadian politicians, the court said that the compiler, if he obtains the information from common, independent sources open to all and does not save himself labor by making a copy of plaintiff's book, will not infringe upon an extant copyright. Remember that the right to copy is the central issue, and therefore, if a photographer or a painter takes a photograph of an object that has already been photographed, or draws an object that has already been drawn, there is no infringement.

In summary then, the Canadian Copyright Act provides that the author of the work shall be the first owner of the copyright except in the case of engravings, photographs, or portraits, where the print or other original was ordered and made for valuable consideration and in cases where the author was in the employment of some other person under a contract of service or apprenticeship, and the work was made in the course of that employment.

The Canadian Copyright Act has adopted *droit morale* in its provision that "independently of the author's copyright, and even after the assigment, either wholly or partially of the said copyright, the author shall have the right to claim authorship of the work, as well as the right to restrain any distortion, mutilation or other modification of the said work which would be prejudicial to his honor or reputation."

Some lawyers say copyrighting in the United States is almost the reverse of copyrighting in Canada, for in the former you have to affix notice or mark the copyright, while in Canada you automatically receive copyright by virtue of creating a work.

CANADIAN REGISTRATION

INFRINGEMENT UNDER CANADIAN LAW

SUMMARY OF CANADIAN COPYRIGHT LAW

DROIT MORALE IN CANADIAN LAW

PATENTS   Protection from copying is, in certain situations, provided by patents.

Dear Ms. Spinner:

Thank you for your recent inquiry about whether you could get a patent for your gerbil-powered spinning wheel and your solar-operated, vegetable-dye-extractor bath. I can't tell if you could patent either of these inventions, but if you will read the enclosed information on patents, you will get some information on patent history, the patent lingo, the steps in obtaining a patent, and where to find legal assistance. Unfortunately, patents are often overlooked by the creative person. Often artists, potters, weavers, and woodcarvers invent processes, equipment, or improvements in doing their work. Sometimes a spouse, lover, housemate, or friend executes the idea, and if it works, pretty soon other artists or craftmakers want to use it.

Beware of patent marketing companies. Don't send your idea to some person or company unless you indicate in writing that the idea is not to be used or disclosed without mutual agreement of the parties. Frequently, early contacts between an inventor and a prospective purchaser of the idea are accompanied by nondisclosure agreements, in which the person to whom the invention is shown agrees not to make it public. If you get a patent, you could sell it to a company or let someone else develop it for you under some profit-splitting arrangement. Some patents are the subject of litigation after issuance and you may want a big company involved in protecting that patent. Good luck.

From
The Chatty Lawyer
Syndicated Column

DEFINITION   A patent is an agreement between an inventor and the public (represented by the government) that permits the inventor to make, use, and sell an invention for a certain

HISTORY   period. Early "patents" were granted around the year 600 B.C. in the Republic of Sibari in southern Italy. There, cooks who invented an especially choice dish were allowed exclusive use of the invented dish for one year in order to encourage others to invent new recipes.

In the fifteenth century the Venetian Republic began a regular system of providing grants and privileges to persons who originated and discovered new techniques. In 1624, the first British statute was adopted; then various colonies in the United States began to issue patents. In 1790, the first American patent statute was adopted.

After a flurry of patent activity in the United States, the first commissioner of patents, Henry L. Ellsworth, in his 1843 annual report stated, "The advancement of the arts from year to year, taxes our credulity and seems to presage the arrival of that period when human improvement must end." Quite to the contrary, patents

PATENTED ITEMS   have run the gamut from A to Z. For instance, patents have been obtained for the zipper (which was discovered by two violinists), the coat hanger, DDT, foam rubber, insulin, solar devices, the incandescent light bulb, television, xerography, steamboats, and the telephone. I saw and talked to a craft street vendor who had a patent on a self-leveling plant shelf.

PHILOSOPHY OF A PATENT   By obtaining a patent, the inventor is granted a right for seventeen years to exclude others from making, using, or selling the defined invention in the United States. In return, the public receives a full disclosure of the invention, which then fosters technical progress.

RECORD KEEPING   First put your ideas on paper and have them witnessed by an outsider capable of understanding them *at the earliest possible moment.*

Keep a bound notebook. Make your entries chronologically. Don't leave blank pages in the notebook. If you have not worked for several days, make an entry to that effect. If you attach a photo or drawing to the notebook, make sure you write the identifying remarks on the additions, so that they are placed on both the addition and in the notebook.

Steps to Obtaining a Patent*

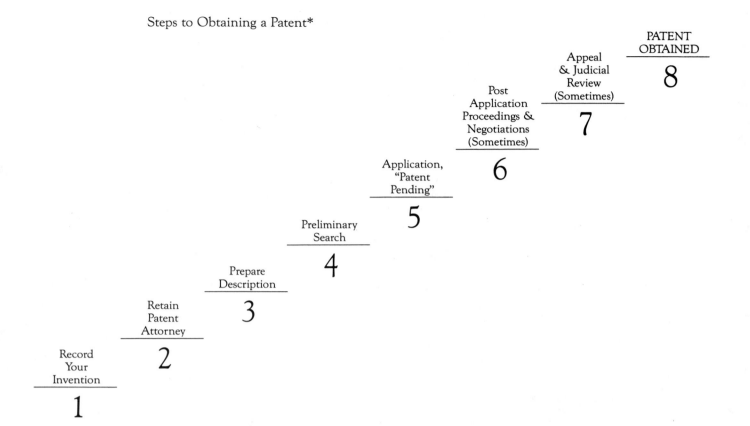

Accurate, on-the-spot record keeping will help you prove you invented the item first. This record keeping gives you evidence of creation plus a basis for the patent search and even preparation of the patent application. Remember the old saying in the patent world: When a man becomes an inventor, he is a dead witness.

RETAIN AN ATTORNEY

Obtaining a patent requires the services of a patent attorney. The attorneys' fees will be considerable. The Patent and Trademark Office as well as your State Bar Association can provide you with the names and addresses of patent attorneys and agents (who are not attorneys) but who are licensed to prosecute patent applications before the Patent and Trademark Office.

IDEA BROKERS

Be very cautious of idea brokers—they have been criticized by the press, involved in numerous lawsuits, and investigated by the Federal Trade Commission. The fraudulent idea brokers give you a glowing report on your invention, ask for $1,000 to $2,000 from you in order to obtain a patent, and do nothing. On the other hand, there are invention brokers who work solely on a contingent-fee basis, with any charge consisting of a part of the patent earnings. Before parting with any of your money, check out the company or person with your Attorney Generals Office and government regulatory agencies.**

WORKING WITH YOUR ATTORNEY

After hiring a lawyer you will need to tell him or her if you know of related devices or whether your invention is an improvement or modification of a prior device, and if so, what the patent numbers are. Also provide the attorney with any literature, articles, and publications relating to the invention, or any other invention like it.

Your attorney should make a preliminary determination concerning the patentability of your invention. Then you and your attorney should decide if you can make

*The U.S. Patent and Trademark Office, Washington, D.C. 20231 has a pamphlet called *General Information Concerning Patents* which you can send for.
**See Chapter 8, "Obtaining Legal Assistance," for a discussion of state and federal regulatory agencies.

enough money from the patented product to make patenting it worthwhile. An automated Tibetan prayer wheel may not have much of a market in the United States, for example.

WHAT CAN BE PATENTED

The subject of a U.S. patent can be "any new and useful process, machine, manufacture, or composition of matter, or any new and useful improvement thereof." It also must satisfy the requirements of *utility, novelty,* and *nonobviousness.* Some classes of subject matter cannot be patented: printed matter, naturally occurring substances such as elements, methods of doing business, ideas, scientific principles, and mental processes.

Even if your invention is a proper subject for patent, you may be denied a patent because you have not met other technical objections to the issuance of a patent, such as anticipation, prior printed publication, public use, on sale one year prior to date of patent application, abandonment, prior foreign patenting, prior inventor, noninventor (applicant did not invent), priority, and obviousness. These are technical terms which your own patent attorney will explain to you.

DESCRIPTION AND SEARCH

Once a complete description of the invention is developed, a preliminary search, called a patentability search or "prior art search," is made at the U.S. Patent Office to determine if the invention is old or obvious. This a search* by a patent lawyer or an associate to determine whether the invention is patentable. The searcher tries to find the patents closest to the invention. Then the patent attorney should be able to decide if the invention is patentable or not; and if patentable, the scope of patent protection. If you can get a patent, then you should reevaluate whether it is financially worth pursuing a patent.

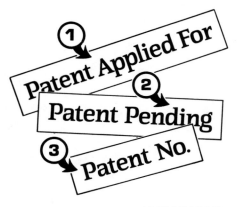

If so, the next step is to prepare and file a patent application along with the filing fees of $300; some of the patent application documents require fine technical writing and illustration. Usually a draft patent application is done by the attorney for the inventor to review, and then the draft is revised for the final application. A "Patent pending" mark may be put on an invention only after the application has been filed.** It only serves to give the public notice that someone utilizing the invention after the patent issues runs the risk of infringement. Before a patent issues, anyone may make, use, or sell the invention without liability. Times for issuance of patent vary.

AMENDMENTS

An examiner with the Patent Office reviews the patent application and often will reject all or part of a patent claim, saying that the prior art teaches the claimed invention. The claim can be amended, and the amendments relate back to the original filing date of the patent application. In about one out of twenty applications, interference proceedings start. This means that more than one inventor has filed a patent application on the same invention. There are two important dates in interference proceedings: the date of conception*** and date of filing the patent application.

INTERFERENCE PROCEEDINGS

APPEALS

About 50 percent of all patent claims are finally rejected by the patent examiner, and often these claims are more favorably received by the Patent Office Board of Appeals. Remember, during the processing of a patent application there is some "horse trading," for often the claim is overly broad in a patent application. This means that the Patent Office will allow you to keep part of your claim if you agree to delete other parts of the claim. The fee is $500 for issuing each original patent.

The patent system added the fuel of interest to the fire of genius ABE LINCOLN, *himself a patentee*

Alice's Allegory #10 or Alices Brainstorm

One day Alice had Romero build her this fantastic potter's wheel that she had dreamt about, and it was like no other. For one thing, it was powered by solar energy and its alternate energy was a motion machine operated by a three-

*There are many kinds of searches done.
**If you put the "Patent pending" mark on your invention before filing, you are guilty of a misdemeanor and subject to a $500 fine for each violation.
***The uncorroborated testimony of the inventor is not worth much as far as the conception date. That is why record keeping is important.

year-old child. Then feeling moved to words, Alice wrote a monograph on developing tools and equipment for craftmakers. At the next craft fair, Alice and Romero sold a lot of pots because they demonstrated their new wheel and gave out copies of their monograph.

Mr. Noit came up to them at the crafts fair and said, "I don't see any 'patent pending' sign on this. Gee, I've had the same idea as this." He talked awhile and left. Alice called her lawyer and said, "How can we protect this?" He gave her the name of a patent attorney, Pat Bond, and Romero and she talked him into doing a trade of pots and half cash for a patent application.

DESIGN PATENTS

You can protect your design by design patent rather than copyright. Design patents have been granted for designs in wearing apparel, fabrics, lampshades, jewelry, a round box with decorative features, a reclining chair, outward configurations of lawn mowers, shoulder rope for a military uniform, and a lamp with metal sleeves. Design patents can be obtained by: "Whoever invents any new, original, and ornamental design for an article of manufacture. . . ." In order to be a valid subject for a design patent, the design must be:

STATUTORY DEFINITION OF DESIGN PATENT

ELEMENTS OF A DESIGN PATENT

- new or novel—a different design from others.
- original—with the author.
- ornamental—the product of authentic skill and artistic conception.
- inventive in character—beyond the skill of an ordinary designer.

The design is the visual features of an object which can be the applied surface ornamentation or the work's shape or both. The purpose of the design patent law is to encourage the decoration of manufactured articles. A design patent application follows the same steps as patents for inventions, but the filing fee is $125, and $175 for issuing a design patent. Design patents have a fourteen-year term of protection.

Sometimes you should get a design patent instead of a copyright. For instance, a court recently concluded that plaintiff's creation of a design for distinctive footwear ("mitten toe socks" and "glove socks") was not infringed by defendant's manufacture of socks with compartments for toes. The court noted that copyright of the legwear drawings protected the expression of the idea, but the general concept could get protection only through a patent. Can you get both a copyright and design patent in one work? Prior to 1978 you could. For instance, the designer of a novelty watch bearing a caricature of Spiro T. Agnew applied for, and finally received, both a copyright and a design patent. It is unclear under the new law if you can still get both.

DESIGN PATENT OR COPYRIGHT?

In a recent case under the old copyright law, the plaintiff developed a kite design that could be manufactured out of only one piece of fabric, and in the process of applying for a patent, the Patent Office printed a written description of the kite in its official journal. A publishing company reproduced the patent text in one of its publications. The plaintiff had not copyrighted the text but argued that he had protection under common law copyright, and the court agreed that he did, for he had not published the work by just describing its use in a patent application. Under the new copyright law there also would probably be no publication, because the patent statutes require publication of patent applications in a government journal, and there is no commercial distribution there for the creator. Since the kite design was unpublished under the new law, it would have copyright protection and there would be infringement.

The following chart will give you an idea of how the two protections compare:

COPYRIGHT	DESIGN PATENT
• courts often find infringement	• courts rarely find infringement
• cheap and simple to get (use for seasonal items)	• long and expensive to get (not good for seasonal items)
• protects against slavish copying	• broader protection from copying
• protects against persons who have access	• protects against persons who each reached idea on own
• no invention requirements	• invention requirements
• term: life plus fifty years	• term: maximum is fourteen years

A test for a design patent is whether the work impresses the ordinary person with its uniqueness of character. Forget a design patent if the design is primarily functional. Consider it if the design is novel and non-obvious.

Generally, for the artist and craftmaker it is simpler and cheaper to get protection with a copyright.*

WHEELING AND DEALING A PATENT

USE A LAWYER FOR SALE OR MARKETING AGREEMENT ON PATENTS

If you do have a patent, you may be stuck in a big-guy/little-guy situation. You may not have the money to market the invention or defend it. For instance, Alexander Graham Bell defended his patent in many suits. If you turn to a big guy with your patent, be sure to use the services of a competent lawyer to negotiate any agreement regarding the patent. Some alternative arrangements would be to:

- sell the patent outright.
- enter into a development and marketing arrangement under a profit-splitting agreement.
- give a company the patent to develop and market for a specific time, with ownership and partial profits (royalty) to come back to you.

PATENT INFRINGEMENT

DAMAGE AWARD

The unauthorized making, using, or selling of your patented invention during its term gives you the right to bring an infringement action. You have six years from the date of infringement to file a suit. It is not uncommon for the validity of a patent to be tested through litigation. The court can stop the infringement and award money damages. You should see a patent lawyer if you have this problem. Patent litigation is costly and complex.

CANADIAN LAW—PATENT

Canadian courts in the patent area tend to follow the decisions of the United States Supreme Court, as the experience of American courts is greater and the United States is Canada's largest trading partner.

TRADE SECRETS

Alice's Allegory #11 or The Sky Blue Trade Secret

Alice's friend, Marlene the Batikist, had long had a secret process for obtaining sky blue in her batiks. It was a carefully guarded secret and all her assistants were warned not to reveal it, but the young man, George, who helped remove the wax, became involved in the process when the batikists had a very large order for a batiked mural for the ceiling of a Moroccan restaurant called Henry-Lamb-Eggplant. Now curious George did not forget the process and showed it to some commercial department store batikists—competitors—who called Marlene when they were drunk and said, "Wow, your sky blue process is great and now we have got the secret from our spy, and have made 100 batiks using it."

Marlene got an injunction from the court to stop her competitors from using her trade secret.

---

*37 CFR Sec. 202.10. Pictorial Graphic and Sculptural Works. "The potential availability of protection under the design patent law will not affect the registrability of a pictorial, graphic or sculptural work, but a copyright claim in a patented design or in the drawings or photographs in a patent application will not be registered after the patent has been issued."

Besides protection under patent law, one may have a common law right in an invention that the state courts will protect through the theory of trade secrets. A trade secret is information generally not known in a trade. Trade secrets which have been protected by the courts are chemical formulas, customer lists, customer credit ratings, blueprints, architectural plans, patterns, unpatentable or unpatented designs, inventions, advertising slogans, and other information. Examples of long-standing trade secrets are the formulas for Coca-Cola® and Smith's Black Cough Drops® (which are over one hundred years old). Trade-secrets protection can last longer than the seventeen years of a patent. Some trade secrets have died away—for example, knowledge of pigment compositions by Old Master painters. The Romans controlled the entire line of possessors of a trade secret by slavery and the Anglo-Saxons used guilds. In modern times you can file a lawsuit against a person who discloses or uses your trade secret without your permission. Usually the person would have acquired the secret improperly either by theft or by receiving the information in confidence with the understanding that he or she would not disclose the information.

WHAT ARE TRADE SECRETS

PROTECTED TRADE SECRETS

If you think your business involves valuable trade secrets, then watch the number of persons you share the secret with and have employees at the time you hire them sign a written contract that they will not disclose the secret.

CONTRACT TO PROTECT TRADE SECRETS

Canada has a civil and criminal law on trade secrets, the Trade Secrets Production Act, with definitive statutory torts and criminal offenses.

CANADIAN LAW—TRADE SECRETS

Another source of protection from misuse of your work by others is the remedy of unfair competition. Unfair competition has been found by the courts in the following cases:

UNFAIR COMPETITION

- passing off a product of another as yours
- false or misleading advertising
- running down your competitor's goods or reputation
- trade secrets in unpatented and unpatentable items
- interference with the business growth of another
- unfair use of written works
- obstruction of competitor's suppliers
- bribing customers of competitors
- unfair usage of imported products
- boycott
- price wars
- unfounded patent litigation
- copying or simulating a trade name or title

EXAMPLES OF
UNFAIR COMPETITION

If you think that you have a claim for unfair competition, ask yourself the following questions:

- has the design of the offending article been taken from yours?
- has the offending work been compared to your original work?
- does the overall appearance of the offending copy strike you as an attempt to pass it off as the original?
- does the copy have the same design but inferior workmanship and are the materials the same as the original?
- has there been trade libel or price cutting?
- would the average person be taken in by the similarity?

An example of unfair competition would be a pumpkin-shaped, machine-woven, quilted tea cozy produced by Palm Off, Inc., that is the exact replica of yours except that it uses synthetic fibers instead of handspun, plant dyed wool. It is advertised as "A $10.95 Exact Replica of the Famous Wovenwork's $49.95 Pumpkin Tea Cozy." If you think you have a case of unfair competition, see a lawyer for advice and assistance.

TRADEMARK AND TRADE NAMES

A clothier in Gloucestershire sold very good cloth so that in London if they saw any cloth of his mark they would buy it without searching thereof; and another who made ill cloth put the clothier's mark upon it without his privity, and an action was brought by him who bought the cloth for this deceit and adjudged maintainable.

Goodwill, trademarks, and trade names have always been closely related. Symbols information about the maker of goods. Examples include the marking of Etruscan cheese with the sign of the moon, marks on pottery found at the ancient sites of Ur, and the granting to George Washington of a trademark for his particular brand of flour.

There are both federal and state trademark and trade name statutes. If your business does not have nationwide scope or potential, then the state registration (if your state has a trademark or trade name law) will be simpler, cheaper, and probably adequate for your needs.

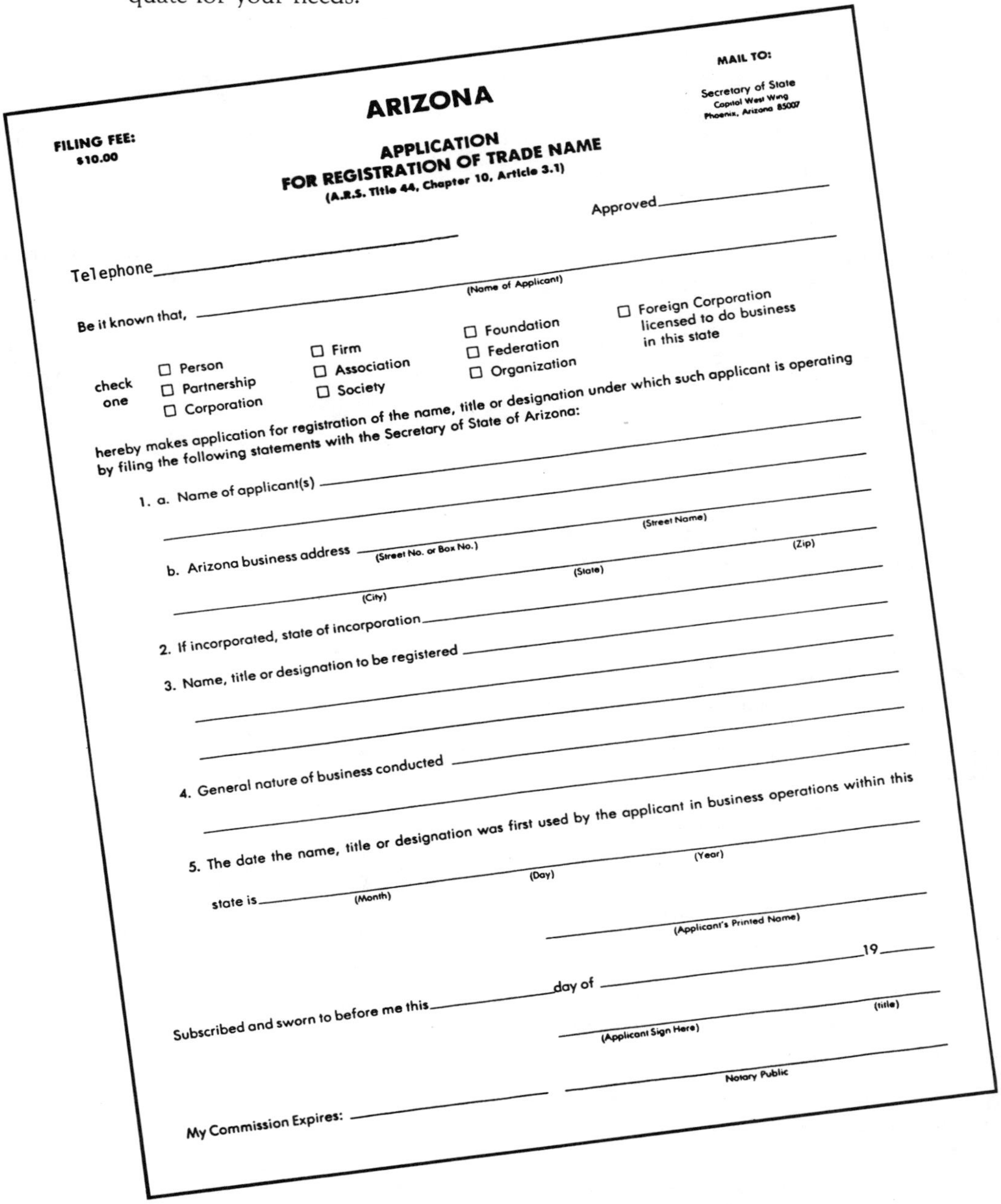

MAIL TO:
Secretary of State
Capitol West Wing
Phoenix, Arizona 85007

FILING FEE:
$10.00

ARIZONA

APPLICATION
FOR REGISTRATION OF TRADE NAME
(A.R.S. Title 44, Chapter 10, Article 3.1)

Approved__________

Telephone__________

Be it known that, __________ (Name of Applicant)

check one
☐ Person
☐ Partnership
☐ Corporation
☐ Firm
☐ Association
☐ Society
☐ Foundation
☐ Federation
☐ Organization
☐ Foreign Corporation licensed to do business in this state

hereby makes application for registration of the name, title or designation under which such applicant is operating by filing the following statements with the Secretary of State of Arizona:

1. a. Name of applicant(s) __________

b. Arizona business address __________ (Street No. or Box No.) (Street Name)

__________ (City) (State) (Zip)

2. If incorporated, state of incorporation__________

3. Name, title or designation to be registered __________

4. General nature of business conducted __________

5. The date the name, title or designation was first used by the applicant in business operations within this state is__________ (Month) (Day) (Year)

__________ (Applicant's Printed Name)

Subscribed and sworn to before me this__________day of __________19____

__________ (Applicant Sign Here) (title)

My Commission Expires: __________ __________ Notary Public

***Figure 3.3** Arizona application, Registration of Trade Name

While a trademark may consist of a name, trademarks and trade names differ technically. The same rules for trademarks, in most respects, govern trade names and both receive the same legal protection.

The advantages of a federal trademark are:

- more protection than under common law.
- nationwide protection.
- coverage for a broad class of symbols.
- possibly a treble damage award if you win a suit for infringement.
- attorneys' fees if infringer acts in bad faith.

A trademark is a visible symbol identifying and distinguishing your goods from similar goods of others. It can be a word, name (Sunoco, Kodak), phrase, sign or symbol (flying red horse, muscular arm with hammer), or all of these. Federal trademarks are available only for marks used in commerce between states, or with foreign nations or Indian tribes. The federal law concerning trademarks is called the Lanham Act.

A mark must be distinctive to be registered, and generally marks that are descriptive, deceptively misdescriptive, surnames, and geographical marks *are not* registrable. "Sawmotor," an oil additive for auto engines, was not registrable. "Old Country," a soap manufactured in the U.S., and "Syrup of Figs," a medicine containing few figs, were not registrable. You establish your rights in a trademark by adopting one that appears, after preliminary research, not to infringe on an existing trademark and by using it on goods in trade for a period of time. Only then may federal registration be sought. An informational pamphlet and applications can be obtained from the Patent and Trademark Office, Washington, D.C. 20231.

After your application is filed, it is examined, and if it is found not entitled to registration, then you are notified that you have six months to respond. There can be reexaminations and interference proceedings, as with patents. However, if you file an affidavit to contestability (a statement that the work has been used for five years prior to registration and that there have been neither adverse decisions regarding the ownership of the mark nor proceedings involving it), then no interference proceedings are allowed. If you achieve trademark registration, it is for a twenty-year term with additional twenty-year renewal terms. Upon receipt of trademark registration, you must put the notice of trademark, an R in a circle ®, or "Registered in U.S. Patent and Trademark Office" or "Reg. U.S. Pat. and Tm. Off." after every use of the trademark word or symbol.*

If you are considering a federal registration of your trademark or a lawsuit for trademark infringement, then you are involved in "big business" and can afford a qualified lawyer.**

Let's use an example illustrating some of the subjects discussed in this chapter. The creator of Free-of-Moths, which professes to keep weavers' wool free of moths, has developed an information card to be attached to the product. A patent application has been filed and is pending before the Patent Office. The card carries the trademark "Free-of-Moths," which is registered as indicated by the™ adjacent to the trademark. The content of the card is the proper subject matter for copyright registration, which copyright is indicated at the bottom of the card and is owned by the sole proprietor, Martha Blue, of the Free-of-Moths business.

Generally speaking, a Canadian trademark is used by a person to distinguish the person's ware or services from those of another, while a trade name is the name under which a business is carried on. Registration of a trademark is *prima facie* evidence of ownership. There are certain requirements, and if the Registrar of Trade Marks decides it should be allowed, then the mark is advertised in the Trade Marks Jour-

DEFINITION

LANHAM ACT

REQUIREMENTS FOR
REGISTRATION OF
A TRADEMARK

APPLICATION PROCESS

TWENTY-YEAR DURATION
PLUS RENEWAL

CANADIAN LAW—TRADEMARKS
& TRADENAMES

---

*The Law (In Plain English) for Craftspeople, by Leonard B. DuBoff (Madrona Publishers, 1984) has an in-depth discussion of trademarks on pages 21 to 29.
**37 CFR Sec. 220.10(c): "A claim to copyright cannot be registered in a print or label consisting solely of trademark subject matter and lacking copyrightable matter."

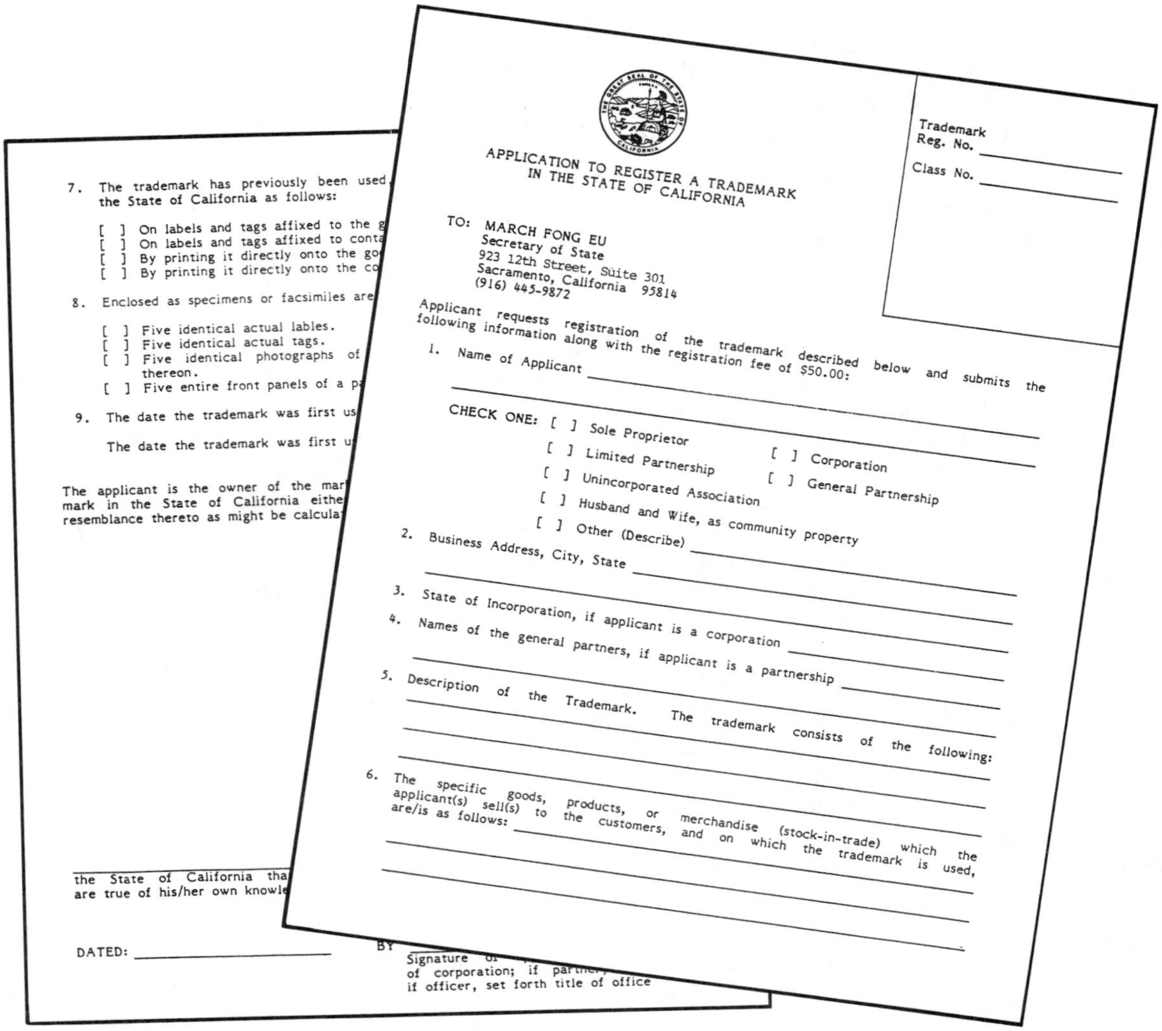

Figure 3.4 California application, Registration of Trademark

nal to allow others to oppose it. At the end of this process, the Registrar may issue a certificate of registration. The owner should maintain the mark and renew it at the end of 15 years.

FAKE OR FORGED ARTS AND CRAFTS

Last, but not least, you should exercise caution if your own work is copied from others' work.

More than collectors are concerned about fake or forged arts and crafts. As a result of the Indian arts and crafts boom, the distribution of forgeries reached epidemic proportions, and many groups—Native Americans, state attorney generals, and so forth—have acted to stem the tide of fakes that flooded the market place. The Zuni Tribe took action to stop a major nationwide department store from selling fake "Zuni" jewelry.

Generally, fakes and forgeries can be divided into three categories:

- deliberately fabricated work—this is work which is created to be sold as the product of another, e.g., Mexican-made rugs sold as Navajo rugs; old ivory carved and sold as ancient Eskimo art.
- exact replicas which are sold as originals—this is work that is executed in the style of a certain artist and sold as that artist's work, e.g., David Stein painted in the style of old masters and forged names to his works.

- altered art—the work is changed in order to enhance its value, e.g., when *The Misses Payne* by Sir Joshua Reynolds was restored, one of the figures was deleted; or a plain old Mimbres pot recently had a design painted on it.

These general federal and state antifraud laws require proof of fraudulent or criminal intent, which is difficult to show for many forgeries because the sellers usually avoid knowledge that the work is forged or faked.

FEDERAL AND STATE GENERAL ANTIFRAUD LAWS

On the federal level, there is the general antifraud law mentioned above and the Federal Trade Commission Act, which prohibits "unfair methods of competition in commerce and unfair or deceptive acts and practices." Under the act it is not necessary to show actual deception. It is sufficient if the activities have a capacity to deceive. The act is violated if there is a misrepresentation as to who created, designed, or manufactured a product. Be careful if you make "Indian goods," for the FTC has specific guidelines for Indian arts and crafts:

FTC GUIDELINES FOR INDIAN ARTS AND CRAFTS

- if sold as "Indian made," "Indian," or "American Indian," then the item must be handmade or handcrafted by Indian residents of the United States.
- if the product is made in part by machinery, then the item cannot be represented as Indian made except for those parts handmade or crafted by Indians. But if Indians played a part in the manufacture, this can be stated.
- if products contain foreign components, the country of origin must then be disclosed.

The FTC will not act unless the unfair competition or deceptive practices occur in interstate commerce* and concern "the public interest," that is, big-time operations. The FTC has declined to act on many of the complaints made to them because the offender's operation is too limited in scope and effect. If you have been victimized, go ahead and send your complaint letter** and ask the FTC to investigate the offender. If the FTC investigates, they may file a formal complaint, which costs you nothing, but even if they find wrongdoing, you will not get money damages. But if you are the violator, the FTC can stop your unfair or deceptive practices, plus you could receive a civil penalty of several thousand dollars for each separate violation.

FTC COMPLAINT PROCEDURES

Specifically directed to the Indian situation is the Indian Arts and Crafts Board*** Act which provides criminal penalties (up to $500, jail up to six months, or both) for representing goods as Indian products when the seller knew the goods were not Indian or were not Indian products of a particular tribe. Besides referring matters for prosecution, the board tries to bring the difference between genuine Indian products and imitations to public attention.

INDIAN ARTS AND CRAFTS BOARD ACT

The Lanham Trademark Act discussed earlier in this chapter can provide some direct relief to a wronged individual. Under this act, a person can recover damages if the offender has falsely represented, designated, or described goods in commerce. Also, you could get an order preventing further unfair or deceptive practices.

Several states have specific legislation dealing with the protection of Native American artists and crafts persons from unfair competition, along with criminal penalties for violations of their laws. However, enforcement of these statutes has proved a problem.

STATE LEGISLATION FOR INDIAN ARTS AND CRAFTS

State laws run the gamut from establishing identification marks for authentic native crafts to holding it unlawful to put out for sale imitation Indian arts or crafts which are not authentic. Some require imitation articles to be segregated from the authentic work or require the seller to label imitation work "not Indian made", "Imitation", "Indian Imitation", and "not genuine American Indian art or craft." Check with your lawyer.

---

*See previous discussion of interstate commerce in Chapter 2, "Legal Restrictions on Content and Materials."
**Send a copy of your letter to your friendly congressman or senator and request congressional attention.
***The board offers a special certification mark to use in marketing for Native-owned craft-marketing enterprises with registered trademarks and high-quality products.

OTHER STATE AUTHENTICITY LAWS

Some states have enacted special laws governing the sale of inauthentic artworks. These laws generally hold the seller of a work to his or her representations concerning the history and authenticity of the artwork. As discussed in Chapter 4, "Making Contracts," several warranty sections of the Uniform Commercial Code would also apply to the sale of fake or forged arts or crafts.

New York State also has a criminal law concerning the making or alteration of objects so that they appear rare, old, or authored by someone else or the issuance of a false certificate of authenticity of a fine work of art.

CHAPTER FOUR

Making Contracts

WHAT IS A CONTRACT

DEFINITION
WRITTEN CONTRACTS
WARRANTIES
CANADIAN LAW
FORMALITIES

A CONTRACT FOR EVERY OCCASION

DIRECT SALES
SALES THROUGH GALLERIES
SALES IN CANADA
COMMISSIONS
CONTRACTS WITH MUSEUMS
PUBLISHING CONTRACTS FOR ILLUSTRATORS AND PHOTOGRAPHERS
AGENTS, REPRESENTATIVES, AND DISTRIBUTORS
SHOWS
PRINTS
SELLING PHOTOGRAPHS

ENFORCING YOUR CONTRACTS

HELP FROM PRIVATE AND GOVERNMENTAL AGENCIES
GOING TO COURT IN THE UNITED STATES AND CANADA

LEGAL ADVICE? NOT ON YOUR LIFE.

WHAT IS A CONTRACT

Alice's Allegory #12 or Find the Contracts Hidden Below

Alice fueled up old Viola the VW for a trip into town to drop off some bowls and mugs at the Artists Coop. She dusted off her going-to-town costume and hoped that the hot-air balloons would be rising along the way.

Alice had breakfast at Mother Nurture and Son with a strawberry smoothie and the revitalizing combination of Mu-Ginseng tea to percolate her through her errands. She dropped off the pottery at the Coop and picked up all the local artsy gossip. Then to Bart's Art Supply, where Alice placed an order for some special glazes that Bart didn't have in stock. With fortunate timing, Alice drove home in the setting sun.

EXORCISE

The first step in understanding the basic law of contracts is to sit up straight, close your eyes, and EXORCISE all prior notions that you have concerning the law of contracts such as: all contracts must be written; you never made a contract in your life; contracts must be typed on white paper and be notarized; all contracts last forever; making a contract involves too much red tape; and so on. The discussion of the law of contracts that follows is a general one. State law varies so check with your lawyer for the provisions of your state's contract laws.

WARNING

Alice made at least four contracts on the day described above: a gas contract with Rainbow Hill Axon, a breakfast contract with Mother Nurture and Son, a consignment contract with the Artists Coop, and a special-order contract with Bart.

DEFINITION

Quite simply, a contract is an exchange of promises between two or more people which is enforceable by law. Had Alice forgotten to pay Mother Nurture, Mother could successfully sue her for the price of the breakfast. Although Alice did not say, "I hereby promise to pay Mother Nurture $1.50 if she delivers to my table a smoothie and tea," and although Alice and Mother Nurture did not sign a written contract, an agreement was made by the conduct of the parties and is legally enforceable.

IMPLIED CONTRACT

The abstract-contract-theory-in-the-sky requires five essential ingredients to make a legally enforceable contract:

- offer
- acceptance
- consideration
- competence
- legality

OFFER

An offer sounds like: "I will pay you $75 for a set of that wonderful green stoneware." An acceptance sounds like: "O.K." In some situations, the only way you can accept an offer is by taking action. A reward for a lost llama is this sort of offer. Consideration is what the parties to the contract promise to give each other, and it usually has a dollar-and-cents value. Sometimes consideration can take the form of refraining from action. "I will give you $10 if you stop smoking cigarettes," for example.

ACCEPTANCE

CONSIDERATION OF AN OFFER

Usually offers may be withdrawn at any time before acceptance. But once an offer is accepted, a contract is formed and the offer cannot be withdrawn. If Alice had changed her mind and decided to order the "Good Morning Special" at Mother Nurture's, she could not withdraw her offer and make a new offer after Mother Nurture had accepted Alice's first offer and put the strawberries in the blender. Of course, if Mother Nurture was agreeable, then Alice could withdraw her offer.

WISH ≠ OFFER

At Bart's Art Supply if Alice said, "It sure would be nice if you would order me some special glazes for that stoneware order," and Bart had said, "O.K.," there would be no contract, because Alice's statement was not an offer, only a wish. To make an offer, you must make a firm, definite promise. If there is a disagreement over whether an offer was made, the courts will look to the demonstrated *intent* of those involved. If Bart ordered the glazes anyway, he could not force Alice to purchase them, nor could Alice force Bart to get the glazes for her, because no contract was formed. However, since Alice made an offer—"I hereby order some special green glazes" and agreed to pay consideration, then the contract between Alice and Bart is enforceable by either party.

Beware of making a contract with the insane or demented, and those rendered mentally incompetent by reason of excessive use of drugs, alcohol, et cetera. These people can break their contracts even though the incompetent's failure to uphold his or her end of the bargain would bring harm and damage to you, the other party. This is because these people do not have the "capacity" to make a contract. If the person ordering the stoneware was a reeling drunk and decided to reject Alice's specially and speedily produced set of green stoneware, Alice could not get a court to enforce her contract.

CAPACITY TO CONTRACT

INCOMPETENTS

In the past, minors were legally able to break their contracts, because of their youth. Today, with the growth in both the rights and responsibilities of minors, some states hold minors to their business contracts. Before contracting with a minor, find out your state law.

MINORS

Contracts to break the law usually will not be enforced by the courts. So don't go to court to collect an outstanding debt from last month's poker game.

LEGALITY

WRITTEN CONTRACTS

If you hadn't noticed, none of Alice's contracts involved much writing. At Mother Nurture's the waiter wrote a bill on a blank piece of paper which Alice gave to the cashier when she paid. The Artists Coop gave Alice a receipt listing the items received and the date. Bart gave Alice nothing. Some contracts do not have to be on paper to be enforceable. Salvador Dali verbally agreed to paint a picture of the Statue of Liberty on live television as a fund-raising gimmick and later thought better of his offer. Dali asked the court to dismiss the case filed against him, saying that the agreement to paint a picture of the Statue of Liberty was not written and therefore not enforceable. The court allowed the case to continue, saying that there could be an enforceable oral contract for personal services in this case.

WRITTEN CONTRACT OFTEN UNNECESSARY

Only in a few cases* must a contract be written in order to be enforceable:

- contracts for sales of goods valued at over $500
- contracts which cannot be completed within one year
- contracts for the sale of land
- leases for longer than one year

CONTRACTS THAT *MUST* BE WRITTEN

There are other situations where a writing is required to make an enforceable contract but these are not relevant to the areas covered in this book.

Under certain circumstances, even oral contracts for the sale of goods valued at over $500 are enforceable. An oral contract for the sale of specially made goods valued at over $500 is enforceable if production of the special order has begun. Also, oral agreements between "merchants" (most artists and craftmakers who are earning a regular income from their work could be considered "merchants") for the sale of goods of $500 or more are enforceable *if* the oral agreement is confirmed in writing and the confirmation is not objected to within ten days of its receipt. This comes from the Uniform Commercial Code (UCC), a batch of laws followed in all the states except Louisiana. This written confirmation, sometimes called a confirming memo, could spell out terms and end with a statement requiring any changes to be in writing and signed by both parties. Even with this memo, you have to prove that an oral contract was made, but the Statute of Frauds won't block the enforcement of the contract. Also, if goods valued at $500 or more are received and accepted by the buyer, pursuant to an oral contract, the agreement is enforceable even though it is not in writing.

EXCEPTIONS TO WRITTEN REQUIREMENTS

The Canadian Statute of Frauds provides that certain contracts, such as those for the sale of land and contracts of guarantee, aren't enforceable unless they are in writing. The Statute of Frauds Acts vary from province to province.

CANADIAN LAW— STATUTE OF FRAUDS

*These rules, called the Statute of Frauds, vary slightly from state to state, so check.

Alice's Allegory #13 or Beware of Woofs in Sheep's Clothing

Nine o'clock Monday morning the telephone rang on Rainbow Hill. "Must be some eager beaver," said Alice as she jumped over the sleeping dog to get to the phone. It was Warp and Woof Woof offering a good deal on a truckload of wool. "Sure," said Alice, thinking of the wool for macrame hangers for her Fabulous Flowerpots. She hung up the phone and forgot all about her conversation while she packed up Viola the VW for a trip to her Great-Uncle's one-hundredth-birthday party.

Home again, two weeks later, Alice found a letter from Warp and Woof Woof confirming her order of wool. Having spent her last dollar on a crate of fresh apricots, there was no way she could pay for the wool.

Old Cautious, the extended family lawyer, told Alice that she did not have a long or a short leg to stand on—oral contracts for goods valued at over $500 are enforceable *if* confirmed in writing and not objected to within ten days—and that Woof Woof had her over a barrel so to speak. Cautious then negotiated a partial trade of pots for the wool bill, and Alice dazedly caught a quick ride home, far away from the maddening crowd.

GET IT IN WRITING

Although a written contract is required only in a few situations, one of the messages of this chapter is to get *all* contracts in writing *now* to avoid trouble later. One reason for getting agreements in writing is the problem of proving the terms of an oral agreement in court. Many times lawsuits based upon oral contracts boil down to one party's word against the other—that is, a swearing contest.

WARRANTIES

Besides laws spelling out the requirements for an enforceable contract, state law sometimes inserts other terms into a contract. The contract terms inserted by state and federal law ("gap fillers") are usually for the protection of consumers or to simplify the law and foster the making of good contracts. Some of these laws affect the contracts discussed in this chapter.

IMPLIED WARRANTIES

Perhaps of most concern to artists and craftmakers are the laws concerning warranties. Although Larry Leatherman does not state to a customer that the leather briefcase he is selling is the "best in the West," the law implies at least three warranty terms into Larry Leatherman's contract of sale of items for personal, family, or household use, that is, consumer goods. One warranty is that the briefcase is "fit for the ordinary purposes for which such goods are used," which in the case of a briefcase is to hold business papers. Another warranty implied by the law is fitness for a particular purpose. If Larry Leatherman receives a special commission for a sword swallower's carrying case, the size should be such to handle assorted swords and other paraphernalia.

"AS IS"

OBVIOUS FLAW

You may be able to avoid the application of these two warranty terms to your sales contracts by including the term that the goods are sold "as is" or "with all faults" in your sales agreement. Also, if a defect is clearly evident upon inspection, a split on the rim of a ceramic mug, for example, the law does not imply a warranty.

WARRANTY OF GOOD AND CLEAN TITLE

Another warranty inserted by law into sales contracts is a guarantee that the seller has the authority to transfer good title (ownership) to the buyer and that the items sold are not burdened by a lien or other clouds on the title. In order to avoid the application of this warranty to a sale, the seller must alert the buyer that seller does not claim to have a good title.

EXPRESS WARRANTY

The law also may turn a little of your fast-talking salesmanship into an express warranty. You may be held to guaranteeing any words, written or spoken, relating to the item to be sold. If you advertise in the *Campus Register* for individually designed and tested flying roof ornaments in all colors of the rainbow, those contraptions better dance with delight in a high wind. Is the best salesperson a mute salesperson, then? The best salesperson is one who offers an *opinion* on the goods to be sold but does not promise or state marvelous things that are not true.

"OPINION"

When you sign your work, you "expressly" guarantee your authorship of the piece. Because of the problem of fakes in art, some states have special laws governing the authenticity of artwork. While Georgia O'Keefe was still alive, a controversy raged over whether works that she directed her house painter to render on canvas could be considered her work.

FORMALITIES OF MAKING A CONTRACT

Contracts come in all shapes and sizes and, with the exception of agreeing to break the law, you have pretty much free rein in drafting the terms of your contract. The language of the contract should be clear and mandatory. Take a tip from Horton and mean what you say and say what you mean. A written contract need not be a formal typewritten document with notarized signatures. A signed, hand-written statement of the essential points of the agreement is a fine contract. In most states, a signed letter containing the terms of the contract binds the signer of the letter. Beware of the fine print on the back of your suppliers' purchase orders. Sit down, put on your reading glasses, and scrutinize each paragraph. If you object to any of these contract terms, make a written objection to the supplier, or you will be held to those terms. Beware of form contracts and negotiate changes, for the terms favor the drafting party.

For some contracts, the assistance of a lawyer will be required. See Chapter 8, "Obtaining Legal Assistance," for more information on when and how to get a lawyer. A cheap way to use a lawyer if you have a contract legal problem is to type up (double-spaced, for editing ease) the agreement which you think you reached with the other party. Then have your lawyer review it with you to suggest additions, deletions, and rewording. If your contract problem is one you routinely encounter, then ask your lawyer to prepare a model form agreement with explanatory annotations. This means that each provision of the model will have an explanation following it, so you understand what you are giving up or gaining when you negotiate changes. Of course, the annotated copy is *not* used as your actual form. The consignment contract discussion later in this chapter and the publishing contract discussion in Chapter 7 follow this format.

A CONTRACT FOR EVERY OCCASION

Many artists and craftmakers prefer to sell directly to their customers. This arrangement is the most lucrative, the least risky, and puts the creator in touch with his or her audience. Direct sales account for the majority of transactions for many artists and craftmakers and take place in a variety of settings—craft fairs, studios, mall shows, in the street—and are contracted with a variety of customers—individuals, museums, galleries, schools, banks, et cetera.

DIRECT SALES DEFINITION

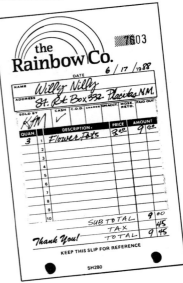

In many cases, the only documentation of a direct sale is a receipt with price, date, and sales tax listed. For the Rainbow Company's sale of three hand-glazed clay flowerpots, the sales receipt shown at right is a perfectly adequate record of the transaction.

Alice's Allegory #14 or Sadder But Wiser

One fine windy fall day, Alice sat dreaming on Rainbow Hill with stars in her eyes and wind in her hair. Since such a marvelous convergence of the elements is apt to produce brilliant inspirations, Alice had one—porcelain bath-towel racks.

Being prone to follow where inspiration leads, Alice found Romero lying under Viola the VW and told him to come and help on this great inspiration.

Alice sold out her entire collection of her handsome porcelain bath-towel racks at the next arts and crafts fair to Knew Contractors, who were producing handcrafted houses and wanted Alice's racks for every nook and cranny of the bathing grottoes. Romero said he wouldn't mind delivering the racks, because he wanted to check out the design of Knew's solar spaces.

Late that night when everybody slept, a tornado whirled out of nowhere and took all of the porcelain bath-towel racks to the land of Oz. Alice was also blown away because she had already spent Knew's check on the beautiful stained-glass window that she had been coveting for years. And she knew that Knew knew that the risk of loss was on seller till receipt by buyer.

Alice's unfortunate loss could have been avoided if the seller and the buyer discussed the various issues involved in the sale and wrote down the terms.

Even a sale or gift to a friend that involves special terms should be memorialized on paper. Better to negotiate now than to lose a friend later over a disagreement on the exact terms of the sale. It does happen, you know.

A direct-sales contract for sales made to customers without a middle person follows:

DIRECT SALE AGREEMENT BETWEEN
ARTIST AND PURCHASER

NAMES Name: ______ ______
Address: ______ ______
______ ______
Phone: ______ ______

Artist agrees to sell and Purchaser agrees to buy the Work described in paragraph 2 below. Artist and Purchaser further agree to the following terms as part of the sale and purchase of artist's Work:

PRICE 1. The price of the Work will be ______. Payment shall be made in the following fashion ______. Title to the Work will be transferred upon Artist's receipt of the full payment price. In the event of any default by Purchaser, Artist will have the rights of a secured party under the Uniform Commercial Code.

DESCRIPTION 2. The Work which is transferred by this agreement is:
Title: ______
Medium: ______
Date: ______
Dimensions: ______

WARRANTIES 3. Artist states that she/he owns the work and that it is an original work created by him/her. If purchaser requests, Artist will provide a written statement of authenticity and a history of the work. Purchaser warrants that any display of the Work will include Artist's name.

CARE OF WORK 4. Purchaser will not permit destruction, modification or damage to the Work. If the Work is damaged, Purchaser shall give Artist the opportunity to repair the Work, if possible.

EXHIBITION RIGHTS 5. Artist reserves the right to borrow the work from Purchaser for the purpose of public exhibition, for ______ days every ______ year(s). Artist will insure the work during the period of the loan and purchaser shall incur no expense as a result of this loan.

COPYRIGHT 6. As provided by the Copyright Revision Act of 1976, Artist reserves all the rights of copyright.

RISK OF LOSS AND DELIVERY 7. Responsibility for delivery of work upon:
______ Artist ______ Purchaser
Insurance of work prior to delivery shall be provided by:
______ Artist ______ Purchaser
Any damage or loss to work prior to receipt by Purchaser shall be at the expense of:
______ Artist ______ Purchaser

RESALE OF WORK 8. If the Purchaser sells, trades, or otherwise transfers the work, she/he must:
______ pay the Artist ______% of the resale profits resulting from the transfer.
______ get the new owner to ratify this contract by signing the attached Ratification Agreement.
______ give the Ratification Agreement to Artist.

BOILERPLATE 9. This agreement represents the entire contract made by the parties. Its terms cannot be modified except by a written document signed by the parties. A waiver of any breach of any form will not be construed as a continuing waiver of other breaches of the same or other provisions of the contract. If any part of this agreement is held to be illegal, void or unenforceable, this shall not effect the validity of any other part of the contract.

ARTIST: ______ PURCHASER: ______
Date: ______

Figure 4.1 Direct Sales Agreement between Artist and Purchaser

Unless you plan to sign a form contract with all the blanks completed by the other party, you will negotiate parts of the contract. Don't tell me you can't negotiate. Remember those dialogues with your parents when, as a teenager, you wanted to do this or that? Negotiate is simply a 50-cent word for the term "bargain." Negotiation is a bargaining process where parties discuss and arrange terms of an agreement to their mutual satisfaction. Various issues should be considered when negotiating a direct sales contract. See page 74 for a suggested checklist.

You need to know your goals—money, credit, control over your work, publicity, whatever. If you can find out the other party's goals before you bargain, all the better. This gallery may always insist on a statewide exclusive representation. If the contract the gallery proposes to you covers the entire Southwest, then you can expect to limit it to Arizona. Always ask for something extra, so you have something to throw away. When negotiating, I use a *key word* checklist in the upper righthand corner of a sheet of paper in different colored ink so that it stands out.

NEGOTIATING A DIRECT SALES AGREEMENT

"Norman Rockwell" types sit in a better bargaining seat, but I don't know of any creative person who wasn't able to negotiate at least one term in his/her favor in a contract.

NAMES AND ADDRESSES

Besides providing the buyer and the seller with each other's name for future reference (contact for shows, Christmas cards, future sales, lawsuits, etc.), it is important to obtain the seller's name and address in the event you need to recall the work or for some other reason notify the purchaser.

PRICE

The price of the work being sold is a basic consideration under the payment terms of the contract. If the customer is going to make payments over time, or trade for the work, then these details should be hammered out and put in writing. If the sale provides for installment payments, the agreement should state that transfer of title will occur upon completion of the payments and that until full payment, the artist retains a security interest in the work. By retaining a security interest, the artist can "repossess" the work if the purchaser fails to make payments. Also, the artist's security interest in the work could protect the work from seizure by purchaser's creditors.

SECURITY INTEREST

RIGHT TO PERCENTAGE OF RESALE PROFIT

Because modern art brings high prices on resale, some artists include in the sale contract a clause which entitles them to a percentage (usually 15 percent) of any increase over the original price at the time of resale.

SALE: Artist hereby sells the Work to Purchaser at the agreed value of $ ______________

RETRANSFER: If Purchaser in any way whatsoever sells, gives or trades the Work, or if it is inherited from Purchaser, or if a third party pays compensation for its destruction, Purchaser (or the representative of his estate) must within 30 days

(a) Pay Artist 15% of the "gross art profit", if any, on the transfer; and

(b) Get the new owner to ratify this contract by signing a properly filled-out "Transfer Agreement and Record" (TAR); and

(c) Deliver the signed TAR to the Artist.

(d) "Gross art profit" for this contract means only: "Agreed value" on a TAR less the "agreed value" on the last prior TAR, or (if there hasn't been a prior resale) less the agreed value in Paragraph 1 of this contract.

(e) "Agreed value" to be filled in on each TAR shall be the actual sale price if the Work is sold for money or the fair market value at the time if transferred any other way.

Figure 4.2 Percentage of Resale Agreement

RESERVATION OF RIGHTS

If you desire reserve rights on resale, you might consider adding the above language to your direct sales contract. Such a serious step requires the assistance of a knowledgeable lawyer.

California passed a law governing the resale of artwork for $1,000 or more, which requires that the artist receive 5 percent of the gross resale price provided that the resale price exceeds the purchase price. Of course, without a contract term expanding the geographic area, this law covers only resales in California or by a California resident.

COPYRIGHT

In the sale of a work, the artist, craftperson, or writer automatically retains the copyright *unless* the contract specifically states otherwise. Also, the creator may sell part of the copyright and retain the balance, which Arnold Artist did when he simply sold the right to produce postcard copies of his work.*

The best sale with the simplest logistics is cash and carry. However, this is not always possible.

*For more information on copyright, see Chapter 3, "Copying."

Memorandum

TO: Wood Shaver File

FROM: MB

RE: Drafting Contract for Client to Use in Sale of Large Cherry Desk

After interview with client, contract for sale of cherry desk should include special terms concerning:

1. delivery
2. risk of loss
3. insurance

Wood Shaver and his buyer have made the following arrangements, which should be included in the contract:

1. Deliver: Since Wood Shaver has truck, he will deliver desk to buyer's home at Peaceful Mountain Top, Vermont, after buyer has paid purchase price.
2. Risk of Loss: Risk of loss to pass to buyer upon delivery of the desk, even though payment received prior to delivery.
3. Insurance: Since risk of loss is on Wood Shaver, then he will insure the desk until delivery.

DELIVERY   If a contract does not state who is responsible for delivery, the buyer would have to make these arrangements, provided the seller made the work available to the buyer and told the buyer how to pick up the work.

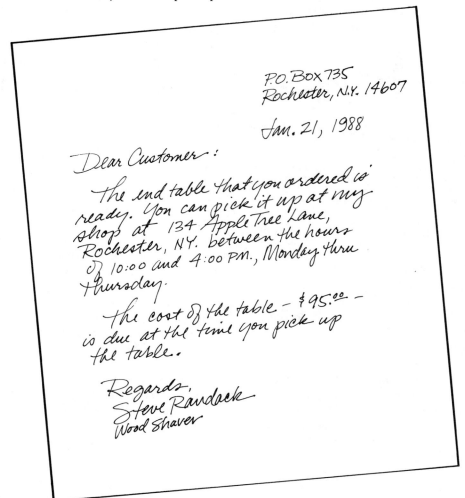

P.O. Box 735
Rochester, N.Y. 14607

Jan. 21, 1988

Dear Customer:

The end table that you ordered is ready. You can pick it up at my shop at 134 Apple Tree Lane, Rochester, NY. between the hours of 10:00 and 4:00 PM., Monday thru Thursday.

The cost of the table — $95.00 — is due at the time you pick up the table.

Regards,
Steve Randack
Wood Shaver

Figure 4.3 Sample notification to buyer

If a contract does not say anything about who is out of luck if the work is damaged before it reaches the buyer, the seller loses. If the seller has agreed to deliver by carrier, then risk of loss is on the seller until the buyer receives or the post office or the shipping company notifies the buyer of the arrival of the goods.

RISK OF LOSS

If the seller agrees to arrange for shipment of the goods, then the seller also is responsible for arranging insurance during shipment even if he or she did not specifically agree to do this. Most shippers do not provide *complete* insurance coverage. If the parties wish to obtain *complete* coverage while the work is being shipped, the sale contract should specify who should obtain and pay for such coverage. Open the package containing your returning artwork from a faraway show at the post office and have the clerk sign a statement description of any damage.

INSURANCE

The final groups of rights that could be included in a sales contract—acknowledgment of authorship, artistic integrity, exhibition rights—are sometimes called artists' rights or *droit morale*. Some of these rights are guaranteed by law in over sixty countries of the world. While one exception,* American artists and craftmakers do not automatically have these rights; for example, unless the contract of sale spells out these protections. Canada recognizes *droit morale*, however, through its copyright law.

ARTIST'S RIGHTS

In several instances where artists have demanded acknowledgment of their authorship, the courts decided that an artist is not entitled to have the authorship attributed to him or her unless the contract of sale so specifies. Some time ago, Vargas sued *Esquire* magazine for carrying some of his drawings without attributing the work to Vargas. He lost.

ACKNOWLEDGMENT OF AUTHORSHIP

A clause in the sales contract conerning artistic integrity would protect an artwork from mutilation or destruction and would give the artist the right to repair or restore a work that he or she sold. Without such a provision, artists have no way, after sale, to prevent their work from being destroyed or probably even mutilated.** The contract of sale should require the artist's consent before any alteration or destruction of the work occurs and provide that the artist be notified in the event of the requirement of repairs or restoration so that the artist has an opportunity to perform the repairs for a reasonable fee.

ARTISTIC INTEGRITY

The exhibition clause could give the artist the right to retrieve the work for an exhibit for certain periods of time, perhaps six weeks, every few years.

EXHIBITION RIGHTS

To prepare for the negotiating session when you are making an agreement governing the direct sale of art or crafts (and to ensure that all the major questions are covered in your agreement), use the checklist on page 74.

If your prospective purchaser wants to rent the work first, make that arrangement subject to an agreement. A model rental agreement which allows the renter to purchase the artwork and apply the rental payments to the purchase price is found in Tad Crawfords' *Legal Guide for the Visual Artist* (Madison Square Press, 1987). Be sure to refer to the incorporation of your direct sales agreement in the rental agreement to cover the renter who becomes purchaser.

RENTER TO PURCHASER

Most artist-gallery relationships are consignment arrangements. Consignment means that the artist retains title to his or her work during the time the work is at the gallery. When the work is sold by the gallery, the title passes directly from the artist to the buyer. Since the gallery both has possession of your work and also acts as your agent to the public, choice of the right gallery is very important and should be carefully made.

SALES THROUGH GALLERIES

---

*The California Art in Public Buildings Act requires that the state respect the moral rights of the participating artists. This includes the requirement that each work "is properly maintained and is not artistically altered in any manner without the consent of the artist." The act also provides that the artist has the right to acknowledgment of authorship.

**An artist sued to remove the paint placed over his fresco commissioned by the Rutgers Presbyterian Church. He lost.

CHECKLIST—DIRECT-SALES AGREEMENT

	Artist	Purchaser
1. Name:	________	________
Address:	________	________
	________	________

2. Payment:
   Amount: ________ Terms: ________ Due Dates: ________
   Right to ________% resale profits: [ ] yes [ ] no
   Security Interest Retained until paid in full: [ ] yes [ ] no
3. Identification of Work:
   Title: ________ Date: ________
   Medium: ________ Description: ________
4. Copyright:
   [ ] Retained by Artist (automatically)
   [ ] Other (explain) ________
5. Delivery:
   [ ] Responsibility on Purchaser
   [ ] Responsibility on Artist
6. Risk of Loss Prior to Receipt by Buyer:
   [ ] On Purchaser
   [ ] On Artist
   [ ] Other (explain) ________
   Provision of ________
7. Full insurance coverage prior to receipt by Buyer on:
   [ ] Purchaser
   [ ] Artist
   [ ] Other (explain) ________
   ____
8. Acknowledgment of Authorship Required:
   [ ] yes
   [ ] no
9. Artistic Integrity:
   a. Restoration and repair rights in Artist:
      [ ] yes
      [ ] no
   b. Protection from mutilation or destruction:
      [ ] yes
      [ ] no
10. Exhibition Rights:
   [ ] Artist's right to regain work at no cost to Buyer for ________ days every ________ year(s), for purpose of exhibition

Figure 4.4 Sample checklist, direct sales

CHOOSING A GALLERY

CHECKING OUT A GALLERY

A gallery should be honest in its dealings, financially sound, and acceptable as your representative to the public. Some artists and craftmakers feel a most important point in a gallery choice is the possibility of an open and comfortable working relationship. Gather this information from other artists and craftpersons. Since it is possible* that an artist's works on consignment at a gallery could be taken in court proceedings brought by the creditors of the gallery, it is important that a gallery be investigated before placing work on consignment there. This is especially important if you are placing works with an out-of-state gallery, because of the added difficulty of resolving differences across state lines. The best reference, of course, for your potential gallery are other artists and craftmakers who have dealt with it. Also, the American Crafts Council in New York City provides a reference service for craftpersons interested in checking out a gallery. The ACC also keeps track of complaints. The local Better Business Bureau may also have information on the gallery, especially if artists had complaints about it in the past.

*Some states have enacted special laws concerning the relationship of the gallery to the artist. These laws specifically exempt works of art on consignment in a gallery from seizure by the gallery's creditors or when the gallery declares bankruptcy. Check with your lawyer.

Since the gallery's records establish the prices paid for the work and the commission taken by the gallery, it is important that the gallery keep accurate and complete records of all its transactions and that these records be available for inspection by the artist.

The size and annual gross of arts and crafts galleries vary as much as the sandal sizes in a Franciscan monastery. In 1975, the art galleries in New York City alone grossed in excess of $200 million. Art means big bucks. Like it or not, the art gallery is the broker of this sometimes lucrative business.

Any business based upon sale of another's work has the potential for abuse. Some art dealers in New York who failed to remit regular payments to their artists caused such an uproar among artists that the state legislature passed special laws to protect artists from art dealers and to prosecute art dealers who wrongfully withhold the artist's portion of the sale proceeds. The legal contests between artists or their heirs and galleries concerning the works of Franz Kline, William de Kooning, and Mark Rothko further illustrate the potential for controversy in the artist-gallery relationship. An ounce of prevention is worth a pound of cure. Don't wait until you are a "successful" artist before you consider negotiating a written contract with your galleries.

Associating with a gallery is a serious step in an artist or craftperson's life. It may take three or four meetings to negotiate a mutually satisfactory agreement. At the final negotiating sessions, be prepared: know what terms you want in the agreement; have a contract with you that reflects your wishes; and if you want the gallery to use a special sales contract when they sell your work, have a copy of that with you too. For many artists and craftmakers, negotiations are easier and more successful if help is provided by a friend or attorney.

After agreeing with the gallery on the terms of the contract, change the form contract* to reflect the negotiated settlement; cross out clauses not applicable and add any additional terms; date the document; and then both parties should initial all changes and sign their names.

GALLERY RECORDS

ART IS BIG BUCKS

ARTIST-GALLERY LEGISLATION

NEGOTIATING A DEAL

CHECKLIST—ARTIST-GALLERY AGREEMENT

Artist   **Gallery**

1. Name: _____   _____

   Address: _____   _____

   _____   _____

2. Appoint of Gallery as Artist's Agent:
   [　] yes   [　] no

   [　] in _____ geographic area

   [　] in _____ media area
   [　] for all works
   [　] for all works except:
   　　[　] commissions   [　] studio sales   [　] trades
   　　[　] juried shows   [　] gifts
   [　] for those works chosen by Gallery
   [　] for those works agreed to by Artist and Gallery
   [　] other _____

3. Delivery and Return:
   a. Responsibility of delivery—costs and insurance on:
   　　[　] Artist   [　] Gallery
   b. Responsibility of return—costs and insurance on:
   　　[　] Artist   [　] Gallery

---

*See also, *The Artist-Gallery Partnership,* by Tad Crawford and Susan Mallan, The American Crafts Council, and *An Introduction to Contracts for Visual Artists,* by Norman Stone, available from CLA.

4. Selling Price Set by:
   [　] agreement between Artist and Gallery with ＿＿＿＿＿ percent commission
   [　] Gallery; Artist to receive agreed-upon net price
   [　] Gallery may discount ＿＿＿＿＿＿＿＿＿ percent from agreed-upon price in sales to museums, galleries, decorators, and architects

5. Commissions due Gallery on:
   [　] all sales by Artist
   [　] all sales by Artist arising from Gallery contact
   [　] Gallery sales only

6. Payment:
   [　] within thirty days of receipt
   [　] within thirty days of receipt of an installment payment; the entire payment to Artist until his or her percentage is paid in full
   [　] Gallery agrees to bear all losses due to the failure of customer's credit

7. Approval Sales:

   [　] yes, for ＿＿＿＿＿ days   [　] no

8. Assurances:
   [　] Artist warrants that work is an original, owned and executed by him/her
   [　] Artist will deliver at least ＿＿＿＿＿ works every ＿＿＿＿＿ months
   [　] Gallery will promote Artist's work

9. Exhibition:
   [　] Gallery agrees to arrange exhibition(s) of Artist's works of ＿＿＿＿＿ days in length, cost of exhibition paid by ＿＿＿＿＿＿＿＿＿＿＿
   [　] Artist shall be consulted concerning the details of the exhibition including other exhibitors, program design, etc.
   [　] ＿＿＿＿＿＿＿＿＿＿＿＿＿ will pay for costs of framing, etc.

10. Statements:

    [　] Shall be made every ＿＿＿＿ months(s) and shall include:
       [　] works sold
       [　] date, price, and terms of sale
       [　] purchaser's name and address
       [　] commission due Gallery
       [　] location of all unsold works not at Gallery

11. Sale Contract:
    [　] special contract for sale of work required

12. Copyright:
    [　] Artist retains copyright (automatically)
    [　] other ＿＿＿＿＿＿＿＿＿＿＿＿＿＿＿

13. Loss or Damage:
    [　] Gallery responsible for providing insurance coverage from date of delivery to date of removal at ＿＿＿＿＿＿＿＿＿ percent of the agreed price
    [　] Gallery insurance covers loss from
       [　] fire   [　] theft   [　] negligence
       [　] acts of God

14. Termination:

    [　] right of either party to terminate within ＿＿＿＿＿＿＿ days of giving notice to the other
    [　] must wait ninety days from date of exhibition to terminate

15. Contract Disputes:
    [　] settled by arbitration
    [　] winner entitled to attorneys' fees
    [　] ＿＿＿＿＿＿＿＿＿＿＿＿＿ state law governs contract

Figure 4.5 Sample checklist, artist-gallery

This checklist presupposes that the gallery will be taking the work on consignment. If you are lucky enough to sell directly to a gallery, use the direct-sale-contract checklist in the previous section (page 74) as well as any of the applicable artist-gallery contract terms.

Not all artists or craftpersons have the luxury of dictating the terms of a gallery agreement. Many times the starving artist will have little choice in the terms of a contract with a gallery, because the bargaining power of the parties is unequal. If you must use the gallery's contract form, isolate three or four key issues and try to negotiate the changes in the contract that you feel are essential. Figure 4.6 is an old Wood Shaver–gallery agreement that has been revised to be a little more favorable to the artist.

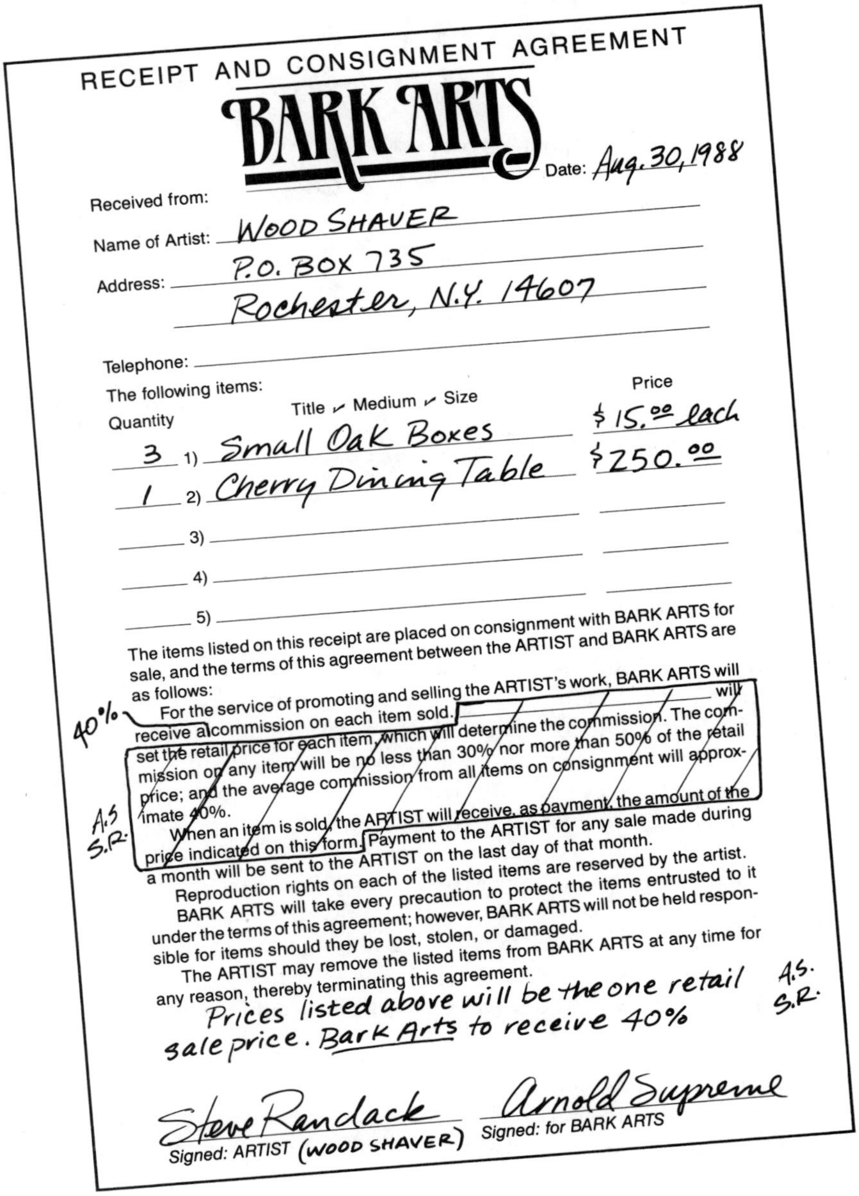
RECEIPT AND CONSIGNMENT AGREEMENT

BARK ARTS

Date: Aug. 30, 1988

Received from:

Name of Artist: WOOD SHAVER

Address: P.O. BOX 735
Rochester, N.Y. 14607

Telephone:

The following items:

Quantity	Title ✓ Medium ✓ Size	Price
3	1) Small Oak Boxes	$15.00 each
1	2) Cherry Dining Table	$250.00
	3)	
	4)	
	5)	

The items listed on this receipt are placed on consignment with BARK ARTS for sale, and the terms of this agreement between the ARTIST and BARK ARTS are as follows:

40% For the service of promoting and selling the ARTIST's work, BARK ARTS will receive a commission on each item sold. ~~will set the retail price for each item, which will determine the commission. The commission on any item will be no less than 30% nor more than 50% of the retail price; and the average commission from all items on consignment will approximate 40%.~~

A.S. S.R. ~~When an item is sold, the ARTIST will receive, as payment, the amount of the price indicated on this form.~~ Payment to the ARTIST for any sale made during a month will be sent to the ARTIST on the last day of that month.

Reproduction rights on each of the listed items are reserved by the artist.

BARK ARTS will take every precaution to protect the items entrusted to it under the terms of this agreement; however, BARK ARTS will not be held responsible for items should they be lost, stolen, or damaged.

The ARTIST may remove the listed items from BARK ARTS at any time for any reason, thereby terminating this agreement.

Prices listed above will be the one retail sale price. Bark Arts to receive 40% A.S. S.R.

Steve Randack
Signed: ARTIST (WOOD SHAVER)

Arnold Supreme
Signed: for BARK ARTS

Figure 4.6 Artist-gallery agreement

Financing Statement

Name of Gallery (debtor): *Arnold Supreme d/b/a BARKARTS*

Address: *P.O. Box 35, New Hope Pa.*

Name of Artist (secured party) *Steve Randack d/b/a WOOD SHAVER*

Address: *P.O. Box 735*
Rochester, New York 14607

This financing statement covers the following types of property whenever acquired

by Gallery: *Wooden furniture and other carvings including boards, boxes, plates, etc.*

Steve Randack
d/b/a WOOD SHAVER   Date *July 30, 1988*
Signature of Artist

Figure 4.7 Sample financing statement

PROTECT YOURSELF WITH
A FINANCING STATEMENT

At the conclusion of all artist-gallery negotiations and contract signing, you and the gallery representative should fill out and sign a "financing statement."* File a copy of the financing statement with the Attorney General, Secretary of State, or the state or county office that records such documents. The financing statement should be filed in the state or county where the gallery is located. Figure 4.7 is a copy of the financing agreement that Wood Shaver filed to protect his works on consignment to Bark Arts Gallery.

This additional step protects the artist's work from seizure by the gallery's creditors. If you don't file a financing statement, your carefully drawn tri-panel might vanish under the arm of one of the gallery's creditors without even so much as a thank-you.

Alice's Allegory #15 or Bald der Dash and His Scented Dome

While at the Fall arts and crafts fair in Tucumcari, a representative of a Dallas gallery saw Alice's handsome porcelain bath-towel racks and was so excited that he hit his bald head on a hanging pot full of scented geraniums. Rubbing his now scented dome, he introduced himself as Bald der Dash and told Alice that he would take all the bath-towel racks that she had and more.

---

*There are certain states in which you may not have to file a financing statement to protect your work on consignment to a gallery. Each of these states has passed a law concerning special treatment for artists' works on consignment. Since these laws vary somewhat from state to state concerning what is covered by the law (crafts) and any requirements for getting this special treatment (special signs, etc.), check this to see exactly what your artwork consignment law is. Chapter 8, "Obtaining Legal Assistance," gives the address of Volunteer Lawyers for the Arts, which should be able to help.

Alice was excited by the gallery's interest and told Mr. Dash that she would be happy to sell him her entire porcelain bath-towel bar supply and even give him a discount. "No," Mr. Dash was not interested in purchasing but rather in a consignment arrangement.

"Well," said Alice, "that changes things somewhat," and sent Romero to look for her good friend Negotiator as she whipped out her handy-dandy-big-gallery-little-artist contract. And after two hours of tea, conversation, frowns, compliments, insults, meaningful glances, et cetera, the three arrived at this:

NAME: _Alice_ _Bubbly Bath Boutique, Inc_

ADDRESS: _P.O. Box 733_ _Big Town Mall_

Albuquerque, NM _Mesquite, Texas_

PHONE: _None_ _214-993-7300_

Artist and Gallery agree to make a consignment contract effective _____

_Oct 15_____, 19 _88___. The terms of the agreement are:

Figure 4.8 Sample consignment contract introduction

For a discussion of the "name" term of the contract, see the section on names in the direct-sales section of this chapter. The parties to a contract usually can insert an effective date before or after the date of actual signing. Most times, the effective date is the same as the date of signing.

NAMES

EFFECTIVE DATE

1. Artist appoints Gallery to act as his/her exclusive agent in the exhibition and sale of Artist's _____ work in the _____ area.
   (medium)   (geographic)

AGENCY

By naming the gallery as agent, several important things are accomplished. First, the gallery must keep the best interest of the artist in mind at all times and act accordingly. As an agent, the gallery must place the advantage of the artist before its own. Also, the agent gallery can make agreements with customers on behalf of its artists.

Alice limits the scope of Bald der Dash's Bubbly Bath Boutique's exclusive agency to the Dallas area and to Alice's ceramic works.

2. The artist will deliver the following number of his/her works in the _____ medium (a) to the Gallery:
   ( ) all works
   ( ) all works except for gifts, trades, commissions, juried shows
   ( ) those works selected by Gallery
   (×) those works agreed to by Artist and Gallery

ARTWORKS COVERED

Your gallery can be the only source for the distribution of your work. If you are giving a gallery such an exclusive in your work, it would be wise to exempt from coverage any works that you wish to give or trade. This term in the contract also exempts commissions, studio sales, and works submitted to juried shows. Although Alice granted Bald der Dash a geographic exclusive, she is not granting him the right to sell all her works. Mr. Dash can sell only those works that he and Alice agree upon.

3. _____ will be responsible for delivery including costs, complete insurance coverage, and risk of loss.
   _____ will be responsible for return of works including costs, complete insurance coverage, and risk of loss.

DELIVERY	Many times, the first delivery of works has already occurred when the contract is signed. However, most artist-gallery relationships extend over a period of time, and the question of who bears the responsibility of future deliveries should be settled at the outset. In Alice's contract, she agrees to provide delivery and the gallery
RETURN	agrees to return all unsold items. In the event that a loss occurs during delivery or return and the insurance does not cover the entire amount of the loss, this term clarifies who bears the loss.

ARTIST'S WARRANTIES

4. Artist states that she/he created and owns all the works delivered to Gallery.
5. Gallery acknowledges receipt of the work described in the List of Works. A supplemental List of Works concerning any additional works delivered to Gallery will be provided by artist and acknowledged by Gallery.

In these two sections of the agreement Alice authenticates her creation of and title* to the works being placed with the gallery and the gallery acknowledges receipt of the works listed on the List of Works.

GALLERY RECEIPT

Once, I picked up work for an artist-client who had terminated his relationship with a nearby gallery. First, I carefully verified with my client that the List of Works included all the works my artist-client consigned to the gallery and the gallery's representive emphatically said that it did. Naturally, he wanted me to sign a receipt that indicated that I had retrieved all the pieces on the list, in other words, the total consignment. Based on my client's assertions, I did. Once my client saw the pieces, he realized there was a missing item or two, but I advised him not to pursue the matter due to the circumstances and to chalk it up to experience. He kept better consignment records after that.

SALE PRICE

6. Gallery will sell the Works at the price listed on the attached List of Works. Gallery may discount _____ percent in sales to museums, galleries, decorators, and architects.

COMMISSION

7. Gallery will receive _____ percent commission on the sale price of:
   (   ) all sales by Artist
   (×) all sales by Artist arising from Gallery contact
   (   ) Gallery sales only

In this provision, Alice sets the prices that the gallery will charge for her work and the gallery takes an agreed-upon percentage as a commission. Another way to reach the price and commission is for the artist to state the amount he or she wants to receive for the piece and to allow the gallery to set any selling price. This "net price" method is usually less beneficial to the artist.

Galleries acting as the exclusive agent of artists many times require that they receive a percentage of *any* of the sales made by the artist. Here Alice and Bald der Dash agree that the gallery will receive a commission on all sales made either by the gallery or by Alice if the sale was a result of the customer's contact with the gallery.

PAYMENT

8. Payment of each party's percentage share will be made within thirty days of the date of receipt of payment from the customer. All proceeds from installment payments will be made first to Artist until his/her share is paid in full. The Gallery agrees to guarantee the credit of its customers, and to bear all losses due to the failure of the customer's credit.

*For more information on warranty of good title and authorship, see the discussion of warranties elsewhere in this chapter.

This clause basically places the burden of credit sales on the gallery by providing that the artist receive his or her entire share of the sale price before the gallery receives its commission. Also, the gallery would be the loser if a customer defaulted on payments, because the artist would be entitled to his or her full share of the sale price regardless of the fact that the customer did not pay the gallery.

9. _____ will pay for the cost of framing or any other expenses necessary in preparation for display or sale of work. The Gallery will make a reasonable effort to promote the Artist and to sell his/her work. The Gallery will hold at least _____ exhibition(s) of artist's work of at least _____ week(s) in length each _____ year(s). Artist will be consulted concerning the details of the exhibition including any promotional materials, other exhibitors, and arrangements. Responsibility for the costs of the exhibition will be agreed upon in advance. Neither party may obtain reimbursement for these costs from the other without prior approval.

PROMOTION AND EXHIBITION

This section is very important if you have signed an exclusive agency contract for a period of time. It protects you from having all your works collect dust in the gallery's basement. Also, this section requires that the gallery arrange a special exhibition of your work. The clause provides that the costs of such an exhibition be divided between the gallery and the artist and agreed upon by both. Further, the section provides that the artist will be consulted concerning the promotional materials used by the gallery.

10. Gallery will give Artist a statement every_____ , beginning with _____ , 19 ___ . This statement shall include:
(×) works sold.
(×) date, price, and terms of sale.
(×) commission due to the Gallery.
(   ) name and address of each Purchaser.
(×) location of all unsold works not at Gallery.
Artist and Gallery will have the right to inspect the other's financial records concerning transactions covered by this agreement.

STATEMENT

The requirement that the gallery provide a regular statement of account ensures that the gallery will maintain orderly records of sales, commissions, and works on hand for the artist. Hotter than New Mexico chilis is the raging argument between galleries and artists about most galleries' policy not to release the name and address of purchasers of the artist's work. Galleries feel that this gives the artist such an opportunity to make his/her own direct sales that the gallery can't take this risk.

ACCOUNTING

11. The gallery will use the sale contract which is attached to this agreement for all sales of artist's work governed by this contract.

SALE CONTRACT

If you wish the gallery to use a special contract for sales of your work, then attach a blank of your direct-sales contract form to the artist-gallery agreement and provide the gallery with copies of the contract. If the gallery uses your direct sales contract, you will get the purchaser's name and address.

12. As provided in the Copyright Revision Act of 1976, the Artist retains all copyrights in the works delivered to Gallery. Gallery will prohibit the public from copying Artist's Works, except for publicity purposes. All reproductions of Artist's Works in Gallery publications and publicity by others will be accompanied by a complete notice of copyright including the copyright symbol, the Artist's first and last name, and the year of first publication.

COPYRIGHT

This section restates the rule of the new Copyright Act which provides that unless a copyright is expressly transferred to buyer, it is retained by seller. This section presupposes that the artist has placed a copyright notice on all the works delivered to the gallery. It also seeks to avoid copyright infringement by requiring that the gallery prohibit the public from copying the artist's works and that the gallery place a complete copyright notice beside any reproduction of the artist's work.*

LOSS OR DAMAGE

13. Gallery is responsible for providing insurance coverage from date of delivery to date of removal. Works will be insured at _____ percent of the retail sale price. Insurance shall cover fire, theft, loss, damage from negligence in the Gallery and outside Gallery premises when under Gallery control.

INSURANCE

Some galleries have no insurance coverage at all, and most gallery insurance policies do not insure the works for the selling price. You could pay for this additional coverage through your own insurance policy. Also, find out if the gallery's insurance covers your work while under gallery control, no matter where it is located—show, home of prospective buyer, in transit, et cetera. Usually, gallery insurance becomes effective when the work is received by the gallery. You may wish to add a provision that any insurance proceeds shall be divided on a certain basis, i.e., the percentages of the consignment agreement, split, and so forth.

TERMINATION

14. Unless already terminated, this agreement will terminate one year from its effective date. Artist or Gallery may terminate the agreement earlier by giving the other party written notice thirty days prior to the date upon which the party wishes to terminate. The agreement may not be terminated for ninety days following a solo exhibition of Artist's work by Gallery.

This term allows either party to be released from the contract after giving thirty days notice to the other. Because of the investment of time and money in an exhibition, the agreement cannot be terminated for three months after such an exhibition. If allowed to run its course, the agreement automatically will terminate in a year's time. At that time, renewal or renegotiation may be in order.

BOILERPLATE

15. This agreement represents the entire contract made by the parties. Its terms cannot be modified except by a written document signed by the parties. Neither party may assign any of the rights or responsibilities contained in the contract without the consent of the other party. Such consent shall not be unreasonably withheld. If any part of this agreement is held to be illegal, void, or unenforceable, this shall not affect the validity of any other part of the contract.

This clause cites terms, normally found in all contracts—integration, nonassignment, and severability. The written document represents the total agreement and can be changed only through another written document signed by the parties. The assignment term prevents either artist or gallery from getting someone else to perform their responsibilities without the written consent of the other party to the contract. The final clause states that if a court rules that one section of the contract is no good, then the contract still stands minus the offending section.

GOVERNING LAW

16. This Agreement shall be governed by the laws of the state of _____ .

Since New York, California, Michigan, Texas, and Connecticut have the most progressive laws concerning artists and galleries, you should provide that the laws

*For more information on copyright, see Chapter 3, "Copying."

of one of those states apply to any disputes arising under the contract, if either of the parties lives or works in one of those states. Otherwise, choose the law of your state.

Signed this _____ day of _____ , 19 _____ .
ARTIST   GALLERY
_____ By _____
                                         (signature of Authorized
                                         Representative)

You could include a provision on arbitration that excepts copyright disputes or disputes over certain sums. Organizations such as CLA offer arbitration services, as does the American Arbitration Association. These services are not free, and if both sides are represented by lawyers, the cost may not be less than court litigation. It is, however, faster and that means less stress. Most states have adopted some rules for binding arbitration.

A sample provision would read as follows:

> The parties agree that should a dispute arise between them in any matter concerning this contract, except copyright, and it involves less than $10,000 exclusive of interest, costs or attorneys fees, the parties will submit the matter to binding arbitration pursuant to state's statutes or rules, and if none, then to the rules followed by the American Arbitration Association, and the decision shall be final and binding upon the parties.

```
+-----------------------------------------------------------------------+
|                                               Medium                  |
|                                               (if contract            |
|  LIST OF ART WORKS                            covers more             |
|                                               than one)               |
|          Name          Size      Retail Price                         |
|   1.                                                                  |
|   2.                                                                  |
|   3.                                                                  |
|   4.                                                                  |
|   5.                                                                  |
|   6.                                                                  |
|   7.                                                                  |
|   8.                                                                  |
|   9.                                                                  |
|  10.                                                                  |
|     Pursuant to contract between Artist and Gallery dated _____,   |
|  19_____. Artist submits this list of Art Works for gallery          |
|  acknowledgment.                                                      |
|                                                                       |
|  _____       _____                           |
|       Artist                    date                                  |
|                                                                       |
|  Gallery acknowledges receipt of the above art works.                 |
|                                                                       |
|  _____       _____                           |
|       Gallery                   date                                  |
+-----------------------------------------------------------------------+
```

Figure 4.9 Inventory Receipt

The Canadian Sale of Goods Act, and the United States Sales Act (superceded now by the Uniform Commercial Code) both developed from the English codification of pre-twentieth century rules on the sale of goods and personal property.

Each province has a Bulk Sales Act which provides some protection to creditors of a vendor who sells all or part of his/her stock beyond the scope of normal business or trade channels, as such sales can lead to a fraud of the creditors. Provincial direct sales laws govern goods over a certain value sold to a consumer—usually at the buyer's residence—and allow the buyer to renege after a cooling-off period. Some provinces have Sales on Consignment Acts which regulate sales through a mercantile agent; these could apply to art sales. Also, pyramid and referral sales are regulated in some provinces. Most provinces adopted a Bills of Sales Act to protect third persons where the property has already been sold. It usually applies when the sale is not accompanied by delivery of the goods.

Most provinces have a Conditional Sales Act, although it's called the Personal Property Security Act in some, which covers those situations where the goods are delivered to the buyer but title doesn't pass till later. All of these require certain formalities.

The Personal Property Security Acts based on the UCC in the United States covers certain commercial transactions formerly dealt with by some of the above acts. It was passed to give uniformity to the law regarding goods.

The Sale of Goods Act has a "fitness for purpose" section.

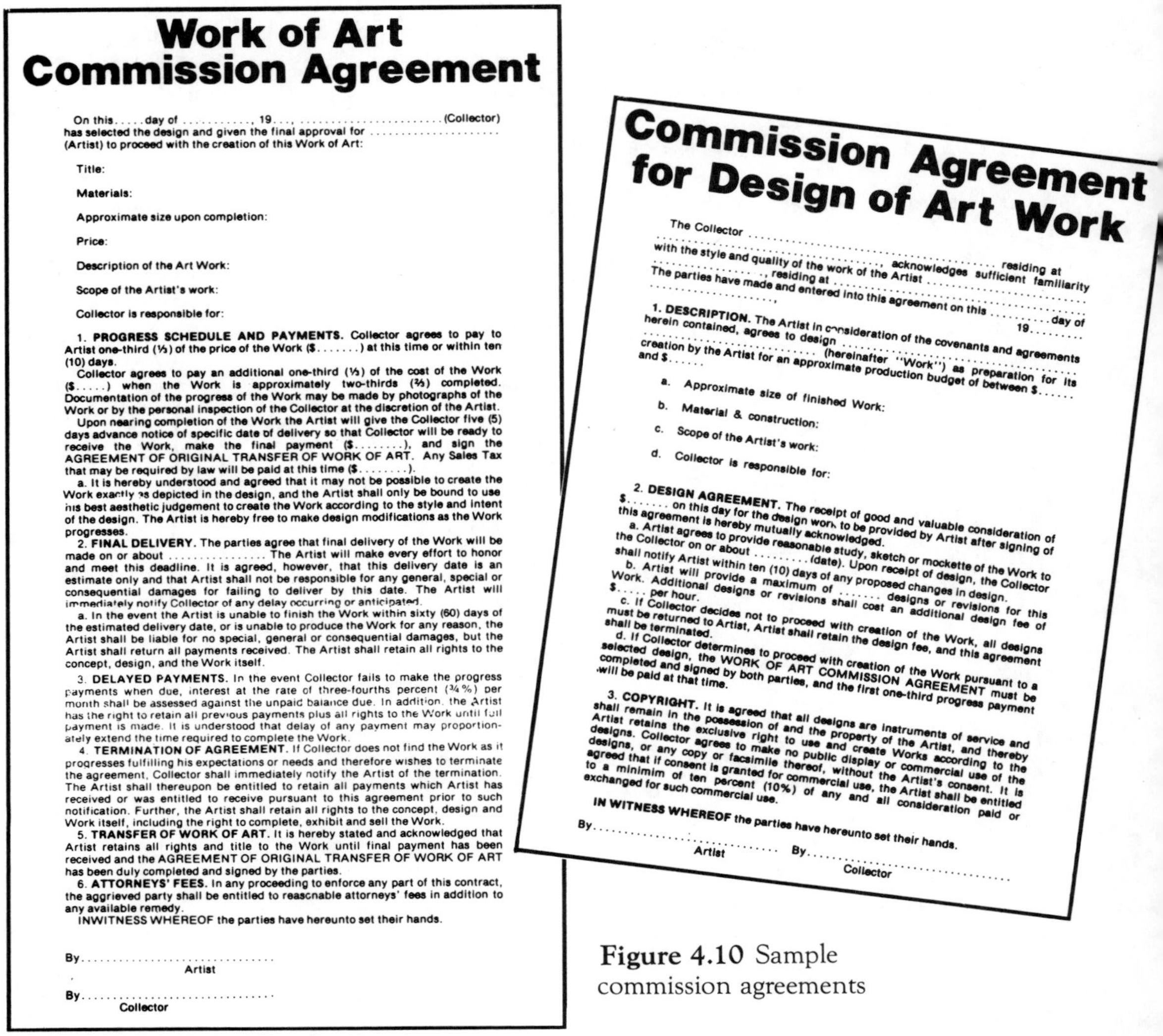

Work of Art Commission Agreement

On this.....day of ...., 19..., ...(Collector) has selected the design and given the final approval for .... (Artist) to proceed with the creation of this Work of Art:

Title:

Materials:

Approximate size upon completion:

Price:

Description of the Art Work:

Scope of the Artist's work:

Collector is responsible for:

1. **PROGRESS SCHEDULE AND PAYMENTS.** Collector agrees to pay to Artist one-third (⅓) of the price of the Work ($.......) at this time or within ten (10) days.

Collector agrees to pay an additional one-third (⅓) of the cost of the Work ($.....) when the Work is approximately two-thirds (⅔) completed. Documentation of the progress of the Work may be made by photographs of the Work or by the personal inspection of the Collector at the discretion of the Artist.

Upon nearing completion of the Work the Artist will give the Collector five (5) days advance notice of specific date of delivery so that Collector will be ready to receive the Work, make the final payment ($........), and sign the AGREEMENT OF ORIGINAL TRANSFER OF WORK OF ART. Any Sales Tax that may be required by law will be paid at this time ($........).

a. It is hereby understood and agreed that it may not be possible to create the Work exactly as depicted in the design, and the Artist shall only be bound to use his best aesthetic judgement to create the Work according to the style and intent of the design. The Artist is hereby free to make design modifications as the Work progresses.

2. **FINAL DELIVERY.** The parties agree that final delivery of the Work will be made on or about .... The Artist will make every effort to honor and meet this deadline. It is agreed, however, that this delivery date is an estimate only and that Artist shall not be responsible for any general, special or consequential damages for failing to deliver by this date. The Artist will immediately notify Collector of any delay occurring or anticipated.

a. In the event the Artist is unable to finish the Work within sixty (60) days of the estimated delivery date, or is unable to produce the Work for any reason, the Artist shall be liable for no special, general or consequential damages, but the Artist shall return all payments received. The Artist shall retain all rights to the concept, design, and the Work itself.

3. **DELAYED PAYMENTS.** In the event Collector fails to make the progress payments when due, interest at the rate of three-fourths percent (¾%) per month shall be assessed against the unpaid balance due. In addition, the Artist has the right to retain all previous payments plus all rights to the Work until full payment is made. It is understood that delay of any payment may proportionately extend the time required to complete the Work.

4. **TERMINATION OF AGREEMENT.** If Collector does not find the Work as it progresses fulfilling his expectations or needs and therefore wishes to terminate the agreement, Collector shall immediately notify the Artist of the termination. The Artist shall thereupon be entitled to retain all payments which Artist has received or was entitled to receive pursuant to this agreement prior to such notification. Further, the Artist shall retain all rights to the concept, design and Work itself, including the right to complete, exhibit and sell the Work.

5. **TRANSFER OF WORK OF ART.** It is hereby stated and acknowledged that Artist retains all rights and title to the Work until final payment has been received and the AGREEMENT OF ORIGINAL TRANSFER OF WORK OF ART has been duly completed and signed by the parties.

6. **ATTORNEYS' FEES.** In any proceeding to enforce any part of this contract, the aggrieved party shall be entitled to reasonable attorneys' fees in addition to any available remedy.

INWITNESS WHEREOF the parties have hereunto set their hands.

By...............................
Artist

By...............................
Collector

Commission Agreement for Design of Art Work

The Collector ....
.... residing at
with the style and quality of the work of the Artist, acknowledges sufficient familiarity
................., residing at ....
The parties have made and entered into this agreement on this ....day of
................., 19..........

1. **DESCRIPTION.** The Artist in consideration of the covenants and agreements herein contained, agrees to design ....
.... (hereinafter "Work") as preparation for its creation by the Artist for an approximate production budget of between $...... and $......

a. Approximate size of finished Work:

b. Material & construction:

c. Scope of the Artist's work:

d. Collector is responsible for:

2. **DESIGN AGREEMENT.** The receipt of good and valuable consideration of $....... on this day for the design work to be provided by Artist after signing of this agreement is hereby mutually acknowledged.

a. Artist agrees to provide reasonable study, sketch or mockette of the Work to the Collector on or about ....(date). Upon receipt of design, the Collector shall notify Artist within ten (10) days of any proposed changes in design.

b. Artist will provide a maximum of .... designs or revisions for this Work. Additional designs or revisions shall cost an additional design fee of $..... per hour.

c. If Collector decides not to proceed with creation of the Work, all designs must be returned to Artist, Artist shall retain the design fee, and this agreement shall be terminated.

d. If Collector determines to proceed with creation of the Work pursuant to a selected design, the WORK OF ART COMMISSION AGREEMENT must be completed and signed by both parties, and the first one-third progress payment will be paid at that time.

3. **COPYRIGHT.** It is agreed that all designs are instruments of service and shall remain in the possession of and the property of the Artist, and thereby Artist retains the exclusive right to use and create Works according to the designs. Collector agrees to make no public display or commercial use of the designs, or any copy or facsimile thereof, without the Artist's consent. It is agreed that if consent is granted for commercial use, the Artist shall be entitled to a minimim of ten percent (10%) of any and all consideration paid or exchanged for such commercial use.

IN WITNESS WHEREOF the parties have hereunto set their hands.

By............................ Artist

By............................ Collector

Figure 4.10 Sample commission agreements

COMMISSIONS

Alice's Allegory #16 or She Had a Dream

The matriarch of the local house of worship Claire Voyant dropped by Alice's hilltop home one wintery day. "I have a dream," she said, "of the most beautiful chalice in all of the country." Alice not being a religious sort wasn't sure just what a commission of the most beautiful chalice in the country involved. "Tell me more," suggested Alice. The matriarch was so enraptured by her chalice fantasy that Alice had to cough a few polite coughs to bring Claire Voyant back to earth. The matriarch pressed her hand on Alice's forehead and said, "Now I shall transfer my vision to your brain." And she did.

Special problems are posed by commissions. On some level the artist or craftmaker must produce a work satisfactory to the customer. It is not always possible to satisfy a customer's wishes, therefore a commission agreement should contain a discussion of what happens if the customer is not satisfied.

Since not everyone has Claire Voyant for a customer, the essential problem in a commission agreement is the customer's communication of his or her idea of the design to the artist. In a large commission, the best way to deal with the problem of satisfying the customer is to provide a design study for the commission proposed by the customer. If a design study would take time and/or materials, it would be best to negotiate a design contract with the customer. This agreement should include means of payment for the design—hourly, set sum for an agreed-upon number of sketches—and who gets the design sample. The contract also should provide that the artist receive payment whether or not the customer decides to order the proposed piece.

As work progresses on the commissioned piece, arrange for a timetable, part payments, and customer's approval of a satisfactory work rather than to "satisfy the purchaser."

Provide for a dissatisfied customer in the commission contract. Determine if the artist can retain the payments already made, the work itself, the copyright, and if the artist can complete and sell the work to another in the event of dissatisfaction by the purchaser. Your commission contract should also contain any special terms of sale such as those discussed on direct sales. If you use a special sales contract, attach a copy to the commission agreement. Even though a commission contract may be for a work valued at over $500, such an agreement should be considered a personal services contract, not one for the sale of goods, and as such, the verbal contract is enforceable. So be careful.

Some artists and craftpersons avoid commissioned work because of the burden of pleasing someone on a piece not yet produced. These creative people feel that it stunts their creativity.

Since the stated purpose of most art museums is to further the education and welfare of the people, museums usually enjoy a preferred legal status. For example, a law in New York state protects from seizure by creditors all fine artworks on loan to any nonprofit art museum there. Most museums are usually exempt from paying sales tax because of the nonprofit status. Because the role of an art museum is to promote the public welfare, certain of their practices are supposed to be more enlightened than those of the art galleries discussed earlier. Keep this special status in mind when dealing with these institutions. It could help.

Contractual arrangements between museums and artists usually involve either a loan of a work for exhibition or sale/gift to a museum. Absent an agreement to the contrary, a museum is only liable to the artist for loss of or damage to a borrowed piece when the damage arises from the museum's negligence. There is no protection for damage to a loaned piece because of non-negligent fire, flood, or acts of God. However, most museums do use contracts that provide added protection to the artist by including a clause that requires the museum to take the same care of a loaned piece as it takes of its own works. Further, many museum agreements insure the loaned work in an amount specified by the lender from the time it leaves the lender's until its return. Unless the artist has extensive insurance coverage, an insurance clause should be required. Other terms customarily contained in a museum contract are receipt, length of the loan, description of the work, any special precautions for preservation and safety of the work, responsibility for return, publicity, reproduction, and framing.

Conditions governing loan of object(s) to The Oakland Museum

...ssion for the time specified on the face of this
...t(s) may be withdrawn from an

(1) Object(s) lent to The Oakland Museum shall remain i...
agreement unless specific arrangements are made...
exhibition only by mutual consent of the lender and...

Care and Preservation

(2) The Oakland Museum will give object(s) left in its...
own. Evidence of damage to object(s) at the time...
be reported immediately to the lender. No alterat...
out the written authorization of the lender. Unless...
are in good condition and will withstand ordinar...

Transportation and Packing

(3) Costs of transportation and packing will be bor...
request or otherwise negotiated. The method...
included in the loan shall be packed for shipm...

(4) Unless otherwise instructed in writing. The (...

Insurance

policy, against all risks of physical loss or da...
during the period of the loan. Insurance will...
agreement, and must reflect fair market va...
lender to substantiate insurance valuation...
damage due to such causes as gradual de...
insurrection, confiscation by order of any...
transportation and/or trade. If a work wh...
repaired or replaced to the artist's speci...
of such replacement. A certificate of ins...
Oakland Museum's insurance coverage...
Museum in event of loss or damage...

Publicity and Photography

(5) Unless The Oakland Museum is notifi...
may be photographed and reproduce...
connected with an exhibition, and th...
for educational use.

Return of Loans

(6) Upon expiration of the loan, object...
ninety (90) days, The Oakland Muse...
special arrangements have been m...
lender's risk and expense, and ins...

(7) It is the lender's responsibility to...
ship of the property on loan. Fai...
nia Civil Code Sections 1899, et...
owner will be required to estab...
satisfactory to The Oakland M...

(8) When the object(s) is (are) re...
RELEASE section is not sign...
the condition of the object(s...
claims for loss or damage.

INCOMING LOAN AGREEMENT

The Oakland Museum
City of Oakland
1000 Oak Street
Oakland, California 94607-4892
TTY 415-451-3322

☐ **Art Department**
415-273-3005

☐ **History Department**
415-273-3842

☐ **Natural Sciences Department**
415-273-3884

Lender:
Institution or Individual

Street
City/State/Zip
Telephone
Contact Person

Exhibition Title:
Exhibition Dates:
Requested Arrival Date:
Requested Return Date:

Description of Object(s) (Accession number, artist, title, date, description, no. of items, condition, credit line) **Insurance Value**

Special handling instructions:
Insured by:
Shipping arrangements:

This loan is agreed to by the undersigned, subject to the conditions stated on the reverse.

The Oakland Museum Representative
Title _____
Date _____

Lender _____
Title _____
Date _____

LOAN RELEASE

The Lender hereby releases the The Oakland Museum from all liability or obligation for the above object(s) and any objects listed on additional CONTINUATION OF OBJECT LIST forms subject to any special conditions noted below and/or on the reverse.
Please sign and return within 30 days when object(s) has (have) been returned to lender.

List any losses, damage, or exceptions:

(If none, write NONE)

Lender's Signature _____ Date _____

White: Registrar's Copy   Yellow: Lender's Copy   Pink: Museum Copy   Goldenrod: Museum Copy

Figure 4.11 Sample Museum Loan Agreement

RESTRICTIONS ON GIFT

A sale or gift to a museum is like any other direct sale discussed earlier in this chapter. The checklist for a direct-sales agreement in this chapter should be consulted prior to negotiating the sale or gift. Unless the artist or craftmaker is quite well known, most museums will not buy or even accept a gift accompanied by restrictions or conditions. If you donate your work to a museum or give the museum a break on the price, consider including a clause in the sale contract that would give you the right to buy back your work if the museum decides to sell it. The Joint Artist-Museums Committee has recommended that a museum not sell or otherwise dispose of a gift without prior consultation with the artist.

BUY-BACK RIGHT

Alice's Allegory #17 or And Yet Another...

Alice's porcelain towel racks were so mind-blowing that *Art Vark* magazine wanted to pay Alice for some photographs of these magical devices to appear in their upcoming article entitled "The Crafty Home," scheduled for the spring spectacular issue.

Soon after Alice had produced the requested photographs, a letter arrived in the mailbox at the bottom of Rainbow Hill containing a "Grant of First-Time Magazine Rights" for Alice's signature. Alice sighed a knee-deep sigh and walked up the hill stopping at Karmic Hollow to meditate over this newest problem in her life.

This section discusses contracts to provide artwork or photographs for a book or magazine. Contracts for the publication of a book are in Chapter 7, "Especially for Writers." Your work may require other types of contracts.

The Graphic Artists Guild has several forms designed for commercial exploitation of work: artist/agent agreement, graphic designer's estimate/confirmation form, illustrator's confirmation form, illustrator's invoice, the textile designer's confirmation form. Consult the Graphic Artists Guild (GAG), 30 East 20th Street, New York, NY 10003.

Negotiating a contract with a publisher is a classic David-and-Goliath situation. With such bad odds to start with, there is no point in worsening the situation by giving up the little protection you have by making an oral agreement with a publisher. It is far better to be aware of the bitter truth from the start than to be surprised and outraged a year later when you see your drawing in an advertisement for breath deodorizer. "Paperback or cover art increases," according to *Publisher's Weekly* (October 2, 1987), quoting Len Leone's introduction to a Society of Illustrator's Catalogue. Leone said that some "paperback houses [were] commissioning 30 to 70 paintings a month and paying fees upwards of $7,000 per cover to illustrate a particular title...."

Ninety-nine percent of the time your publisher will present you with a form contract for your signature. You can negotiate changes. Some artists' groups have worked on form publishing contracts for graphic artists.

Before you sit down at the negotiating table, scrutinize the publisher's form contract and note your suggestions for changes.

Usually an initial clause of a publishing contract describes the work to be done by the artist. This contract clause should contain a *clear* description of the work required by the contract—the size, number, medium, and subject matter. Also, the deadlines for delivery of the preliminary and final work and any penalties for delay are usually set forth here. This clause or term usually specifies that the work be "satisfactory" to the publisher. If possible, insert the word "reasonably" before the word "satisfactory" to avoid a publisher's rejection of the work for no good reason.*

This term also should require that the artist consent to any changes in the work made by the publisher, but the publisher probably will want to require that the artist not withhold consent unreasonably.

The next term describes exactly what rights the publisher receives from the artist. Traditionally, the publisher got "all rights" sometimes described as "exclusive world rights in perpetuity." These rights fall into two categories—the basic right of the publisher to publish and sell the work and the subsidiary rights to the work. Subsidiary rights include paperback, book club, foreign, reprint, and performing rights.

Several limitations are now being placed on the grant of "all rights" by those negotiating with publishing companies. Nowadays, artists try to retain the copyright to their work so they can control the publisher's use of their work.** Also, artists usually include a term guaranteeing the return of their work after its use by the publisher, or within an agreed-upon period of time if not used. Another clause limiting the publisher's rights is one which retains for the artist all the rights that are not specifically transferred to the publisher. Another limitation that could be placed on the grant of all rights to the publisher is that the use of the work be only for purposes related to the publication of the book or magazine, thereby reserving subsidiary rights to him- or herself.

Many times magazine publishers only want the first-time magazine publication rights, with the artist retaining all other rights. Other magazine contracts provide

*For more information on the "satisfactory" problem, see the section of this chapter on commissions and Chapter 7, "Especially for Writers."
**For more information on copyright, see Chapter 3, "Copying," and Chapter 7, "Especially for Writers."

that all the rights granted by the contract will revert back to the artist after the first publication of the work.

PAYMENT

Payment for your work is either by means of a one-time fee or an advance and royalties. Your contract should state that any advance by the publisher is not refundable and also is not chargeable against other work contracted for by the same publisher.

ADVANCE NONREFUNDABLE

If a publication contracts for work that is subsequently not used, then many magazines will pay the illustrator a "kill fee" for the effort required to produce the work.

"KILL FEE"

ROYALTIES

If you will be getting royalties, it is important which dollar figure your royalty percentage will be based on—the retail price or the publisher's net price. If the royalties are based upon the lower figure—the publisher's net price—your royalty percentage should be greater than those royalties based upon the retail price. If it is possible that the work will be reproduced in another form, you should agree both on the basic royalty percentage and on the percentage of income from sale of subsidiary rights.

WARRANTIES

Most contracts will contain a clause whereby the artist agrees that the work produced is original and neither libelous, nor obscene, nor invades the subject's privacy. Here the artist usually agrees to pay any costs of the publisher resulting from lawsuits contesting the artist's work. If lawsuits arise concerning any of the matters covered in the warranty clause, most contracts provide that the artist will pay *all* the publisher's costs. The Authors Guild's model contract limits the author's liability only to the publisher's costs arising from final court judgments after appeals have been taken. Since you agree to indemnify the publishing company for any costs, include a term giving you the right to have a lawyer of your choosing participate both in any litigation concerning your work and any settlement offers.

INDEMNIFICATION

EXCLUSIVE CREDIT

Some contracts will prohibit the artist from selling artwork to competing publishers. Don't agree to that. You should also establish whether or not you will be given credit for your work and the manner in which credit will be given.

TERMINATION

If the publisher does not publish the work within an agreed-upon period of time or does not maintain the work in print, the artist should have the right to terminate the contract and regain all the rights transferred to the publisher. Also, the artist should be able to terminate in the event of the publisher's bankruptcy or insolvency.

AGENTS, REPRESENTATIVES, AND DISTRIBUTORS

Photographers, illustrators, artists, craftmakers, and writers all may use agents to sell their work. The relationship with an agent is very similar to the artist or craftmaker's relationship with a gallery. For information on author-agent relationships, see Chapter 7, "Especially for Writers."

BEWARE OF FLY-BY-NIGHT AGENTS

Choice of an agent is *very* important. Many artists and craftmakers have been taken by a fast-talking agent who is here today and gone tomorrow with all the aritst's work. And it is hard to track them down because an agent usually doesn't have a gallery or a showroom. Get the names of other people your agent has represented and check the person out before you place yourself in his or her hands. Larry Laidback has nothing but praise for his agent who sets up shows and sells Larry's work ten times faster than Larry can. Different strokes for different folks. The Society of Photographers and Artist Representatives, Inc. (SPAR, P. O. Box 845, FDR Station, New York, NY 10022) is a source for finding an agent.

AGENT CONTRACT

An agent usually takes a percentage on the work he or she sells for you. Many times representatives will want their percentage (10 to 50 percent) before the customer has paid the bill, which could pose a problem.

The individual requirements of each type of business have resulted in customary terms for agency contracts in that business. The best way to discover the special points in an agency contract for your area is to contact someone who has already dealt with an agent. The Graphic Artists Guild also has a model artist-agent agreement.

Issues arising in any agreement with an agent include: commission, exclusivity, and method of payment. Make sure the figure upon which the commission is based is clear; if the sale price includes special costs to the photographer, for example, does the agent still get a commission based upon the total sale price? Does the agent have the exclusive right to sell all the artist's work or can the artist or someone else also sell the work? Can the agent handle other work that competes with the work already represented by the agent? Does the customer pay the agent or the artist? Be sure that the exact powers of the agent are spelled out, because absent limiting language, an agent can make agreements on your behalf that bind you. See the checklist for an artist-gallery agreement in this chapter for other issues that should be considered when contracting with an agent.

SHOWS

Art shows run the gamut from craft fairs to museum-sponsored competitions, mall shows, street fairs, juried shows, and others. Each show has its particular way of doing things, so read all the promotional literature carefully and obtain answers to any questions that you might have.

PROMOTER'S ADVERTISING

Any organizer of an art show—juried or not—is bound by the guarantees made in the show's promotional material. If you arrive at a mall show only to discover that the "free" both space requires a $50 rental fee, the Consumer Fraud Department of the State Attorney General's Office should be contacted, since a large group of people was misled by the false advertising of the promoter. Suing the show's organizers is also available as a remedy but is usually too expensive and time consuming for this sort of problem.*

INSURANCE

Another special consideration for shows is who bears the costs and insurance for items shipped to a show for judging and/or sale and also for those items returned. Stories of damage to works shipped to a show are plentiful, so make sure that someone insures your creation in transit and while in the show. Also agree that if a piece of your work is damaged, you will have the right to substitute another for the duration of the show. Besides the considerations discussed above, sales at a show are like any direct sale, and that checklist should be consulted. Many artists and craftpersons prefer selling at shows because they can keep the middle man out.

Another problem that comes up at shows is payment by cash, credit card, or personal check. Make sure any check is made out to your "bank account" name for the exact amount of the sale. Be sure that the customer's address is on the check and that the correct amount has been written in. Verify address and identity with a driver's license and one other ID—not one that can be easily forged. Ask for a check-guarantee card. Note the date and the maximum amount guaranteed. Watch the person sign the check and compare the signature with other ID signatures. Don't take third-party checks, which are checks made out to someone else and signed over to you. Never cash a check. Finally, for big sales with an unknown person, you might want a cashier's check.

Be careful to avoid large bills and if there is a counterfeit alert in the community, pay attention to the bills you get.

For credit card sales, be sure to compare the signatures and follow precisely credit card company's procedures or you may get stuck.

PRINTS

WILL THE REAL FINE PRINT PLEASE STAND UP

FINE PRINT LAWS

In recent years, a special wrinkle has developed in the area of fine print sales. A booming art market resulting in an astronomical rise in both the price and sales of prints and the development of sophisticated photomechanical reproduction techniques has caused John Q. Public to wonder just what is behind those high price tags—etching, woodcut, lithography, seriography, engraving, or what? In some instances unscrupulous dealers grossly overcharged for reproductions, or peddled editions said to be limited but which contained as many prints as the stars in the sky. As a result,

*For more information on remedies for rip-offs, see the section in this chapter on enforcing your contracts.

legislation regulating the advertising and sale of prints passed some states.* A careful record of the printing process for each edition will protect the artist from complaints of fraud.

The states which passed laws governing the sale of fine prints vary in some of these particulars:

- any alteration of plates
- application to charitable organization
- if artist is deceased, whether the print is a restrike edition or if plate has been reworked
- name of printer
- penalties
- prior or other editions
- status of plate
- total size of limited editions
- type of print
- what constitutes a signed print
- what work is covered, i.e., definitions of what is a fine print, multiples

Some states require (and some artists desire) the use of a print documentation form.

Since the artist's signature indicates the artist's approval of the print as authentic, an artist could be held liable for signing a print which defrauds the public either as to the printing process or the number in the edition.

Because of the booming print market, many artists find themselves contracting for the production of prints of their work. Generally, there are three ways to have your work printed:

- contracting with a printer
- co-publishing with a print workshop or gallery
- accepting a commission for a print

CONTRACTING WITH PRINTERS

The first arrangement is fairly straightforward with the artist retaining all the rights and making all the payments. Be sure that the printer keeps sufficient records so that you can properly document the print upon sale as required by the laws of various states. Most importantly, the artist wants the print to satisfy him or her. Any printer's agreement, order form, and so forth should set out the specific materials and methods to be used and the artist's approval at each step of the process.

Under the co-publishing arrangement, the artist provides the original image and time in the printshop and the print workshop provides the equipment, each party taking a share of the prints. With gallery co-publishing arrangements, the parties must agree on the size of the edition, the prints kept by each, the consignment terms on the prints the gallery keeps, the term of the agreement, the sale price of the gallery prints, and what happens to the gallery prints at the end of the agreement.

The commission arrangement is similar to the commission contract discussed earlier in the chapter. Payment is either by flat fee or a royalty percentage. Under this arrangement, the artist usually gets a few artist's proofs.

Whether doing it alone or with another party, decisions regarding the number of prints, the division of them if other parties are involved, and whether to sign them or not will need to be made.

Ownership pivots around the prints themselves, the plate or other image, and ownership of the copyright. Under any of these arrangements, be sure to reserve the right to approve the final print. Also provide in the agreement that the print contain a copyright notice and, if possible, that you retain the copyright.

---

*Check with a knowledgeable attorney about print laws in your state. In 1982 New York adopted a new law called the Visual Arts Multiples Law which governs transactions in art prints and photographs. This law requires disclosure of information in certain categories.

For those artists who are lecturers, a short and long model lecture agreement for artists is found in Tad Crawford's *Legal Guide for the Visual Artist*. ARTIST-LECTURER

SELLING PHOTOGRAPHS

INTRODUCTION

Selling a photograph is essentially like selling a painting or weaving or other form of art or craft. This section on contracts for photographers supplements the information presented earlier. Whether you are a photographer or a potter, the basic terms of a commission agreement are the same. Ditto contracts with galleries, museums, agents, and publishers. A helpful "Working Arts" publication, entitled *Photography and Copyright, Film Contracts,* is available from CLA.

Minimally, when you submit photos, indicate what you are submitting; that it's for selection purposes only; that images are returnable in "X" days; that if lost, there will be a fee of "Y" dollars; and if images are selected and a fee is negotiated, you must be provided with a proper copyright notice. On selection, you grant them one-time, non-exclusive North American rights to use (describe) photo, size in use, color or black and white, where and when used (only 1990 *Southwest Art* Magazine, for example) and again, a proper copyright notice must be provided.

The special terms contained in a contract for the sale of a photograph arise from the nature of the photographic medium—the photographing of a subject and the subsequent making of prints from the transparency. A body of law and custom has grown up around the handling of both the print and the negative as well as the subject matter.

The basic question that must be clearly answered in any agreement concerning the sale of a photograph is what *exactly* is the photographer selling and the customer buying. The problems that occur in this area usually result from too vague a sales agreement—"Sure, I'll sell you this photograph." So be very clear about exactly what you are selling.

The magic words used to express the sale of *all* rights to a photograph are the words *exclusive* rights. The customer then has the right to unlimited use of the photograph including the right to: EXCLUSIVE RIGHTS

- the photograph itself.
- reproduce the photograph.
- crop or retitle the photograph.
- copy the photograph in another medium.
- make any other use of the photograph.

It is not clear at this time if copyright would be included in the list of "exclusive rights." If you do not wish to sell the copyright when you grant exclusive rights, indicate in your contract that "artist retains copyright." COPYRIGHT

Most times a customer only receives the right to a limited use of a photograph—basically the right to rent the photograph. Magazines will usually buy "first rights"—the right to be the first to publish the photograph. Similarly, when a customer buys "one-time rights," the photographer retains all rights to the photograph except for the right of the customer to use the photograph one time. If the photograph is sold as part of a limited edition, then the customer has the right to possess one print out of the total number in the edition—no more and no less. FIRST RIGHTS ONE-TIME RIGHTS LIMITED EDITION

Without a contract concerning the sale of photographs, the courts look to the relationship between the photographer and customer for guidance in determining who owns what. If the photographer is "employed" by the customer, then the customer has all the rights to the photographs taken, except for the possession of the negatives. Only if the photographer is free-lancing and covering all expenses does he or she have full rights to the photographs taken. CUSTOMER'S RIGHTS

Other items in a photography contract that limit the customer's use of the photograph could be a term requiring that the customer give the photographer credit for the photograph and a clause prohibiting the customer from cropping, retitling, or otherwise changing the photograph. CREDIT LINE CROPPING RETITLING

Two other legal questions that occur in photography contracts arise from the possibility of a lawsuit based either upon the invasion of the subject's privacy or upon the libelous use of a photograph. If you wish to read more about invasion of privacy, libel by photography, exceptions to or obtaining a release from the subject, see the sections on these topics in Chapter 2, "Legal Restrictions on Content and Materials." A word about releases. Keep them written. Make them as broad as possible, get one from every individual, group, or entity whose name, likeness, image, photograph, performance, or story is being depicted or recorded. A release is an agreement where one releases a right, claim, or privilege and insulates the other party from claims asserted after the work is finished. There may be state laws covering the use of child models. Contact your state department of labor or your lawyer.

INDEMNIFICATION

Because of the possibility of lawsuits, many magazine publishers will require that the photographer indemnify (pay any costs) incurred by the publisher in defending a lawsuit brought because of the photograph. This puts a heavy burden on the photographer, who can least afford such an expense. The photographer should make sure that, if he or she is sued because of the customer's use of the photograph (retitling, placement, etc.), the customer will indemnify the photographer.

VALUE OF LOST PHOTOGRAPH OR TRANSPARENCY

Another special problem for photographers is establishing liability and valuing a photograph or transparency should the customer lose or damage the work prior to purchase. First, the parties should agree that the risk of loss is on the customer while the photographs are in the hands of the customer prior to sale or approval. Without this agreement the risk of loss remains with the seller until the sale is completed. So as mentioned above, when submitting photographs or transparencies to a customer on approval, obtain a receipt which lists the number of photographs or transparencies delivered and states that the customer is liable for any loss. Also agree on a dollar value before the prints or transparencies are released, because of the difficult task of placing a value on the lost photographs. Without such an agreement the value would be based upon the selling price of a similar work by the photographer or if there is no similar photograph, the cost to the photographer (transportation and materials) to replace the lost photograph. Man Ray received $15,000 for eleven transparencies lost by The American Museum of Natural History. Today, value is often set at $1,500 per image. A similar valuation problem occurs when film is lost or damaged by the processor or shipper.* The American Society of Magazine Photographers (ASMP), 419 Park Avenue South, Room 1407, New York 10016, has publications with information and forms of benefit to photographers including a model submission/holding form, sometimes called a delivery memo. This could be used for any art work, not just photographic negatives, transparencies, and so forth. Its provisions include:

- insurance
- objection to terms in so many days
- fees for keeping the material too long
- specified damages for loss
- no use without transfer of cash
- ownership

This is directed to situations where a person is looking over an artist's, craftmaker's or photographer's work but no sale decision has been reached.

CONTRACTS CONCERNING "OBSCENE" MATERIAL

A final area of problems for photographers concerns the enforcement of a contract deemed by the courts to concern the production of "obscene" material. Many courts will not enforce a contract which is considered to deal with obscene materials. For a discussion of the current legal definition of the word *obscene,* see Chapter 2, "Legal Restrictions on Content and Materials."

*Also beware of the processor's contract clauses, which attempt to limit their liability for lost or damaged film to the cost of the unexposed film itself.

In summary, with photos, you must answer three questions in the affirmative: can you take it, can you use it, and do you own it? There are prohibitions against photographing a scene or subject without permission. Some of these are secret military installations, money, a photo that requires you to trespass on private property, and a copyrighted performance such as a jazz concert. You probably own it, if it is not shot as an employee or work for hire. You can probably use it with a model release, but if the presentation distorts the subject, the risk may go beyond the release. For a discussion of some of these questions relative to Canadian law, see Chapter 3, "Copying."

Memorandum

TO: Bigodi Bigthumb File
FROM: MB
RE: Letter Received from Client
DO: Contact client to come in as soon as possible to discuss strategy of locating adverse party and regaining jewelry or its equivalent.

Hiring a lawyer and rushing to court is not the only way to deal with a problem like Bigodi Bigthumb's. The Better Business Bureau of Winslow may be concerned about the town's image and could be helpful. The State Attorney General's Office in Phoenix may have a new attorney who is especially concerned about the illicit practices of Indian traders. Maybe the trader met with a fatal accident on the Interstate and his estate will take care of all the business debts.

Sometimes a problem may arise from a simple misunderstanding or lack of communication. If the problem is fairly straightforward or too insignificant to warrant the assistance of an attorney, start the enforcement process with a telephone call to the person in charge of the business.* Have the documents (receipts, contracts,

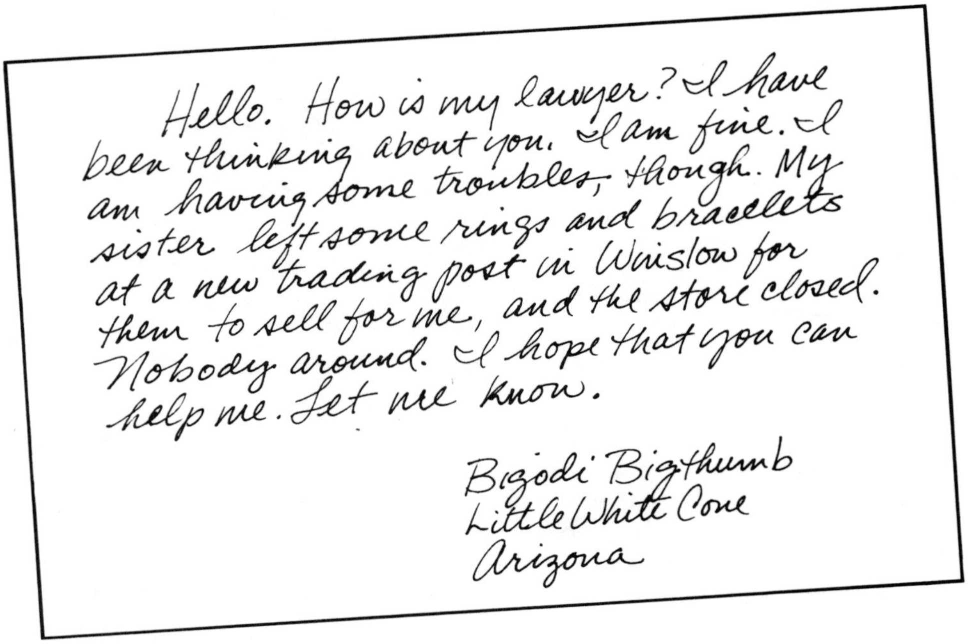

Hello. How is my lawyer? I have been thinking about you. I am fine. I am having some troubles, though. My sister left some rings and bracelets at a new trading post in Winslow for them to sell for me, and the store closed. Nobody around. I hope that you can help me. Let me know.

Bigodi Bigthumb
Little White Cone
Arizona

Figure 4.12 Bigodi Bigthumb letter

*Douglas Matthews' book, *Sue the B#st#rds*, (Dell, 1975), has a good chapter on the steps to take before you go to court. Don't do what one of my clients did. She was faced with a copyright infringement claim against some local businessmen who were known for being tough. When she talked with them they threatened to punch her out. Then she wrote a demand letter for $200 and got no response, and she came to see me and wanted to recover several thousand dollars. A tough case!

```
                                    37 Starlit Acres
                                    Espanola,  NM  87342

                                    April 27, 1988


Jack Splatte
Mirror Image
24 Hyperson Mall
Albuquerque,  NM  87125

Dear Jack,

     I have called several times to talk to you about the
payments that you owe me for the work that I did for you.
I agreed to take half up front and the balance when the
job was done.  To date I have not received the second half
- $150 - although I finished the work over a month ago.

     I need the money that you owe me and would appreciate
payment within the next two weeks.  Please call me immediately
if this is not possible.

     If I do not receive the money owed me by May 15, 1988,
I will take any steps necessary including legal action to
get the money that I am owed.

     I do hope we can resolve this without too much trouble.


                                    Sincerely yours,

                                    Skip

                                    Skip Reynaldo
```

Figure 4.13 Sample demand letter

etc.) concerning the problem in front of you during the telephone call so that you can refer to them. State your case and listen carefully to the response and take notes. Remember that your presentation of the facts can be crucial to your case. If a telephone call does not take care of the problem, immediately send an "I am serious about this" letter. In the letter, state the facts of your case and what you want from your opponent. Save copies of this letter as well as *all* other documents relating to the transaction in question, no matter how spindled, torn, or mutilated. See Figure 4.13 for a sample demand letter.

DEMAND LETTER

TIMING

In contemplating your strategy, you should not wait so long to go to court that it is too late. All states have laws concerning the time within which a lawsuit must be filed. This is called a statute of limitations. A suit for the breach of a written contract must be filed within two to ten years from the time of the breach, depending on your state's law. For the breach of a contract involving the sale of goods, the lawsuit must usually be brought within four years of the breach.

If you still have no success, then consider the possibility of filing a complaint with an agency that handles the sort of complaint that you have. Agencies that provide assistance to shortchanged consumers can be grouped into three basic categories:

- private organizations
- local and state government agencies
- federal agencies

You will find the Better Business Bureau and a Chamber of Commerce in most fair-sized cities. How effective these organizations are depends on local staffing, membership, and about whom you are complaining. The Better Business Bureau might be helpful in arbitrating a disagreement with a gallery concerning the correct amount of the gallery's commission because the BBB's basic concern is to maintain a good image of local business. In over one hundred cities, the Better Business Bureau provides free arbitration services for aggrieved consumers. However, the adversaries must voluntarily submit themselves to the arbitration proceeding because the Bureau has no powers to require a merchant to submit to arbitration.

PRIVATE ORGANIZATIONS

Sometimes an effective place to make a complaint, especially concerning a practice that affects a group of people, is the consumer "hotline" affiliated with the local television or radio station. This would be a good place to complain about a sales representative who showed up at the last arts and crafts fair and took your whole line of leather belts and disappeared into thin air. The television station might help you track down the thief. Also, the local Nader-supported Public Interest Research Group may be helpful for a group gripe.*

All states have passed laws to protect the consumer from fraud or "deceptive sales practices." The laws authorize state funds for investigation of fraudulent practices and usually give the state Attorney General power to seek an order halting such practices. Some state laws also give consumers a right to recover cash damages if they can show that they were victims of deceptive sales practices. In most states, the state Attorney General's Office is responsible for administering these laws and would be the agency to contact for help. A mall-show promoter who did not provide the mass prepublicity campaign that had been agreed upon, or a clay distributor selling clay loaded with lime are good targets for the state consumer protection laws. Figure 4.15 is a consumer complaint that would be completed by Bigodi Bigthumb for submission to the state Attorney General's Office.

LOCAL AND STATE AGENCIES

Many federal agencies have departments concerned with some aspect of consumer protection. The General Services Administration staffs the Federal Information Center in key cities across the country. These centers serve as the public's directory to the federal bureaucracy for the purpose of both making complaints and obtaining information. The United States Postal Inspection Service operates a consumer-protection program which assists in any mail-fraud problems. A Navajo weaver I know was helped by the U.S. Postal Inspection Service in regaining a rug she had sold through the mail to a Connecticut couple who never paid the balance due. A coordinating Consumer Affairs Office is presently located in the Department of Health, Education, and Welfare.

FEDERAL AGENCIES

Sometimes it is just not worth bringing a lawsuit, even though right and justice are on your side. If the only people liable for the disappearance of the best in your line of batiks are applying for food stamps, it may not make sense to file a lawsuit against them. Size up the situation—be cagey. The chart on page 99 will help you size up your prospects for a successful court suit.

GOING TO COURT

SIZING UP YOUR LAWSUIT

*Check your local telephone book for PIRG's address and telephone number.

State of California
Office of the Attorney General
DEPARTMENT OF JUSTICE
CONSUMER COMPLAINT

JOHN K. VAN DE KAMP
Attorney General

Public Inquiry Unit
Office of the Attorney General
P.O. Box 944255
Sacramento, CA   94244-2550
(916) 322-3360
Toll Free—California Only:
800-952-5225

I wish to file a complaint against the company named below. I understand that the Attorney General does not represent private citizens seeking the return of their money or other personal remedies. I am, however, filing this complaint to notify your office of the activities of this company so that it may be determined if law enforcement or legal action is warranted.

PLEASE TYPE OR PRINT LEGIBLY

1. Party Complaining

Name

Address

City ___ State ___ ZIP

Home Phone ___ Work Phone

2. Complaint Against

Name

Address ___ State ___ ZIP

City

Home Phone ___ Work Phone

NAME OF PRODUCT OR SERVICE INVOLVED:

If product or service advertised (attach copy of ad if possible): When ___ (date)

Where

Was a contract signed? Yes ☐ No ☐

Have you contacted another agency for assistance? Yes ☐ No ☐

What agency? ___

DATE OF TRANSACTION:

Have you contacted an attorney? Yes ☐ No ☐

If so, list the attorney's name, address, and phone number:

I will sign a sworn statement regarding these charges if needed: Yes ☐ No ☐

This complaint may be sent to the company complained about: Yes ☐ No ☐

Attach two copies of contract in addition to copies in duplicate of other pertinent papers. (PLEASE DO NOT SEND ORIGINALS; DOCUMENTS CANNOT BE RETURNED.)

Briefly describe events in the order in which they happened. Indicate dollar amount in dispute. If additional space is required, attach pages in DUPLICATE.

Dated ___

Signed ___

PLEASE RETURN BOTH COPIES OF THIS FORM

PIU-3 (REV. 3-87)

87 82017

Figure 4.14 California consumer complaint form

"YOU CAN'T SQUEEZE BLOOD OUT OF A TURNIP"

Whose name and address are you going to put on the complaint? You might have to find out who really owns the gallery by checking with the city business-license department or the state corporation commission. If the owners live out of town or out of state, this adds to the difficulty of the suit. Poor defendants are the worst kind because it is usually impossible to collect a judgment from them.

THE WINNINGS

What amount will you get if you win? The amount you sue for in a contract suit is your dollar loss resulting from your opponent's failure to uphold his or her end of the bargain. If money cannot replace the loss, then sometimes a court will order that the loser perform some action like returning Bigodi Bigthumb's jewelry.

EXPENSES OF LAWSUIT

How much will the lawsuit cost? Will you use a lawyer or can you represent yourself in the local small claims court?* Is the case too big for a small claims court? Can you get legal help free from a local organization?** What is the filing fee for a lawsuit? How do you serve the papers on the adverse party and what is the fee for service of the papers? You may have to take time off from work. This also costs money.

*All states have a small-claims-type court. In some states these courts are called justice or magistrate court.
**Chapter 8, "Obtaining Legal Assistance," lists sources of free legal help for artists, craftmakers, and writers.

File No.: _____

Remarks:

Category: PS ___ V ___

By:

(PLEASE TYPE OR PRINT IN BLACK INK ONLY)

State YOUR Name and Address: _____

State Name and Address of FIRM complained against: _____

_____

_____

_____

Zip _____   Zip _____

Home Phone_____ Bus. _____   Phone_____

Please indicate which of the following age categories applies to you: (For statistical purposes only.) Under 19 ( ); 20-39 ( ); 40-59 ( ) or 60 & over ( )

May we send a copy of this to the person or FIRM you are complaining against? ( )Yes ( )No (If your response is no, we may be prevented from taking any action on your complaint.)

We may send a copy of your complaint to another government agency for their review or investigation. May we also send a copy to any private agency which resolves disputes like those raised in your complaint? ( )Yes ( )No

Did you sign any documents? ( )Yes ( )No

Date of Transaction _____ *(Please attach copies of each document)*

Was an oral or written warranty given? ( )Yes ( )No

Place of Transaction _____

Name of Salesperson _____

Witness to Transaction _____

Have you complained to the FIRM? ( )Yes ( )No   To Whom? _____

What was their response? _____

Was product or service advertised? ( )Yes ( )No   If Yes, indicate how advertised and indicate date:

_____

Do you have an attorney? ( )Yes ( )No   If Yes, give attorney's name and address: _____

_____

Is any legal action pending? ( )Yes ( )No   Explain _____

Other consumer agencies contacted: _____

Please explain the entire circumstances surrounding your complaint below and on the reverse side. Please fully describe any oral or written misrepresentations made to you:

_____

_____

This statement is true and accurate to the best of my knowledge.

Date _____

Signature _____

AG/FFD #10

Figure 4.15 Arizona consumer complaint form

At this point, you should consider the possibility of getting a lawyer to send a letter to your opponent for you. Since the time and expense of sending a lawyer's letter is far less than going to court, this step makes good sense in many cases.

If, after calculating all the angles, a lawsuit still seems sensible, it is likely that your case will never see the inside of a courtroom. Eighty to ninety percent of the suits filed in small claims court are settled before a trial is held.

LAWYER'S LETTER

Figure 4.16 Utah small claims form

The partial left form reads:

INSTRUCTIONS TO [cut off]

1. **Filing Suit.** To begin an action in Small Claims Court, come to [cut off] necessary papers for you. The maximum amount you may ask for is [cut off] cannot be used to sue for possession of property or to put a tenant ou[cut off] ... Small Claims Court is located, or a person living elsewhere i[cut off] treated as a "person." Bring with you the following information:

(1) Amount of claim and what it is for; and

(2) Name, street address, (not P.O. Box) and telephone number [cut off]

The debt must be owed to you; you may not bring an action on b[cut off] an employee to be his representative. The clerk will prepare the [cut off] A filing fee of $12.50 will be charged, as well as a service fee a[cut off] directing him to come to the court to answer your claim.

2. **Trial.** A trial date will be set by the clerk. The clerk will g[cut off] date entered on it. It will be your responsibility to appear at [cut off] notice, and to bring with you any papers and witnesses to pro[cut off] tions, below.) **IF YOU FAIL TO APPEAR AT TRIAL, YOUR CAS**[cut off]

INSTRUCTIONS T[cut off]

1. **Trial.** You have had a lawsuit filed against you. If you [cut off] court date and bring with you any papers, evidence, or [cut off] "Witnesses" under General Instructions, below.) **IF YOU** [cut off] **AGAINST YOU.**

2. **Payment.** If you do not dispute plaintiff's claim, yo[cut off] judgment. Include the court costs shown in the affidavit [cut off] court, additional court costs will be charged to you.

GENERAL [cut off]

1. **Attorney.** Small Claims Court is informal. Parties u[cut off] if you wish.

2. **Settlement.** If the claim is settled prior to court [cut off]

3. **Witnesses.** If there is someone you need as a [cut off] issue a subpoena, which will compel the person to [cut off] than 10 days before the trial date.

4. **Judgment.** If the judgment is for plaintiff, pl[cut off] along with a letter of demand for payment. If the [cut off] judgment. The procedures for doing so (garnish[cut off]

5. **Appeal.** By law, the plaintiff cannot appeal [cut off] within 5 days, and a new trial will be held in Di[cut off]

The right form reads:

CASE NO.	PLAINTIFF	DEFENDANT
DATE FILED		VS.
	ADDRESS	ADDRESS

CIRCUIT COURT, STATE OF UTAH

SAN JUAN **County,** MONTICELLO **Department**

STATE OF UTAH) ss.
COUNTY OF SAN JUAN)

SMALL CLAIMS AFFIDAVIT

The affiant undersigned, being sworn, states:

1) DEFENDANT OWES PLAINTIFF THE FOLLOWING SUM: $ _____

PLUS COURT COST: FILING FEE . . . . . $ _____
ESTIMATED SERVICE . . . $ _____
ESTIMATED TOTAL . . . . _____

2) THE PARTIES LIVE AT THE ADDRESSES SHOWN ABOVE. DEFENDANT HAS BEEN ASKED TO PAY THE CLAIM, BUT HAS NOT DONE SO.

3) THE CLAIM AROSE ON THIS DATE _____ BECAUSE OF THE FOLLOWING:
_____
_____

SUBSCRIBED AND SWORN TO BEFORE ME ON _____

AFFIANT'S SIGNATURE   CLERK OR DEPUTY CLERK

ORDER TO DEFENDANT

YOU ARE DIRECTED TO COME TO SMALL CLAIMS COURT FOR TRIAL AT THE DATE AND TIME SHOWN:

DATE OF TRIAL	TIME OF TRIAL	ADDRESS OF COURT
		SAN JUAN COUNTY COURTHOUSE COURT ROOM MONTICELLO, UTAH

YOU SHOULD BRING WITH YOU ALL WITNESSES, PAPERS, EVIDENCE AND BOOKS YOU NEED TO SUPPORT YOUR DEFENSE.

IF YOU FAIL TO APPEAR AT THE TRIAL, JUDGMENT MAY BE ENTERED AGAINST YOU FOR THE AMOUNT CLAIMED BY PLAINTIFF (SHOWN ABOVE, PARAGRAPH 1) PLUS COURT COSTS. PLEASE READ THE INSTRUCTIONS ON THE BACK.

DATE   CLERK OF COURT OR CIRCUIT JUDGE

ENDORSEMENT OF SERVICE
SERVED BY SIGNATURE _____
TITLE _____
ON DATE OF _____
FEE FOR SERVICES $ _____

Small Claims Affidavit & Order

SMALL CLAIMS COURT

The next step is to decide if you can and want to file suit in small claims court. Sometimes this is a quicker and cheaper (lower filing fees and no attorney's fee if you represent yourself) way of getting the courts to help you with your problems.* Find out if your case can be handled by the small claims court. Telephone the clerk of the court and ask what is the maximum amount that can be sued for in small claims court. Tell the clerk the current business and home address of your adversary and ask if the small claims court would cover his or her location. Stroll around

CHECK IT OUT

the courthouse when you go down to fill out the forms. Sit inside a courtroom to see what's happening there, who's there, what they are saying, who's winning, what sort of judges, and so on. If you feel comfortable with the small claims court, fill out the complaint form, file it, and pay your money. Figure 4.16 is a sample small-claims-court complaint form. The clerk will tell you how to serve the right papers

*Free or inexpensive lawyer's advice may be available for assistance with making a claim in small claims court. Also, the state Attorney General's Office may have a pamphlet with instructions on small-claims-court procedures.

on your opponent. Don't forget that your opponent will file an answer to your papers and in that answer can charge you with any debts that you may owe him or her. This procedure is called a *counterclaim*.

COUNTERCLAIM

After you file the lawsuit, your opponent may finally realize that you are serious and will make a settlement offer. Carefully consider taking an offer. If you can't file your lawsuit in small claims court or you decide for some reason not to, then you will need the service of a lawyer. Read Chapter 8, "Obtaining Legal Assistance," before you shop for your lawyer. Also consult that chapter for information on sources of free legal help.

FREE LEGAL HELP

SIZING UP A LAWSUIT

		YES	NO
Adverse Party			
Available for service or papers:		☐	☐
Has Assets:		☐	☐
Recovery Expected Estimated Damages (or value of items regained):	_____		
Plus Filing, service and lawyer's fees (if available from adverse party):	+ _____		
Minus Filing, service and lawyer's fees (if NOT available from adverse party):	− _____		
Minus Other expenses (witnesses, discovery, et cetera):	− _____		
Minus Counterclaim (if any):	− _____		
Equals Total Estimated Judgment:	= _____	☐ (if higher than total estimated expenses)	☐ (if lower than total estimated expenses)

The *Law Society of Upper Canada Bar Admission* Course Materials Creditors and Debtors rights 1985-1986 supplement discusses these procedures. If you are forced to a lawsuit to collect an account, you need to remember that obtaining a judgment does not by itself guarantee collection, and that the collection of a judgment debt can be very difficult and frustrating. Be sure that you have all the necessary documentation and that you calculate the amount owed correctly. The Ministry of Consumer and Commercial Relations can give you "after a search" the debtor's proper name or legal status so that you can determine how to caption the case and who to serve. You will also want to check and see if the debtor is in bankruptcy or if there are any outstanding writs against the debtor. Debts in Canada can be pursued in either Supreme Court, the District Court, or Provencial Court (also known as a Small Claims Court). The District Court has jurisdiction over claims up to $25,000 and the lower court will probably have cases come to trial sooner.

GOING TO COURT IN CANADA

If your letter demanding payment hasn't gotten any results, you should check to see if there is a form entitled "Statement of Claim for Debt" in your District Court which you can use. There are companies within the United States and Canada that print forms which are available for sale through catalogs or business supply stores. You can check with the courthouse to get the addresses of these particular companies.

If the defendant is going to defend a lawsuit, then the matter proceeds through some steps to trial and judgment. If not, then a default may be posted. Once a judgment is obtained, a writ of seizure for sale is used for enforcement and it directs the sheriff to seize a portion of the judgment debtor's property which, when sold, will satisfy the amount of the execution. There are also garnishment proceedings, which can attach the debtor's salary directly at the employment level.

SMALL CLAIMS COURT

The Courts of Justice Act streamlined some of the smaller courts and created a new Provencial Court, also known as a Small Claims Court, for use where there is a claim for payment of money or the recovery of property not exceeding $1,000, exclusive of interest and costs, generally.

The Small Claims Court in the Judicial District of York has a jurisdiction up to $3,000. These Small Claims Courts have great latitude in the administration of justice, and therefore, a plaintiff-creditor or the creditor's solicitor commences the action by making a claim and filing it with the court clerk, along with a filing fee. The place of filing is where the cause of action arose or where the defendant lives or does business. The claim should be stated in simple, non-technical language and attached to it should be any documents required to support it. The court bailiff will serve the plaintiff for the defendant-debtor. If the defendant-debtor doesn't file a statement of defense within twenty days after receiving the claim, the defendant is in default and a default judgment can be entered. If the defendant defends, then there can be a pretrial conference, but the actual trial pursued is inexpensive and traditional rules of evidence are not strictly enforced.

Once the court orders payment by the debtor, that is, the creditor gets the judgment, then the same steps will follow to enforce the order, that is, a writ of seizure and sale of the property or land; an examination of the debtor to determine what assets the debtor has; or garnishment, if that's possible. There are other procedures in Ontario.

ARBITRATION

Arbitration allows parties to choose their own forum to resolve disputes, and in some provinces, such as Ontario, there is an Arbitration Act. The use of arbitration should depend on the issue and amount of money.

CHAPTER FIVE

Federal Income Tax

LEGAL ADVICE? NOT ON YOUR LIFE.

TAX BACKGROUND

Historically, taxes consisted of money, services, or payment in kind demanded by a government for its support. The normal Roman land tax was one-tenth of annual yields; the Bible speaks of the tithe (one-tenth) as the annual tax; European serfs satisfied their taxes by working a certain number of days for their lords; the Chinese paid entry and exit fees at their ports of entry; and nobles levied tolls on goods transported by roads or rivers that crossed their lands.

HISTORY

TAXATION WITHOUT REPRESENTATION

Taxes triggered some revolutions. Some say the stamp tax, plus other British duties levied by the British Parliament, started the American Revolution.

These old forms of taxation left untouched the wealth resulting from the Industrial Revolution. Taxation could recapture some of the accumulated wealth and redistribute it to the poor. Even in the Middle Ages government recognized the unfairness of taxing the rich man and the peasant at the same rate and utilized one's ability to pay: the 1377 poll tax taxed the Duke of Lancaster at a rate 520 times that of the peasant. The root of modern income tax was a 1799 English 10 percent income tax which was passed as a temporary wartime measure. The first personal income tax law enacted in the United States was passed during and after the Civil War. The second United States income tax law was held unconstitutional in 1895 by the United States Supreme Court. It took a constitutional amendment, the sixteenth, in order to pass our income tax law.

TAX ROOTS

THE SIXTEENTH AMENDMENT TO UNITED STATES CONSTITUTION

Memorandum
TO: Rose Weaver File
FROM: MB
RE: Tax Confusion of Client

During a discussion with Rose Weaver, I asked the amount of income reported on her 1987 federal tax return. She told me she had never filed any tax returns on her craft business as wholesalers told her that she did not have to pay any taxes as long as she was wholesaling.

I explained to her that the tax the wholesalers referred to was not the federal income tax, but the state sales tax. I also explained different kinds of taxes.

The three general categories of taxes that concern craftpersons, artists, and authors are depicted in this chart:*

AN ASSORTMENT OF TAXES

- Federal
    Personal income tax
        Estimated Tax—self-employed
        Withholdings—employee
    Self-employment tax—(social security tax for self-employed)
    Unemployment tax
    Corporate tax
    Estate and gift tax
    Federal excise tax
- State
    Personal income tax
    Unincorporated business tax
    Sales tax
    Estate and gift tax
    Personal property tax
    Licenses
    Inventory tax

The art of taxation consists in so plucking the goose as to obtain the largest amount of feathers with the least amount of hissing.
—A SEVENTEENTH-CENTURY FRENCH STATESMAN

*Not every person would be subject to all these taxes and not every state or local government has these taxes.

- Local
  - Real property tax
  - Income tax
  - Sales tax
  - Business license tax
  - Unincorporated business tax
  - Inventory tax

The average taxpayer's yearly bite from earnings to pay federal, state, and local taxes is substantial. Average Q. Taxpayer works from January 1 to May 4 of the year to pay this tax bite.

Don't wait until April 15 to read this. The overview of taxes in these two chapters unravels a confusing tax-work quilt so that you glimpse the tax consequences of certain transactions, know what records to keep, take advantage of tax planning, and generally make some sense out of the tax-work quilt. Keeping proper records means that you can get all the tax deductions and benefits that you have coming.* Organized and detailed records mean a savings on any tax preparer's charge and your time. Further, it gives you, if audited, the necessary information to back up your return. Learn at least this—keep complete, accurate records and a good diary.

I will not discuss line by line each tax form because tax forms and tax laws change like a chameleon's color. What is a deduction or credit one year may not be the next year.

WARNING

KEEP RECORDS

You pay federal income tax on most income, property, or anything of value you receive in a sale or exchange. A simple tax formula is to calculate the income you *get* (money and fair market value of property received) *minus* certain money spent (expenses or costs) and *minus* deductions for certain situations (i.e., dependents) equals taxable income. If you apply the applicable tax rate to your taxable income and subtract any tax credits, then you find your tax liability.

FILING

your income (money and fair market value of property)

− certain money spent (expenses, costs, personal exemptions)

taxable income

× tax rate

tax

− credit for certain situations (general business credit, child-care credit, etc.)

final tax liability

If you are self-employed, you prepay taxes in the form of estimated taxes. If you are employed, tax is withheld from your check. You may pay additional taxes when you file your federal income tax return.

HOW DO YOU PAY TAXES?

Filing an income tax return means you fill out the various tax forms, sign the return, enclose a check if you owe taxes, and send to the proper service center. The basic filing form is Form 1040. Usually your tax return (including any of the more than thirty special forms which may be part of it) should be filed at the Internal Revenue Service Center named in the directions to your personal Form 1040 or at the service center listed for your place of residence on the 1040 instruction sheet.**

FILING YOUR RETURN

*The person who "does" your taxes, whether you or someone else, must have checks, receipts, sales slips, diary, etc., in order to do your return.

**Nonresident aliens and U.S. citizens living abroad, check instructions to 1040 form for further information.

WHEN DO YOU FILE?

Most people file by April 15.* The postmark date on your mailed return is the date of filing. If you file a late return, then the date IRS received the return determines the penalty. You can get an automatic extension** for filing your federal tax return without even an excuse, if you fill a request on or before April 15 on Form 4868 and enclose a check for your estimated or "calculated guess" tax bill. Catch 22: If what you sent as the estimated tax owed is less than the tax liability computed on your late return, then you have to pay a .5 percent penalty on the unpaid tax. The penalty increases to 1.0 percent per month after demand is made by the IRS for payment. Interest on the unpaid taxes is also assessed.

HOW MUCH DO YOU PAY?

You use tax-rate schedules to figure your tax. The tax-rate scale is graduated and increases as taxable income increases. Whether you must file depends on how much money you make.

Taxes should be proportioned to what may be annually spared by the individual.
—THOMAS JEFFERSON

Generally, you must file return if you are:	If your gross income is at least: 1987
Single	4,400
Single, sixty-five or over	5,650
Married	7,560
Married, one spouse sixty-five or over	9,400
Married, both spouses sixty-five or over	10,000
Self-employed	400

WHO MUST FILE?

FILE TO GET REFUNDS

If your gross income is less than above figures, you must file to get a refund of any taxes withheld from your wages. You must file with even less than $400 self-employment income if certain regulations apply.

Filing a return does not mean you always have to pay taxes. Your tax liability depends on your deductions, exemptions, and so forth, but you must file before a tax liability or nonliability can be established, or before a refund is made. We can hear you now, "Well, I won't file a return, and since I am a self-employed printmaker, who will know the difference."*** There are several reasons for "going legit" and filing:

GOOD REASONS FOR GOING LEGIT

- to establish a financial record to obtain financing, loans, credit.†
- to get a refund for overwithholding from a salary job.
- because *if* you owe tax, the IRS can levy on your property and wages without getting a court judgment.
- because the IRS can find out that you have earned income and have not reported it, particularly through computer tracking.
- because the three-year statute of limitation (time for the IRS to take action against you) does not start running until you file, and under certain situations there is no statute of limitations for tax evasion.
- because there are penalties for not filing, including prison time.

Remember, there are ways to minimize your tax load. This is called *tax avoidance,* and it is legal. *Tax evasion,* though, is cheating and involves a fraudulent intent to evade taxes. The tax evader gets heavy interest, penalty charges, and maybe jail.

---

*A business electing other than the calendar year files on the fifteenth day of the fourth month following the end of its fiscal year.
**Since state income tax returns are tied to federal returns, you will need a state extension also. State income tax extensions sometimes require a reason. Check with the tax department of your state.
***Newsweek, April 10, 1978, pp. 85-86, discussed the underground economy, giving examples of persons who do not report their income. This underground economy of jobs, services, and business transactions that are never publicly recorded exists, but you take a serious chance in not reporting. Indeed, one of the people discussed in the Newsweek article was later behind bars.
†In applying for credit, loans, etc., the lender *always* requests from self-employed persons a copy of their financial statement and/or tax returns.

There are numerous publications available free from the IRS, including one subject publications, plus Publication 334, "Tax Guide for Small Business"; Publication 552, "Recordkeeping For Individuals"; a List of Tax Publications; Publication 583, "Recordkeeping, Information for Business Taxpayers"; and Publication 17, "Your Federal Income Tax for Individuals." These incorporate completed forms.

Remember, these publications *do not* discuss views contrary to the IRS's official position or ambiguities in the tax law. Other useful non-IRS publications are the Volunteer Lawyers for the Arts *The Art of Filing** and J. K. Lasser's *Your Income Tax*, published yearly by Simon and Schuster. The latter is excellent, widely distributed (e.g., in supermarkets), dull, and reasonably priced. For readability, my favorite is Kamoroff's *Small Time Operator.*

Alice's Allegory #18 or "It's all there, but ..."

Spring came to Rainbow Hill mingled with March winds. Alice, who was busy wedging clay, stopped and thought, "Oh my dear, April 15 is only one month away. My taxes!" She left her studio and went to the house to frantically and unsuccessfully search for her records. Alice quieted herself with some mu tea and deep breaths.

Romero was not very interested in the search, saying, "Why go legit?" but Alice said, "Because I sell to an IRS agent, and besides how will we get the loan for our Tibetan prayer wheel if we can't prove what we make?"

"I know," she said rejoicing, "the only logical place, the Thai rise storage basket." She located the basket between raw cashews and the herb jars and dumped the contents on the meditation mat. She looked at the IRS 1040 and the mass and jumble of receipts on wrapping paper, paper bags, sales slips, bank statements, and her expense diary, which was a rolled Japanese scroll written from right to left.

She exclaimed, "I can't do it!" as she gathered it all up and trucked into town to see a Certified Public Accountant recommended by Wood Shaver.

"What's your usual charge for preparing a tax return for a potter?" she asked.

Mr. Figure said, "Well, about two hours at $40 an hour if you are organized."

"Great," and she opened her Thai basket and gracefully spread the contents on the south half of his otherwise clean desk, saying, "I've been real organized this year and kept everything."

Mr. Figure gasped and proceeded to explain what he meant by organized, but admitted he was pleased she had kept records.

Although the charge ended up to be more than $80, Alice talked Mr. Figure into a trade for a ceramic wall plaque to add luster to his rather dull office.

Tax preparers charge for time, so the better organized you are, the less it costs. It's estimated that an average tax return** takes two hours, and tax preparers charge $20 to $100 per hour. Tax preparation charges are *deductible*.*** Some states have an organization of accountants, similar to VLA, called Accountants for the Public Interest, which does free work for nonprofit organizations and those without money.

There are several categories of persons who do tax returns:

- local or national chain tax preparers who may just provide a quickie service and are not specialists
- uncertified accountant, public accountant, or a bookkeeper

---

*Write to Volunteer Lawyers for the Arts (VLA), 1285 Avenue of the Americas, 3rd Floor, New York, NY 10019; the cost of this updated volume is $12.95.
**If your return involves a partnership, business return, or unusual transactions such as the sale of a residence, capital gains income, or investment credit, this fee range will be too low.
***Deductible as miscellaneous itemized deduction on Schedule A, subject to the new 20% floor on adjusted gross income for 1987 and thereafter.

- a certified public accountant (CPA)
- tax attorneys
- enrolled or ex-IRS agents—these people have passed an IRS exam. Check with the national IRS office for a list.

Some tax preparers agree to accompany you to an audit at no extra charge or to pay any extra tax liability incurred because of an arithmetic error on their part, and some agree to nothing. A good tax preparer usually will know how to accurately and quickly fill out the forms to be filed with your return and should be able to direct you to tax savings based on your individual situation. Because of past abuses, the 1976 Tax Reform Act imposes certain requirements and various penalties on income-tax-return preparers. Do choose your tax preparer carefully.

TAX ADVICE

While the IRS itself provides assistance in preparing tax returns, on very detailed questions they may not be helpful. An IRS inspection team posing as taxpayers found the wrong tax advice was given 72 percent of the time by IRS taxpayer-assistance workers! Warning: If an IRS employee gives the wrong tax advice, the IRS isn't bound by that advice. A 1976 General Accounting Office study also found a very high rate of error on returns prepared by a national chain of tax preparers. Uncertified accountants should be more accurate than national or other local tax services. The best bet is a certified public accountant. He or she can set up your bookkeeping system so that tax preparation will be simplified (and cheaper), and is qualified to represent you at an audit and can do tax planning. Most of my clients who use a CPA save more than the CPA's fees as a result of a lower tax obligation.

STEPS PRIOR TO FILING A RETURN

You need to decide three basic things when you start your business: your accounting period, record-keeping methods, and method of accounting.

ACCOUNTING PERIOD

Use the calendar year, from January 1 to December 31, for your accounting period.

RECORD-KEEPING

The second task is setting up a general record-keeping system. Record-keeping is simply the way you record business activity. First, keep *any* documents indicating income or expenses including:

PRIMARY RECORDS

- invoices
- vouchers
- bills
- receipts for both expenditures and sales
- register tapes
- canceled checks
- deposit slips
- diary entries

These are referred to as "primary" or "first" records of individual transactions.* If these documents do not contain a designation of the transaction, date item was purchased or sold, business purpose (if not apparent), and cost; then put that information on the document. These primary records should be accessible in a place like a file folder, shoe box, or cookie jar. Sort these records at least once a year, at tax time, into categories: rent, supplies, travel, medical, insurance, salaries, and so forth.

*No particular form is required, but records must be kept thoroughly and accurately, accessible and available, in a safe and convenient place. Artists are often self-employed individuals, and tax laws require self-employed persons to "keep such permanent books of account or records, including inventories, as are sufficient to establish the amount of gross income, deductions, credits, or other matters to be shown" on the tax returns.

How long should you keep your records? Since the government can challenge (audit) your tax return up to three years after your return is filed, keep all the supporting records, both primary and secondary, for at least that period. Contracts, government documents (e.g., trademarks, copyrights), advertising materials, claims and papers regarding legal suits should be kept permanently.

You enter and total primary transactions in secondary records often referred to as books—a journal, ledger, single-entry book.* These records provide a handy way to review your financial affairs—the money that comes in and the money that goes out. Record-keeping methods range from the very simple to the complex. I'll discuss just three—two simple journals and a file-folder system—which can be used in a do-it-yourself program. Samples of two very simple single-entry income-expense journals appear in Figures 5.1 and 5.2.

WOVENWORKS JUNE 1988		INCOME				EXPENSES
6/4	Dead Duck Gallery	300 –	6/1	Studio Rent		100 –
6/9	Sale Mr. Verona	35 –	6/6	Yarn - Yarn Depot		60 –
6/17	State Income Tax Refund	44 –	6/7	Entry Fee/ADC Show		15 –

Figure 5.1 Single-entry income-expense, Sample #1

WOVENWORKS June 1988		CHECK NO.	CASH IN	CASH OUT	SALES	OPERATING EXPENSES
DATE						
6 1	Mr. Wall - Studio Rent	101		✓		100 –
6 4	Dead Duck Gallery		✓		300 –	
6 6	Yarn Depot - Yarn	102		✓		60 –

Figure 5.2 Single-entry income-expense, Sample #2

Or you could mark a double-pocketed file folder for each month and put sales or other documents indicating income on one side and the documents showing the monies paid out on the other. At the end of the month write down on one sheet the items and amounts paid out, and in another column the items and amounts received. At a glance, you have a summary of the month's activities, that is, profit or loss. This is essential for business planning. Note that most business advisers suggest that you plan a year at a time—say you decide $100 a year is your budget for advertising, then if you spend that $100 on advertising in the first four months, you may be in trouble.

Separate your business income and expenses from your personal income and expenses by using separate bank accounts. Pay all business expenses by check. Establish a petty cash fund for small expenses but support those cash payments by documents—

*If you use a double-entry system, which according to accountants is the only way to tell whether your books are in balance, see an accountant to set these up. Recently the government hassled a client about a National Defense Loan he had paid off 19 years ago—no proof of payment survived. An old car I traded recently showed a lien. The bank had failed to clear the lien six years earlier. I quickly proved I had paid it, and even quicker, the bank released the lien.

for example, a $2 receipt from hardware store for nails for picture frames. Note on all checks what item is paid for (it may not be self-evident that a check to Acme Art Supply for $22 is for canvas) and on all deposit slips the source of income. When you want money for your personal use, then write a check to yourself from your business account and deposit it in your separate personal account. Use your personal account to pay personal, nonbusiness obligations. I mean what I say—keep separate checking accounts and record your withdrawals for personal use from your business account.

For example, Crazy Mary's Quilts was audited by IRS, and her use of one checking account without any secondary records led to a large tax liability. Then Crazy Mary set up two bank accounts. On December 10, 1987, she had the following transactions: she had $1,000 in her business account, $10 in petty cash, $200 in her personal account and $400 of personal bills to pay. Of that, $100 was rent and half of that rent was for studio space. For the thread (47 cents worth) that Mary needed that day at T.G.I.F., she used petty cash and saved the receipt. She wrote a business check to herself for $300, marked "Withdrawal—Crazy Mary" and put it in her personal account. She paid her personal expenses, including all the rent (part personal, part business) from her personal account. In her secondary records she reflected that portion of the rent that was the business share.

Some accountants recommend voucher checks—when you write a check, it automatically makes copies. The original check goes to the creditor, one copy gets attached to the receipt, and the other copy is kept in chronological order. There are also other types of checking account systems you could discuss with your accountant.

SUFFICIENCY OF CANCELED CHECKS

Are canceled checks sufficient documentation of an expense? Some IRS offices say it depends on the item of expense and the amount of information on the check. The government tax guide states that a canceled check standing alone is not by itself sufficient to support a business deduction. Accountants say no, for you can put whatever purpose you want on a check. However, canceled checks are better than nothing.

DIARY

Another important record-keeping method is a diary. A diary is a calendar, account book, or booklet where you can put down relevant expenditure information as it occurs regarding travel and entertainment expenses. It documents business trips and expenses not documented by receipt. If you are audited, the diary entries must show the purpose, business reason for the expense, the date, the place, business relationship, the cost and mileage if it involves travel. If the diary entries have insufficient information, the diary-based deduction may be disallowed.

In deducting your travel and entertainment expenses, follow these rules (check each year, as these rules are subject to change):

- travel—22½ cents per mile for the first 15,000 miles, and 11 cents per mile over that for use of your personal automobile. You may choose the regular method with ACRS or MACRS depreciated, which means that, you deduct your actual operating and maintenance expenses and depreciation, or if you qualify, you can use this optional method of deducting a mileage allowance.
- lodging—receipts or itemized paid bills regardless of the amount
- other travel-entertainment expenses—need receipt if in excess of $25
- meals—while away from home on business
- business meals or entertainment—dining or entertainment with business associates for a business purpose. Starting in 1987, the deduction for unreimbursed meals and entertainment is limited to 80% of expenses.

108

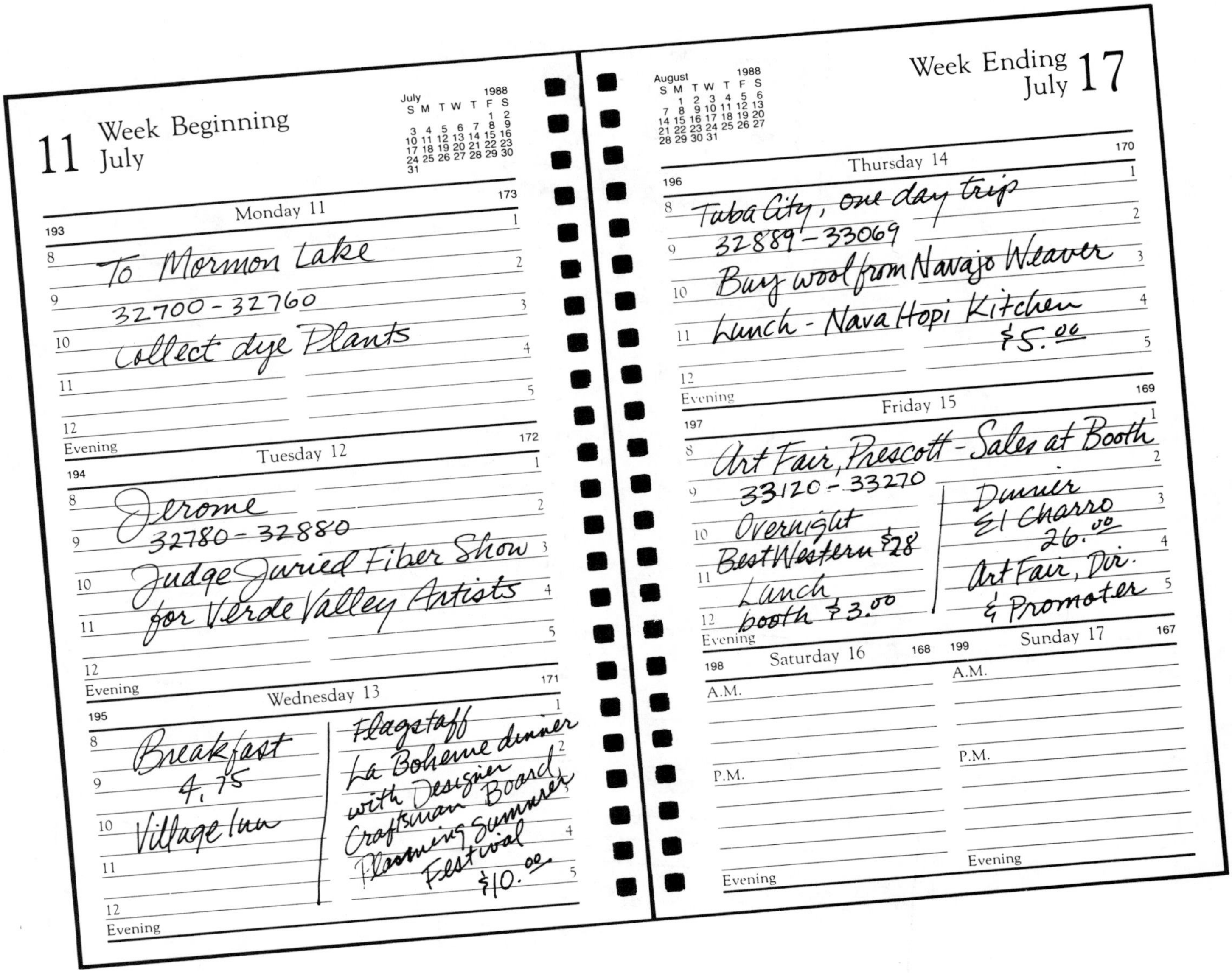

11 Week Beginning July

July 1988
S M T W T F S
1 2
3 4 5 6 7 8 9
10 11 12 13 14 15 16
17 18 19 20 21 22 23
24 25 26 27 28 29 30
31

Monday 11

8 To Mormon Lake
9 32700 - 32760
10 Collect dye Plants
11
12 Evening

Tuesday 12

8 Jerome
9 32780 - 32880
10 Judge Juried Fiber Show
11 for Verde Valley Artists
12 Evening

Wednesday 13

8 Breakfast 4.75
9
10 Village Inn
11
12 Evening

Flagstaff
La Boheme dinner
with Designer
Craftsman Board,
Planning Summer
Festival
$10.00

Week Ending July **17**

August 1988
S M T W T F S
1 2 3 4 5 6
7 8 9 10 11 12 13
14 15 16 17 18 19 20
21 22 23 24 25 26 27
28 29 30 31

Thursday 14

8 Tuba City, one day trip
9 32889 - 33069
10 Buy wool from Navajo Weaver
11 Lunch - Nava Hopi Kitchen $5.00
12 Evening

Friday 15

8 Art Fair, Prescott - Sales at Booth
9 33120 - 33270
10 Overnight Best Western $28
11 Lunch booth $3.00
12 Evening

Dinner El Charro 26.00
Art Fair, Dir. & Promoter

Saturday 16
A.M.
P.M.
Evening

Sunday 17
A.M.
P.M.
Evening

Figure 5.3 Daily records

K. Lasser's *Your Income Tax* has lengthy discussions about these deductions. Some credit cards, such as American Express, already have a record expense form on the back of the cardholder's copy of the charge slip which you can complete.

Remember a receipted bill or voucher must show:

- cost
- date
- place
- nature of expense (business purpose and business relationship to the taxpayer of each person entertained)

Another record-keeping method is a job work card. Have you ever asked yourself "What did I do last year? How many pieces did I do? What did I name that orange-white wall hanging?" Keep a work record of each major piece, job lot, or series that you create. A job card can be used for this purpose. The cards should describe the work, date finished, materials (cost and amount), exhibit information, hours of labor, photograph information, and sale information. If possible, a slide of the work and sales receipt should be attached. Use a 4″ by 6″ card or make duplicate job cards.

RULES FOR TRAVEL AND ENTERTAINMENT EXPENSES

RECEIPTS

JOB WORK CARD

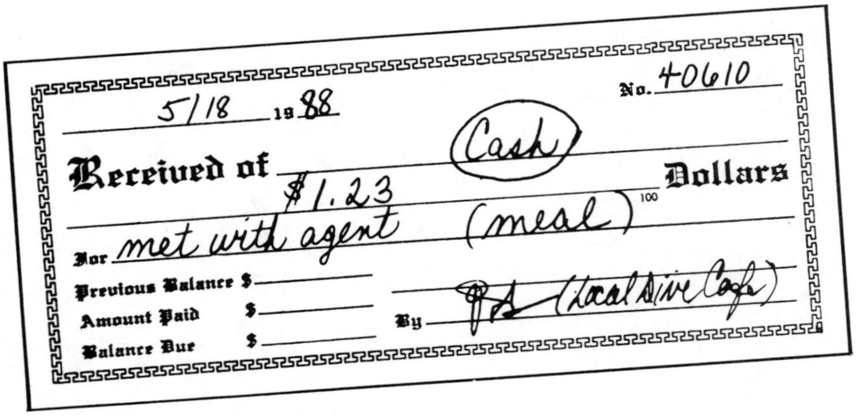

Figure 5.4 Receipt for breakfast on overnight business trip

A sample card is shown below. Modify the card to suit your needs. If you create small items, treat them as a series and use one card for the entire lot.

Refer to the copyright chapter for a discussion of the publication date and when you should file your copyright application. You want the sales information for your mailing lists, but in California you also need it to pursue resale royalties or if you have contractual provisions for resale royalties.

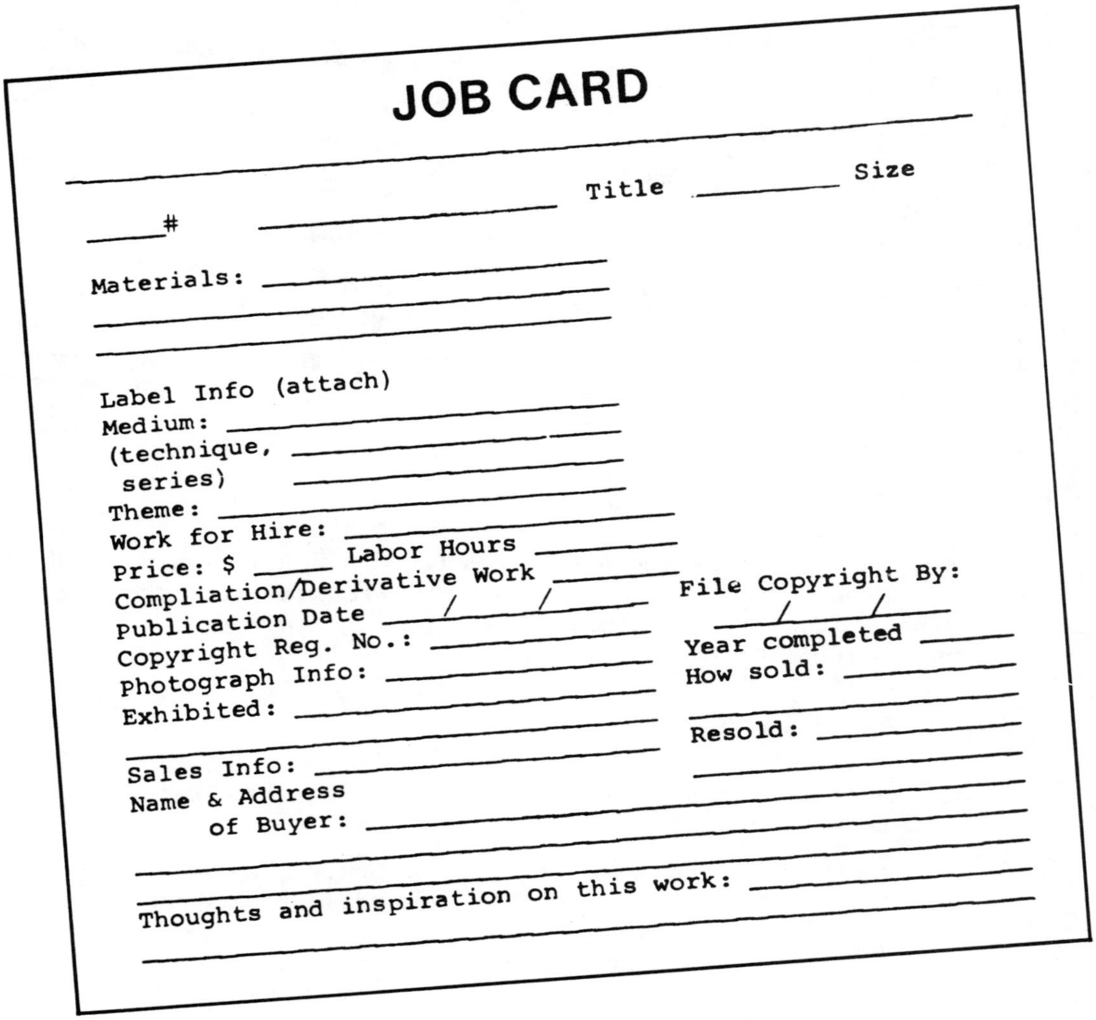

Figure 5.5 Sample job card

A job card serves many purposes:

- to provide evidence of professional attitude toward your work to meet IRS hobby challenge*
- to measure the number of your works produced
- to record information for insurance or proof of casualty loss
- to give you information you may need to fill out copyright forms and tell you the copyright status of the work
- to provide information for restoration
- to provide a track record of exhibition/sale
- to record your inspiration
- to provide a reference source after work leaves your possession
- to indicate labeling attached to work

Another handy record-keeping device is the in-out record. This records your major works in the order they are completed along with some identifying information. From this list you can tell at a glance where your work is located, what has sold, and whether the piece was damaged prior to return to you. If you keep job cards, then you won't need as much identifying information regarding a piece on the in-out record. A simple in-out record is shown in Figure 5.6.

IN-OUT RECORD 1988

OUT	NO.	TITLE	WHERE	IN	PRICE
1-4	42	Noon (TPY)	Lame Duck Gallery		250 —
1-11	43	Desert (TPY)	Sale to FNB		100 —
1-22	44	April (B)	ADC (damaged feathers)	3/2	400 —
1-31	45	Moon (TPY)	Sale to Ms. Lawyer		300 —
2-3	46	Lunch (TPY)	Show at Univ.		2000 —

(K) = Contract form I use   (TPY) = Tapestry
(B) = Basketry   (CST) = Consignment

Figure 5.6 In-out record

Job cards, in-out records (neither is required by IRS), and the income-expense file or journal will help you organize your daily artcraft work for your own information. These records show you are in business to make money and not as a hobbyist, and help plan and budget your business operation.

*See later discussion of business and hobby loss in this chapter.

ACCOUNTING METHOD

ACCRUAL METHOD

When you start your business you choose which method of accounting to use—the "cash method" or the "accrual" method. With the cash method you include all income received during the year and deduct all expenses paid. With the accrual method you include all income *earned* whether received or not (e.g., bills sent) and deduct expenses when *incurred* (e.g., bills received). You may figure your business income on the accrual basis even if you report your nonbusiness income on a cash basis. If you have inventories or your gross receipts exceed five million dollars, you generally must use the accrual basis in your business.* Once you choose a method, you must get the IRS's consent before changing to another.

CASH METHOD

The cash method records all income received** during the tax year and deducts all expenses actually paid during the tax year. A tax-saving device for the cash-basis taxpayer is to pay many expenses in December (assuming you are on the calendar year) and put off sales until January. Payment of those expenses at the end of the year reduces your taxable income for that tax year. If you can use the cash basis, income and deductions can be shifted between years. Thus, you could structure your transactions to create income in three out of five years in order to help you meet a hobby-loss challenge by the IRS. If you show a profit three out of five years, your activities are not usually considered a hobby and you can deduct your losses against

CASH BASIS—PAY EXPENSES AT YEAR'S END

any income received.*** If you mail your check for expenses no later than December 31, then you can deduct the expense that year. Many businesses customarily send bills out in December reminding their cash basis clients that debts paid before the end of the year are deductible that year.

Under the accrual method you report income that has been earned whether or not received, and you deduct costs and expenses incurred whether or not you paid them,†—for example, Mr. Silk Screenprinter, who was on the accrual basis, sends a bill for $800 for a silk screen to Minby Co. and gets a bill for $200 from Exotic Paper Co. on December 30, 1987. Neither were actually paid until the next year. The income is reported and the expense deducted on the 1987 tax return because Mr. Screenprinter is on the accrual basis.

INVENTORIES

INVENTORIES AND THE ACCRUAL METHOD

Many sales and manufacturing businesses must use inventory in calculating their taxes. So must a service business that stocks and sells parts.†† The tax law provides that "in any case in which it is necessary to use an inventory the accrual method of accounting must be used with regard to purchases and sales unless otherwise authorized. . . ." The phrase "necessary to use an inventory" may be interpreted to mean that it is necessary to use inventories to clearly reflect income. If you consistently use a method that accurately reflects income, then you probably wouldn't be required to use the accrual method. If you have a small number of handcrafted works on hand and low material costs, it is likely that the cash method of accounting would be acceptable. Potters who are using natural clay dug for free and creators of "found art" are obvious examples because the major cost of producing their work is their labor. On the other hand, if you are producing in volume, have a substantial number of works on hand, and high material costs, then the use of inventories would most clearly reflect income.

---

*See discussion which follows concerning inventories.
**This may include income not actually received if the income has been credited or set apart so as to be subject to your control. This is called *constructive receipt of income,* and would include a check received and not deposited, or royalties reported to you and credited to your account but not paid out to you.
***A discussion of the hobby loss challenge can be found at the end of this chapter.
†However, accrued interest, salaries, and other expenses paid to family members are deducted when accrued only if paid within two and one-half months after the close of tax year.
††Service businesses usually do not involve inventories but businesses involving the production, purchase, or sale of merchandise or materials used for sale do.

What happens if you've used a cash basis and the IRS says you have to use the accrual method? If the cash basis reduced your income, then the IRS may find a tax liability.

But why all this fuss about inventories? Simply this: Cash expenditures won't reflect your true financial picture where inventories are involved. For example, if you spend $1,500 on wool your first year and sell only three pieces at $100 each that year, the IRS would say that you haven't put several hundred dollars of weaving supplies into those three weavings; rather, you have put it into raw materials, works in progress, and unsold finished products. Thus, you must spread this supply cost over all the unsold and unfinished weavings and you cannot deduct the $1,500 from the $300, for you have really made a profit on the three weavings. To deduct the $1,500 would distort your real income from that work.

MATCHING COSTS
AGAINST REVENUE

Inventories include:

- merchandise or stock in trade
- raw materials
- work in progress
- finished products
- supplies (which will become a part of sale items)

DEFINITION OF INVENTORIES

You do not include tools, equipment, office supplies, vehicles, or anything else purchased for reasons other than resale. Only the cost of those inventory items sold is deductible. This means that only a part of your inventory purchases can be deducted as yearly expenses. The cost of unsold inventory at year-end is an asset of the business and will not be a deduction until it is sold or becomes fully depreciated. So this inventory concept involves measuring the changes in quantity and value of your stock in trade from the beginning of the year to the end to get the costs of goods sold.

UNSOLD INVENTORY IS ASSET

Page **2**

Schedule C (Form 1040) 1987

Part III Cost of Goods Sold and/or Operations (See Schedule C Instructions for Part III)		
1 Inventory at beginning of year. (If different from last year's closing inventory, attach explanation.)	1	42,843
2 Purchases less cost of items withdrawn for personal use	2	240,252
3 Cost of labor. (Do not include salary paid to yourself.)	3	— 0 —
4 Materials and supplies	4	— 0 —
5 Other costs	5	— 0 —
6 Add lines 1 through 5	6	283,095
7 Less: Inventory at end of year	7	43,746
8 Cost of goods sold and/or operations. Subtract line 7 from line 6. Enter here and in Part I, line 2	8	239,349

Figure 5.7 Form 1040 Schedule C-1: Cost of Goods sold

You can see from this that determining the ending inventory is a key step in establishing the cost of goods sold:*

cost of goods available for sale

− ending inventory
_____

= cost of goods sold

The ending inventory must be determined by actually counting the merchandise on hand at the end of the year. You should do it when your business is closed, so that you can be accurate. It is common practice in counting inventory to have two persons do it. One person counts and calls the description and quantity of the item to another, who lists the information on an inventory sheet. When all the goods

TAKING INVENTORY

*See IRS *Tax Guide for Small Businesses,* latest edition.

have been counted and listed, the items on the inventory sheet are priced at cost, then the unit prices are multiplied by quantities to get a dollar value, and these are added together to determine inventory value. Be sure to count all your inventory regardless of its location.* Or you could set up ongoing inventory cards. Perhaps you could use an envelope with cards by each item so "in" items could be marked on one card and "out" items on another.

PRICING THE INVENTORY

There are various methods of pricing inventory, and the method you choose will affect the amount of income tax you pay. Generally, the cost of an item to you is the basis for valuation. This cost includes transportation (to bring item to point of sale), materials, supplies, and *paid* labor but not the value of your labor. If you are a "manufacturer" then you must include overhead in your costs, which is called full absorption accounting.

PRICE FLUCTUATION ON MATERIALS

Where identical materials are *purchased* at *different prices during the year*—for instance, truckloads of clay—what price shall be used as the cost of the merchandise remaining at the year-end inventory? In this situation, there are four valuation methods commonly used:

- specific identification
- average cost
- first-in, first-out (FIFO)
- last-in, first-out (LIFO)

Stop. If you will be involved with price fluctuation for materials and/or full-absorption accounting, then you should have the assistance of an accountant.

RECAP

Now let's recap. A few pages ago we were talking about using the cash or accrual method. Let's look at a simple example using the accrual method.**

Memorandum
TO: Weaver's Attorney
FROM: Mr. Figure
RE: Inventory of Ms. Weaver (Elected Accrual Basis for Accounting)

Ms. Weaver's inventory on December 31, 1987, consisted of ten tapestries which cost her, figuring all costs, $200 each to produce. Her cost of production for 1988 (including her overhead, labor, raw materials, insurance, etc.) came to $7,500. Her total receipts for the year were $22,000. Her year-end inventory for 1988 was three tapestries which cost her, figuring all costs, $200 each to produce, and she had $300 worth of wool left.

total receipts		$22,000
beginning inventory 12/31/87	$2,000	
cost of production	7,500	
net cost	$9,500	
less year-end 12/31/88 inventory (three tapestries and wool)	− 900	
cost of goods sold	$8,600	− 8,600
profit		$13,400

INCOME—THINGS OF VALUE YOU GET

For visual artists, income results when you sell your works for cash or for a trade of property or for services. So most swaps are taxable.*** The fair market value of the property or service is what you count as income.

*Goods in transit are the inventory of the seller if the terms of shipment are FOB destination. Also includes goods on consignment.

**Assume all identical material was purchased at the same price throughout the year so method of valuing materials with fluctuating costs is not a consideration.

***See accountant for information on tax-free trades which involve business in like-kind properties, i.e., real property for real property. Artist wares are not considered business property.

Memorandum

TO: File of Ms. Queentrade
FROM: CPA
RE: Unreported Trade Income

Ms. Queentrade traded a walnut, circular end table with an epoxied, multicolor, beaded, sequined, feathered, tropical-rain-garden motif to her dentist for dental work for her much-neglected teeth. The dentist billed her $1,200 for the dental work, and the parties agreed that the fair market value of the table was $1,200. The dentist both counted the table's value as income and deducted it through depreciation as a business expense, since he kept the table in the waiting room of his office. He was audited, and the audit trail led to the flagstone walkway of Queentrade's two story dome, because she failed to report the income from the sale. Explained to client audit steps and worked out installment payment of delinquent taxes because the swap was income to her under these facts.

You must report money, property, or receipt of anything of value as income. It is presumed that anything of value received is income unless it falls within a specific exception. Refer to the yearly edition of Lasser's *Your Income Tax* for a lengthy checklist of what must be counted as income. Listed below are some common examples of income:

INCOME

- fees received as election official or juror
- forgiveness of a debt
- gambling and lottery winnings
- gross wages, salary, other employee compensations
- hobby income
- illegal income*
- income from a business or farm
- installment payments
- interest and dividends
- net gain from sale or exchange of capital assets
- pension, annuities, rents, royalties, trusts**
- per diem payments of more than $44 a day
- prizes and awards for past accomplishments
- punitive and exemplary damages
- state and local tax refunds (if tax previously claimed as tax deduction)
- tips
- trades—the fair market value of property or services received for yours

The following are *not* considered income:

NOT CONSIDERED INCOME

- accident and health insurance paid by your employer
- certain prizes and awards (special rule discussed later)
- child support, *usually*
- compensatory damages for personal injuries
- employee death benefits up to $5,000
- federal tax refunds
- gain of up to $125,000 from sale of residence, if over 55
- gifts, under certain conditions
- income earned abroad (up to $70,000)
- interest on qualified bonds***

*Al Capone and other persons engaged in criminal activities were caught on this one.
**See Schedule E and instructions to Form 1040 if you have this income. It varies. There are fully taxable pensions and annuities not reported on Schedule E.
***Often, income from municipal and state bonds is not taxed. See Lasser's *Your Income Tax* for a specific list.

Income

Please attach Copy B of your Forms W-2, W-2G, and W-2P here.

If you do not have a W-2, see page 6 of Instructions.

Please attach check or money order here.

7	Wages, salaries, tips, etc. *(attach Form(s) W-2)*	**7**	
8	**Taxable** interest income *(also attach Schedule B if over $400)* . . .	**8**	
9	**Tax-exempt** interest income (see page 10). DON'T include on line 8 **9**		
10	Dividend income *(also attach Schedule B if over $400)*	**10**	
11	Taxable refunds of state and local income taxes, if any, from worksheet on page 11 of Instructions .	**11**	
12	Alimony received	**12**	
13	Business income or (loss) *(attach Schedule C)*.	**13**	
14	Capital gain or (loss) *(attach Schedule D)*	**14**	
15	Other gains or (losses) *(attach Form 4797)*	**15**	
16a	Pensions, IRA distributions, annuities, and rollovers. Total received **16a**	**16b**	
b	Taxable amount (see page 11)		
17	Rents, royalties, partnerships, estates, trusts, etc. *(attach Schedule E)* .	**17**	
18	Farm income or (loss) *(attach Schedule F)*	**18**	
19	Unemployment compensation (insurance) (see page 11)	**19**	
20a	Social security benefits (see page 12) **20a**	**20b**	
b	Taxable amount, if any, from the worksheet on page 12		
21	Other income (list type and amount—see page 12) _____	**21**	
22	Add the amounts shown in the far right column for lines 7, 8, and 10–21. This is your **total income** ▶	**22**	

Figure 5.8 Form 1040: Reporting Income

- life insurance proceeds
- money received from an estate
- return of capital (e.g., selling house for same price plus cost of improvements)*
- some scholarships and grants
- unemployment compensation, social security (over a base amount), workers' compensation, government payments under certain conditions

SCHOLARSHIPS

In order for scholarships or grants to be nontaxable, you must be a degree candidate at an educational institution and receive a scholarship *along* with no obligation to teach or perform services. The exclusion is limited to only the amounts spent on tuition, fees, books, supplies, and equipment. Otherwise, all scholarships and grants granted after August 17, 1986, are taxable.

ALIMONY

Alimony must be taxable to the person who receives it to be deductible by the person who pays it. The rules for agreements made or modified in 1985 differ from earlier rules. See your lawyer or tax consultant for the tax consequences of alimony, property, and child support.

MONEY YOU SPEND

Don't feel discouraged that every dollar you make is counted as income. Remember, it is only *net* income that is *taxed*.

Over and over the courts have said that there is nothing sinister in so arranging one's affairs as to keep taxes as low as possible.

Everybody does so, rich or poor, and all do right, for nobody owes a public duty to pay more than the law demands. Taxes are enforced exactions, not voluntary contributions.

—JUDGE LEARNED HAND

income
- adjustments (moving expense, alimony, etc.)
= adjusted gross income
- itemized deductions
- dependent and other exemptions
= net taxable income
× tax rate
= tax
- tax credits
= tax liability or refund due

*Record retention for home improvements should be from date of purchase to at least three years after the tax return is filed where the sale or exchange of residence is reported.

Thus, to get to your net income you subtract all the legally allowable deductions and any adjustments to income.

In 1976, about 20 million Americans found themselves in the 25 percent or higher tax bracket. For those persons every dollar of deduction and adjustment that they are legally entitled to saves them at least 25 cents which would have gone to Uncle Sam.

ADJUSTMENTS TO INCOME

Following the gross income section of the 1040 form is a section called Adjustments to Income. After totaling your income, you can subtract certain items right off the top whether you itemize other deductions or not. These are adjustments to income: certain employee business expenses, payments to an individual retirement plan or Keogh plan, alimony paid, and so forth. This information is put on the 1989 Form 1040 in the portion reproduced below and subtracted from your gross income.

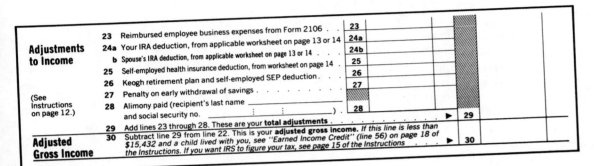

Figure 5.9 Form 1040: Adjustments to Income

EMPLOYEE BUSINESS EXPENSE

Employee business expenses are those expenses ordinary and necessary to earn salary or wage income. These words *ordinary* and *necessary* are magic words to the IRS. For an employee, travel business expenses away from home, auto expenses, and certain entertainment expenses are deducted from gross income as adjustments to income.

You can use Form 2106, Employee Business Expenses, or you can write up your own employee-business-expense statement.

Other job expenses, in excess of those reimbursed by your employer, such as certain business gifts up to $25, union dues, uniform and work clothes (only if unacceptable for street attire) are deductible, if you itemize, under *miscellaneous itemized deductions*, Schedule A, but are reduced by 2% of your adjusted gross income. Self-employed persons or independent contractors deduct those business expenses from business income on Schedule C.

BUSINESS AUTO EXPENSE

For cars placed in business service after January 1, 1987, there is a five-year depreciation maximum with dollar amount and percentages for each year as follows:

1st year	$2,560 or 20 percent
2nd year	$4,100 or 32 percent
3rd year	$2,450 or 19 percent
4th & 5th year	$1,475 or 11.5 percent
6th year or thereafter	$1,475 or 5.8 percent

The optional method mileage allowance may be utilized only if you satisfy certain requirements. See IRS Publication 917, "Use of Car," for further information. However, most people don't use a vehicle solely for business purposes and the business auto expense then needs to be prorated against the nonbusiness use.

A LITTLE LOOPHOLE: PAYMENTS TO RETIREMENT PLANS

By depositing income you don't need into a qualified retirement plan, you avoid paying taxes on this money now. You pay taxes later when you draw on these funds during retirement. After retirement, most people are in a lower tax bracket. This is another adjustment to income. You must be sure you don't need the money, because if you withdraw it before age 59½, you pay tax plus a penalty.

You may contribute to the plan each year the lesser of $2,000 or 100 percent of your earnings, or $2,250 if married and your spouse had $250 or less of earned income that year. There are limitations placed on IRA deductions if you or your spouse, starting in 1987, are active participants in an employee retirement plan like a Keogh. Check IRS Publication 590,"Individual Retirement Arrangements."*

Under a Keogh Plan for self-employed individuals, you contribute and get a tax deduction for up to 20 percent of your net self-employment income or $30,000 in one year.

In certain situations, you can make contributions to an IRA after the end of the tax year, but it is treated as if made during the tax year. This area is complicated, so see your accountant, banker, or lawyer.

ALIMONY PAID

Good news for ex's—if you are divorced, or separated under a written agreement incorporated in a decree, or there is a decree of spousal support, then cash payments are deductible to the person paying the alimony and whoever receives it counts it as income, provided the agreement does not say otherwise and the parties live apart in separate households. If you qualify, you enter alimony paid in the adjustment-to-income section. This is a complicated area—see your lawyer and accountant *before* signing an agreement.

HEALTH CARE, ETC.

If you are self-employed, you may sometimes qualify to deduct 25 percent of your health care insurance payments as an adjustment. The remainder goes to Schedule A, deductible as a medical expense. Office-in-home expenses, if they qualify, can be adjustments to income if an employee, or for the self-employed deducted on Schedule C or F.

You are finished now with the most common adjustments. Subtract your adjustments from income to get your adjusted gross income.

DEDUCTIONS—SCHEDULE A

The other place that you subtract employee expenses as well as your personal deductions is on Schedule A, Itemized Deductions. Beginning in 1987, the standard deduction (replacing the zero bracket amount) is taken from the adjusted gross income if you do not itemize. So, roughly figure your Schedule A itemized deductions to see if it is more than the standard deduction. You might review your financial situation toward the end of the tax year, and if your unpaid deductions won't help you top the standard deduction, wait and pay those deductions the next year when they may help.

In 1987,** the standard deduction (if there is no eligibility for age or blindness) was:

- $3,760 married, filing joint return
- $1,880 married, filing a separate return with spouse itemizing.
- $2,540 single or unmarried head of household

If you itemize your deductions, remember that the tax tables have already incorporated the standard deduction, so you use the tax rate schedules.

This area is subject to change, so check the Schedule A deductions each year.

MEDICAL EXPENSES

A thorough chart of deductible medical expenses is in the yearly edition of Lasser's *Your Income Tax*. Items such as medical equipment, prescribed hot tubs, swimming pools, air filters, and saunas have been deducted as medical expenses. Such equipment must be depreciated.

*The Internal Revenue has approved for IRA investments government bonds (special retirement bonds), IRA savings accounts, certain insurance plans (retirement endowment plan and retirement annuity), and certain mutal funds.

**Only medical expenses of 7.5 percent of adjusted gross income are deductible on your federal return, but many states allow a full deduction.

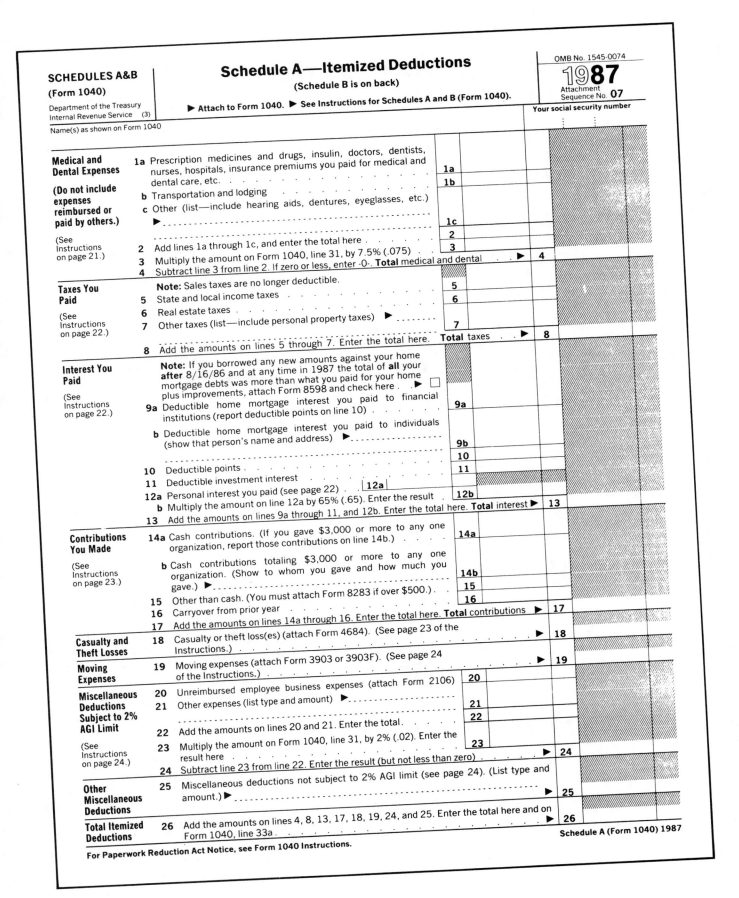

Figure 5.10 Form 1040: Itemized Deductions

SALES TAX The 1986 Tax Reform Act wiped out the sales tax deduction. Some states allow the deduction, however.

CHARITABLE DONATIONS Cash contributions to charitable organizations approved by the IRS are deductible. Unfortunately for charitable institutions and creative persons, since 1969 artists and craftmakers who donate work they have created to charitable institutions can only deduct the cost of materials used in creating the work, if on the accrued basis, while those noncreators who own such works can donate them to a charitable, educational, or cultural institution and receive an income tax deduction for the total value. Creative persons are trying to regain the charitable deduction for donor-created works through tax reform. See the Internal Revenue Service Publication 526, "Income Tax Reductions for Contributors." Some states do allow the artist to deduct the fair market value of contributed work.

If you have a loss due to fire, theft, storm, accident, or any act of God, you deduct the property loss (less $100 per casualty) for property used for personal purposes to the extent the loss is not covered by insurance. Unusual casualty losses can be the result of flooding, electrical blackouts, snow accumulation, freezing, et cetera. Be sure to report thefts to the appropriate authorities so that you have proof of the loss in case of an audit. The federal floor is 10 percent of adjusted gross income, but most states allow anything over $100.

MISCELLANEOUS DEDUCTIONS ON SCHEDULE A If you are an employee, you can claim the following as miscellaneous deductions on Schedule A if you have not been reimbursed and if they are ordinary and necessary for performing your job:

- computers used at qualified office in home are 5 year recovery property
- unreimbursed entertainment expenses
- country club dues
- business gifts (not in excess of $25 per person)
- business association dues
- union dues and cost of bond
- special uniforms and work clothes (can't be adjustable to normal wear), protective items
- expenses in looking for a new job
- educational costs
- investment expenses
- other ordinary and necessary expenses relating to your job not paid by employer (see Deductible Job Cost Chart in Lasser's *Your Income Tax*)

In order to deduct educational expenses you must be employed and already meet the minimum educational requisites for your job. Further, educational activity must improve your job related skills—for example, Isabel Illustrator employed at McDuck's Magazine takes a class in calligraphy; it's deductible.

EXEMPTIONS Everyone gets at least one personal exemption—one exemption as a taxpayer, one for a spouse, and one for each dependent. Beginning in 1987, you were entitled to deduct $1,900 for each exemption claimed on your return. It increases to $1,950 in 1988, then $2,000 in 1989, and after that, will be indexed for inflation. Don't laugh, but you lose the tax benefits of these exemptions if your taxable income for a single person exceeds $89,560 by a 5 percent surtax. Married persons and heads of a household can have more taxable income before the surtax kicks in.

To qualify as a dependent, five tests must be met:

- The dependent can't earn more than the exemption unless your child is under 19, or a full-time student. Children five years old or older will need a social security number.

120

- You must contribute 50 percent or more to the dependent's support.*
- The dependent must be a member of your household or related in certain ways.
- The dependent must be a citizen or national of the United States or resident of the United States, Mexico, or Canada.
- If the dependent files a joint return with someone else, then you can't claim him/her.

H & R Block's yearly *Tax Guide and Workbook* has a clear lengthy discussion of the exemption process and the tests, for instance, to determine who is entitled to claim a child where the parents are divorced.

Figure 5.11 Form 1040: Exemptions

The following expenses may be deductible if ordinary and necessary to your business. "Ordinary" means that the similar expenses are common or accepted in your particular business. A "necessary" expense is one that is appropriate and helpful in developing and maintaining your trade or business. Any expense incurred in the furtherance of your business and its economic goals should be deductible.

All cash payments are not necessarily counted as a business expense. For example, payments made for assets used in business (land, buildings, equipment, car, etc.) are not deducted all at once but rather over a period of time. The list that follows is not exhaustive for business expenses; rather common ordinary and necessary business expenses are listed to give you an idea of deductible expenses in your business. Check Lasser's *Your Income Tax*. Of course many of these payments must be prorated between business and personal use.

Beware — uniform capitalization of expenses under the new tax law adversely affects all creative persons. Since legislative reform is in the process, these complex rules are not covered in the text.

CHILDREN OF DIVORCED PARENTS

SELF-EMPLOYED
BUSINESS EXPENSES**

ALLOWABLE BUSINESS
DEDUCTIONS, ETC.

- Accounting fees—tax preparers' fees
- Admissions—to theater, films, or other events that relate to your work
- Agency fees—for jobs or commission work
- Air fares
- Art and craft supplies—for materials (check earlier inventory discussion)
- Automobile expenses—discussed in adjustments
- Bad debts—must have resulted from normal course of business. On cash accounting method you cannot claim uncollectible bills, fees, etc., as bad debts.

*If two or more persons pay in combined payments more than 50 percent of a dependent's support, then either may claim the person, provided the person not claiming signs a Multiple Support Declaration, Form 2120. Example: Alice and Kate contribute together more than 50 percent of the support of their mother and they switch mother's dependent exemption from year to year and fill out proper forms.

**This section discusses the expenses deductible by a self-employed person. Some of these expenses can also be deducted instead as an adjustment to income or as a miscellaneous deduction.

- Books, publications, professional journals—fully deductible if in your field, or necessary to keep abreast or maintain skills for your job. If useful for more than one year, then it is a part of a professional library and must be depreciated.
- Business gifts—deductible up to $25 per year per business associate or customer.
- Business machines and equipment—having useful life of one year or less.
- Business meetings and entertainment—cost of meals with actual or potential customers, clients, partners, professional advisers if it is in a clear business setting involving planning, discussion, negotiation, etc., of business. If entertainment for reasons directly involved with active conduct of your business or trade, then you can deduct meals, drinks, tickets, and home entertainment; starting in 1987, this deduction is limited to 80 percent.
- Cleaning costs
- Commuting costs—generally not deductible. If your business is at home, then you can deduct travel costs starting with your first call.
- Convention trips—complicated, see Lasser's *Your Income Tax*
- Depreciation
- Display samples, display space
- Driver's license—remember to prorate
- Dues—membership, fees
- Educational expenses
- Food and lodging
- Furniture
- Home studio/office expenses—see later discussion
- Insurance
- Interest—deductible on business loans and mortgages
- Legal and professional fees—must be for business purposes, related to tax matters, or to protect income-producing assets
- Magazines
- Meals—overnight rule bars the deduction of the cost of meals on one-day business trips. Business lunch is allowable.
- Moving expenses
- Office supplies and postage
- Protective clothing
- Rent on separate studio/office
- Repairs
- Research for current projects or teaching your classes
- Retirement-plan payments
- Salaries, tips, and fees to performers and staff
- Taxi fares
- Tax-return-preparation books
- Telegrams
- Telephone and answering service—a separate business phone—total deduction allowable: otherwise prorate basic service charge plus all long-distance business calls
- Tips
- Toll charges
- Tools
- Training—regular training such as cost of writing, drawing classes. Any classes that you need to maintain or improve your skills.
- Transportation and travel expenses—if the reason for your trip is primarily business,* then you can deduct the ordinary and necessary travel costs including transportation—air, bus, train, your auto expenses, telephone, tips
- Tuition
- Uniforms, costumes, protective or special clothing—includes cleaning and repairing of same

*If your trip is primarily personal, then no traveling expenses are deductible, except for expenses incurred directly relating to business.

Remember, there are many other ordinary and necessary business expenses not listed here which you may deduct—so you will have to analyze some of your transactions to see if they qualify.

HOME STUDIO
1. EXCLUSIVE-USE TEST
2. REGULAR-BASIS TEST

There are very strict rules concerning the home studio/office expense which require that a home studio or office be used *exclusively* and on a *regular basis* as your principal place of business or place where you meet or deal with customers in the normal course of business.* You can't take a home studio deduction if you use the guest room as a weaving studio.**

One exception to this exclusive-use test is when you sell products and your home is the "sole fixed location" of your trade. Although you may have a mixed use, the deduction is allowable provided the space is identifiable. Example, you sell yarn and use part of your basement to store it.

There are two kinds of home studio/office expenses:

- *direct expenses* are work-related costs peculiar to your studio or office, such as painting your studio, repairing the studio ceiling.
- *indirect expenses* are those that apply to your whole house but have a relation to your work. These must be prorated on the basis of your business space to your house space using the number of rooms or percentage of space. Among indirect expenses are utilities, rent, taxes, and insurance.

Even if you meet all the tests, there is an overall limit on your home-office business expense deduction. These expenses cannot exceed the amount of net income that is derived from the home studio.

OVERALL LIMIT ON HOME OFFICE/STUDIO DEDUCTIONS

Worthless debts arising from sales, professional services, unpaid salary or rent are *not deductible* unless they were previously included in your gross income. Other business bad debts are deductible up to certain limits.

BAD DEBTS

If an item of expense is used for both personal and business use, then the expense must be prorated.

PRORATE CERTAIN DEDUCTIONS

Examples:
- Ms. Weaver uses her basement to store all of her weaving fibers. The basement represents 20 percent of her house space, so she could deduct 20 percent of house-related expenses.
- Mr. Candlemaker residing in Phoenix attended a two-day arts and crafts fair in Tucson and stayed an extra two days (he transacted no business those two days) to visit friends near Tucson. He deducts his expense during the fair plus his total mileage to and from Tucson.
- Mr. Candlemaker pays $200 a month rent for his house and studio. The studio is one-fifth of the total space. So he then deducts this as a business expense of $40 a month only for the studio.

So far we have discussed several ways to legally cut your taxes—exemptions, deductions, and exclusions of certain income. There are other ways.

CUTTING YOUR TAXES (WITHOUT CUTTING YOUR THROAT)

If you have a small business, you can shift some income to other members of the family by hiring your children, paying them up to $1,300 per year without the children paying tax on that income while you keep the dependent exemption of $1,000. Be sure to make all the proper withholdings and pay fair market value for the labor

SHIFTING OF INCOME IN FAMILY

*If you are employed, the part of your home must be used in connection with your employer's business or for your employer's convenience, if your employer provides no office or work space.
**The exclusive use condition is excepted if you use the space for storing of inventory or day care for children.

CHILDREN MUST BE BONA FIDE EMPLOYEES	performed. The 1986 Tax Reform Act discourages splitting family income where the children are under 14, and the use of trusts to shift income. Discuss what income-splitting opportunities are left with your tax advisor.
FAMILY PARTNERSHIP	If you form a family partnership, management and financing burdens must be shared, otherwise IRS disallows income shifts on the basis that it is a sham partnership.
GIFTS TO MINORS	If you have interest-bearing bank accounts, disperse the interest to family members. Custodian accounts, opened in the child's name with the parent as guardian/custodian, can be set up at a mutual fund or brokerage firm. If the interest from a custodian account exceeds $1,000, for a child under 14, then the excess is taxed at the parent's rate.
INSTALLMENT SALES	If you sell some hefty priced works in one year, you may want to enter into an installment sales agreement with the buyers which staggers payments into different tax years. This reduces your gross income in that year and you pay less taxes. Do not do this without a contract that secures your interest in the property. Check with your tax advisor on the general and special rules which govern installment contracts. Form 6252 is used to report installment sales.

BUYING A HOUSE AND OTHER TAX SHELTERS

Buying a house can be your biggest tax shelter. By spending your housing money on deductible mortgage interest and real estate taxes, you shelter or remove some of your income from the tax collector's grasp.

Taxpayers 55 years of age or older can exclude up to $125,000 in gains arising from the sale of their residence. Under the new rules, interest paid on loans received before August 16, 1986, is fully deductible, but after that, it depends on the residence's cost basis, the existing mortgage debt, and sometimes how you use the loan proceeds. See Form 8598, Computation of Deductible Home Mortgage Interest, if you took out a home mortgage after August 16, 1986.

FORM OF DOING BUSINESS

Sometimes your business form saves you taxes, that is, sole proprietorship, partnership, or corporation. If your business generates earnings that can be retained, see a lawyer or an accountant for advice.

CAPITAL ASSETS—A TYPE OF BUSINESS PROPERTY

A capital asset* is business property with a useful life of over one year. Depreciable capital assets include buildings, machines, equipment, furniture, and fixtures. For artists, capital assets could be cameras, kilns, looms, framing devices, pug wheels, spool racks, and so forth. These are more or less permanent equipment used in, but not consumed by, the process of creating the artist's work.

CAPITAL GAINS: TAXED AT A REDUCED RATE

The profit from the sale of your capital assets was known as a *capital gain*. This capital gain was part of your income for tax purposes, but if you held on to your capital asset for twelve months, you paid a 50 percent long-term capital deduction, which meant that you paid tax on one-half of your gain. The capital gain deduction was repealed under the Tax Reform Act of 1986, but as the maximum income tax rate is 28 percent, it may still provide tax savings. Form 4797 is used to report the sale or exchange of property used in trade or business.

DEPRECIATION

As I stated above, a purchased asset which has a "useful life" of more than one year cannot be deducted as a business expense in the year you buy it. Instead you get an annual deduction based on the asset's total useful life. First you subtract the salvage value** from the cost and then divide this figure by the useful years. This method of deduction is called *depreciation*. The theory is that equipment used in trade will not wear out in a year, thus it should, for tax purposes, be depreciated over its useful life.

---

*Small tools of low value are treated as ordinary and necessary business expenses even though they may last for more than one year.
**Salvage value is generalized to pre-1979 items.

Depreciation is an expense deduction for your capital investment in automobiles, buildings, machinery, and other property used for business. The depreciation deduction is prorated.

cost of asset (easel)	$2,000
− salvage value	− 500
net cost	$1,500
÷ useful life	÷ 5 years
Yearly Depreciation	$300

Choose one of several different methods for depreciation. The straight-line depreciation method is the simplest. It distributes the depreciation expenses equally over the useful life of the asset. A potter buys a kiln for $3,000 and estimates the useful life at ten years and salvage value at $400. The kiln is calculated with the additional first-year expensing (for pre-1981 purchases), explained next.

cost of kiln	$3,000
first-year additional depreciation	600
estimated salvage value	400
ten-year property	10 years

$$2,000 \div 10 = 200$$
yearly depreciation for 10 years = $200

Don't worry if your asset outlives the tax "useful life." But don't take any more depreciation on it.

The year you get a capital asset, you can deduct as an ordinary and necessary business expense up to $10,000 of the cost of business equipment, i.e., personal property, and then depreciate the remainder of its useful life. There are many limitations, so check with your accountant.

Starting in 1987, the new law lessens the write-off advantage of ACRS (accelerated cost recovery) with a new method, MACRS (modified accelerated cost recovery); property placed in service after 1986 falls in a 3-, 5-, 7-, or 10-year class. A 3-year property includes property with a 40-year or less life under the Asset Depreciation Range (ADR), which includes, among others, breeding hogs. Fancy words for what IRS now determines as the life of property. The five-year class includes computers, typewriters, cars, light-duty trucks, and so forth. Your tax preparer can help you in this area.

Section B.—Depreciation

(a) Class of property	(b) Date placed in service	(c) Basis for depreciation (Business use only—see instructions)	(d) Recovery period	(e) Method of figuring depreciation	(f) Deduction
6 Accelerated Cost Recovery System (ACRS) (see instructions): *For assets placed in service ONLY during tax year beginning in 1987*					
a 3-year property					
b 5-year property					
c 7-year property					
d 10-year property					
e 15-year property					
f 20-year property					
g Residential rental property					
h Nonresidential real property					
7 Listed property—Enter total from Part III, Section A, column (g)					
8 ACRS deduction for assets placed in service prior to 1987 (see instructions)					

Figure 5.12 Form 1040, Schedule C: Part III Depreciation is carried over from form 4562.

Tax credits, subtracted from your bills, are advantageous. This is not a business deduction but rather, a dollar credit directly against your tax liability. Check special computations and limitations with your accountant. A tax discount for business equipment purchases, called an investment tax credit, used to be available. Except for some oddball properties (transition property, qualified program expenditures, and qualified timber products), the investment credit is no longer available.

The general business credit scoops in the regular and energy investment credits, the alcohol fuels credit, the research activities credit, the credit for low income housing, and the targeted jobs credit—each has its own form.*

Warning: This chapter suggests ways to reduce your final tax bill with specific exemptions, credits, adjustments, and deductions, but your qualifications for these must be checked. If you look eligible for one of these, then check other sources or consult with your tax preparer.

OTHER TAX CREDITS

There are several other tax credits available to individuals. With the exception of the earned income credit, these are entered in the credit section of the 1040 return. Please note the various credits on the tax return below, for I discuss only the child and dependent care tax credit.

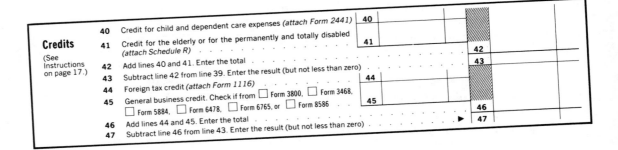

Figure 5.13 Form 1040, page 2: Tax Credits

CHILD- AND DEPENDENT-CARE TAX CREDIT

To be eligible for a child- and dependent-care credit,** Form 2441, you must incur the sitter expenses to earn money, look for a job, maintain a household for the dependent (furnishing over half the cost), and file a joint return if married. Certain expenses qualify for this deduction. The maximum amount of qualified expenses for one qualified person is $2,400 and $4,800 for two.

EARNED INCOME CREDIT—A BONUS FOR LOW-INCOME FAMILIES

The earned income credit or the "negative income tax" is very important, for you may get money even if you don't pay taxes. It is available to low-income workers with a dependent child or children (even if over eighteen) living with them in a household maintained in the United States. It equals up to 14 percent of the first $6,015 earned, but is reduced by 10 percent of excess earnings over $6,975 adjusted gross or earned income, so the credit disappears at $15,432. The maximum credit is $851.

Check each year for new tax credits, or changes in the old ones.

If credits reduce your taxes too much, then the government slaps you with an alternative minimum tax.

*See Lasser's *Your Income Tax* for further details.

**This can include a disabled dependent of any age or a spouse who because of a physical or mental condition cannot take care of him/herself. See Lasser's *Your Income Tax*.

A loss from a *business* can offset income from other sources. If you have more than one source of income, your combined net profits and losses are reported as income (loss) on your return. Commonly the taxpayer who has a salaried job and a part-time craft business. If the business shows a loss, the taxpayer applies that loss against his income from the salary source—for instance, Mr. Potter substitute-teaches for $8,000 a year. He also incurs a $1,000 craft business loss, so his adjusted gross income is $7,000.

If your loss exceeds your income for the year, then it carries backward three years and then forward seven years. Carrying a loss back entitles you to a refund, and a loss forward reduces your taxes. See your tax advisor for business losses.

When losses are routinely incurred, then the IRS may raise the question of whether your activity constitutes a legitimate business or a hobby. If your work is ruled a hobby, the income is taxable but net losses (excess of expenses over income) are deductible only against hobby income. The IRS is concerned when a salaried taxpayer has a part-time "business" which shows a loss or when a couple filing a joint return uses a business loss to offset salaried income. In both cases the tax liability is reduced. If you consistently lose money in a sideline business, you court an IRS challenge that the activity is a hobby. Often artists and craftmakers face a hobby loss challenge, for even though dedicated, they may show losses for several years.

The test distinguishing a business from a hobby is whether the activity engaged in is done with the bona fide intention and expectation of making a profit. The profit motive is checked by IRS when it applies the three- out-of-five-year test. If you show a profit three out of five consecutive years, the activity will be presumed to be a business with profit intent and expectation. Maybe plumbers, lawyers, and handymen can be judged by that test, but an artist, craftmaker, or writer usually does not achieve instant approval, recognition, and sales. Lesson: Arrange your affairs to show some profit some years. But even if you don't show profit in three out of the last five years, you can successfully beat an IRS challenge that you are a hobbyist, if you can show a profit motive. Some of the factors to consider in evaluating the profit motive are:

- the time and effort you expend in the activity.
- methods by which you record business activity—keeping receipts, journals, in-out records, job cards.
- your expertise and experience—steady professional notice (gallery shows, prizes, mention in books).
- expectation that your work will increase in value.
- your success in related and unrelated activities helps to show you can make a go of it.
- profit/loss history—increasing income is helpful, but a continued large discrepancy between the activity income and expenses isn't.
- your financial status—if you have independent income, this goes against finding of a profit motive.*
- the extent to which you do the work for personal pleasure.

Throughout this chapter are suggestions for doing your work in a businesslike fashion—if you have good record keeping, get into galleries and juried shows, win prizes, show an increase in income, study or achieve recognition, sell to people other than friends, then hopefully you can meet an IRS challenge.

One artist, Gloria Churchman, engaged in painting, designing, sculpting, and drawing for twenty years, and her art-related income never exceeded her art-related expenses. The tax court held that she could deduct her art-related expenses because the facts showed that she engaged in the art activities with an intent to make a prof-

BUSINESS OR HOBBY?

HOBBY LOSS CHALLENGE

TEST: PROFIT MOTIVE

FACTORS TO EVALUATE PROFIT MOTIVE

---

*Several cases have held that where persons of independent wealth consistently had expenses in excess of income from the artwork, then the activity was a hobby and there was not the necessary profit motive.

it.* To obtain the 1970 and 1971 tax deductions for her art studio and studio office, Ms. Churchman argued that the Internal Revenue Code should allow her deduction because the activity was engaged in for profit. Even though she had a history of losses, she did not depend on the art income for her livelihood, and though there was a recreational element in her activities, there was still a profit motive. The profit motive was shown by her professional qualifications and commitment, her art training and experience at colleges and workshops, her effort to sell her work publicly, and her businesslike record keeping of art-related expenses and sales.

COMMON TAX RETURN ERRORS

Some of the most common errors that crop up on returns completed by individuals are:

- entries placed on wrong lines
- failure to attach necessary schedules, a check for tax due, W-2 forms
- failure to have joint returns signed by both spouses
- failure to claim tax credit such as the earned income credit
- confusion over the medical deductions and charitable gifts
- failure to include the previous year's deducted state and local tax refund as income
- putting casualty losses together and deducting the $100 exclusion only once
- failure to take 12 cents per mile for driving done for charitable or 9 cents for medical reasons.
- taking a partnership loss as an itemized deduction rather than a reduction in income.

AUDITS

WHO GETS AUDITED

An audit is a review of your return by a revenue agent. About 2 percent of all returns are audited. The more money you make, the greater are your chances of being audited. Other factors making an audit more likely include your self-employment and payment in cash, if your alleged self-employment looks like a hobby, if your deductions are way out of line with the average itemized deductions, if you have high deductions for business and travel, and if it is unlikely that you can support the family on the income you state. Some returns are randomly picked for an audit. The IRS audited one family three years running, because of the wife's craft ventures and publishing efforts. She failed to separate these transactions from the general family business and failed to keep records.

COMPUTER CHECKS

Now computers match your tax return with computerized information on wages, interest, dividends, et cetera. A few months after filing your return you may receive a correction-to-arithmetic notice or a letter asking for fully completed related forms or other information which calls your attention to an obvious blunder. This is not an audit notice but rather is a notification of a glaring error that appeared on your return when it was checked. In this case, most people pay any tax liability or accept a refund as indicated on the correction notice because the goof is usually obvious.

Even if you get a refund or if you pay an IRS demand for additional tax, the IRS has three years to audit a return, unless fraud is involved. Fraud leaves the door open longer for an audit (three years from the date the fraud is discovered). An audit

MODERN-DAY BOUNTY HUNTERS

can be triggered by an angry neighbor, ex-lover, ex-spouse, an employee turning you in—they can get a bounty of up to 10 percent of the taxes and penalties collected.

NOTICE LETTER

If you are chosen for audit, you get a letter setting up an appointment. The letter will also indicate what items are questioned and what supporting evidence you will need. *Don't ignore the letter.* You can request a change of location or a postponement, but again, don't ignore the appointment. Usually a Form 5714, Confirmation of Appointment, is attached to your notice. On that form you indicate if you will keep the appointment or want another date. If someone prepared your return, ask him

---

*Churchman v. Commissioner, 68 T.C. 696 (1977).

or her to go with you. If you did your own return and don't think you can handle an audit or if you have evaded taxes, then take a certified public accountant or attorney with you.* You will need to sign a 2848-D Authorization and Declaration form before information can be given to them.

Prepare yourself thoroughly for the meeting—review your return, accumulate and organize your canceled checks, receipts, diary, and so on.** Don't overdress for the meeting. For example, if you have claimed $200 yearly income from your printmaking and you show up for the audit wearing a beaver-skin hat, alligator boots, and a genuine leopard vest, the auditor will be suspicious of your income. It won't help for you to be either hostile to the agent or overly friendly. Don't volunteer informaton. Let the agent set the pace and just answer questions asked. Be firm and positive if you know you are entitled to a deduction. You may have to talk to someone higher up. During my recent audit, I took book contracts, an agent agreement, royalty statements, and published books and magazine articles to meet a hobby loss challenge to my writing business.

If you agree with the findings, the IRS agent will figure your additional taxes and ask you to sign an agreement form. After signing you lose your appeal rights, so wait until you get the Report of Individual Income Tax Examination Charges, Form 1902A. The report spells out amounts and reasons for the charges. In hardship situations you can make installment payments.

Remember in dealing with the agent that horse trading on issues is possible, for this avoids paperwork and litigation for all. The agent has authority to settle the questioned parts of your return. Occasionally, at the end of an audit, a taxpayer will even have a smaller tax bill.

His horse went dead, and his mule went lame,
And he lost six cows in a poker game;
Then a hurricane came on a Summer day,
And blew the house where he lived away;
An earthquake came when that was gone,
And swallowed the land the house stood on.
And then the tax collector came around,
And charged him up with the hole in the ground.

If you and the agent disagree, you have several alternatives: an appeal within the IRS; litigation in the tax court; and/or a combination of these. You will be sent Publication 5, "Your Appeal Rights and Preparation of Protests for Unagreed Cases." Generally, once you receive the written report you can submit additional information, discuss the findings with an examiner, or request a district conference. Or you could use the new small claims division of the tax court for amounts under $5,000. You file only one petition. The court usually is more lenient in accepting evidence than the IRS, and you can represent yourself. There is no appeal from the tax court small claims division if the IRS is upheld.

If you allegedly owe IRS a lot of money, if it looks like a fraud situation, or if you have decided to litigate, get professional help.

You've had a pretty exhausting trip through the federal income tax maze. Maybe reform is around the corner and maybe it's not—but you've got the idea of keeping records so you can reconstruct your business and personal activities to determine the money you got, and the money you spent. Some friends, an English professor and his wife, filed recently not only for his salaried income, but for his sideline handyman business and her pottery business (they built a beautiful double hexagon studio and huge kiln). With a very commendable doggedness, our friends used to do their taxes themselves using mainly the IRS "Business Tax Kit," Lasser's *Your Income Tax*, and calls to the IRS. It took them about thirty-five hours, but now the new partnership information form, Schedule K (which has no instruction sheet and is a rat's maze) forces them to use the services of an accountant for part of their return.

The Canadian federal government, under the Excise Tax Act, imposes a tax on all goods produced or imported into Canada. The Canadian Income Tax Act covers

---

*There is an IRS manual that instructs agents on what to look for during an audit. You might look at it at a library. There is a summary of the manual called *How to Survive a Tax Audit* available from Reymont Associates, 29-S Reymont Ave., Rye, NY 10580 which may be worth getting.
**Keep all your notes and scribbles that go into making up your return. If audited, this will help piece together the basis for the deductions you claimed, i.e., if you claim $300 for professional books, then you keep the worksheet where you listed the books and totaled their price.

taxation of rental and royalty or license payments to non-residents with respect to copyright and the rights thereunder, but the current Canada-U.S. States Tax Conversion may alter the Canadian taxpayer's obligations in this situation under the Income Tax Act. See a knowledgeable lawyer.

Most goods imported into Canada are subject to a custom duty imposd through the Customs Act. Some provinces have a Retail Sales Act, which imposes a percentage retail sales tax on the sale, rental, or lease of particular kinds of tangible personal property with certain exceptions. Sometimes, services to install, adjust, repair, or maintain tangible personal property are also subject to tax.

CHAPTER SIX

Other Taxes

SELF-EMPLOYMENT TAX
ESTIMATED TAX
SALES TAX
STATE AND LOCAL INCOME TAX
PROPERTY TAX
ESTATE AND GIFT TAX

LEGAL ADVICE? NOT ON YOUR LIFE.

INTRODUCTION

This chapter is a catchall for taxes not covered in the previous chapter—self-employment taxes, estimated taxes, sales tax, and various property taxes. Two of these, the self-employment and estimated taxes, are related to the previous chapter.

SELF-EMPLOYMENT TAX

WHEN DUE

You are liable for self-employment tax (your payment into the Social Security system), if you have an annual net income of $400 or more from self-employment. In 1988, you pay the Social Security tax rate of 7.51 percent if an employee and 12.30 percent for self-employed persons to maximum earnings of $43,800. This is added to your income tax liability, and the two taxes are paid as one. You compute the self-employment tax on Schedule SE, and pay it with your yearly tax return. Of course, in order to be self-employed, you must be selling your work for a profit; that is, if you sell only one pot or magazine article during the year, you may not qualify as self-employed.

IF BOTH EMPLOYED AND SELF-EMPLOYED

If you work full- or part-time as an employee and are self-employed on the side, then you pay that tax on the *lesser* of your net self-employed earnings or the difference between your wages subject to the self-employed tax and the $43,800 maximum. There's also a nonform optional method for self-employment tax. You cannot receive Social Security benefits until you attain *insured status*, which you get by contributing tax for a certain number of quarters of work. Social Security has a variety of benefits (all with special qualifying rules): retirement, Medicare, disability, and survivor benefits. See your Social Security office for free copies of numerous Social Security information pamphlets.

ESTIMATED TAX

PAY-AS-YOU-GO PLAN

Since the law requires that you pay taxes owed on your income at the time you are paid, partially or totally self-employed persons (which would include artists, craft-makers, and writers) have to fill out and file quarterly a Form 1040-SE, Estimated Tax Declaration Voucher and pay estimated taxes, if your estimated tax for 1988 is more than $500 and the estimated tax withheld that year is less than 100% of tax for 1987 or 90% of tax for 1988. This means you act as your own employer and send in taxes quarterly on your income as it's earned.

To pay the estimated tax, estimate your tax for the year, complete the voucher, and mail it by April 15 of that year. Other installments are due June 15, September 15, and January 15. The remaining estimated tax owed can be paid along with your regular 1040 form, filed on or before April 15. If you overestimated your taxes, the excess can be deducted from next year's tax. If you underestimate your tax but generally pay what you paid last year, then you won't be penalized. It's easiest to figure your estimated tax on the basis of your previous year's income tax and self-employment tax liability. For example, if your 1988 tax is $2,400, by fixing your 1989 estimated tax at $2,400 you will not be subject to a penalty as long as your quarterly payments are timely.* Of course, if you have reason to believe that your income will be over last year's, then you should pay additional estimated tax.

Alice's Allegory #20 or Enshrined for Eternity

Alice on filing her 1987 tax return paid a lot in taxes plus a penalty for failure to pay her estimated tax, which meant staying up nights throwing pots and selling her wares on the street to get the cash together for the local tax agent. She said, "Wow, I can't go through that again. Show me how to do it."

The local tax agent, who had turned on to Alice's fantastic stoneware Oriental soup spoons in Maltese blue glazes said in March 1989, "This is it. Do you know how much you are making this year?"

"I don't know but I paid $1,000 in taxes in 1988."

---

*Failure to make timely quarterly payments of your estimated tax can subject you to a penalty.

He said, "You'll need the amount of your last year's tax liability to figure your estimated tax for this year. Take notes."

She got a stylus and said, "I will enshrine this information for eternity." And on the slab she had just rolled she took dictation.

"On the voucher form, figure you'll pay $1,000 in taxes. File the voucher form and your first quarterly installment of $250 by April 15, 1989. Then pay $250 on June 15, September 15, and January 15, 1990—or pay $1,000 before January 15, 1990, because that's what you paid last year."

"I got it," said Alice and she promptly popped the slab in her kiln, then bisqued, glazed and fired it again for a beautiful wall hanging in her studio.

One day the tax agent returned, and said, "I have an order for five hundred of those estimated tax slabs. By the way, you better amend your estimated tax voucher or you'll be caught with a huge bill at the end of the year."

SALES TAX

A sales or gross receipts tax is a tax imposed by most states and some cities on retail sales to customers.* Only a few states do *not* have a sales tax. In some states, sales tax is also placed on services. If the seller pays the tax, then it can be deducted as a business expense. For example, Mrs. Duffy wants to buy a flowerpot from you priced at $10. You add a 4 percent sales tax (the rate for your state) to the pot's price, selling it to her for $10.40. You report that $10.40 as income, send the $.40 to the state sales tax department, and deduct the $.40 on your tax return.

Check with other business people or your state tax department to see if your state has a sales tax. If it does, make an application for a sales permit, and you will get a resale number.** Some states require you to post a bond prior to the issuance of the permit. The reason for this is if you don't pay the sales tax either by pocketing the tax paid by your customer or by failing to charge the tax, recovery for the amount of the tax obligation can be made against the bond. If you don't collect or fail to forward the tax for whatever reason, you may be liable for not only the tax but also interest and a penalty.

Sometimes at fairs, the management will get a sales tax permit, or the craftmaker (if the maker is from out-of-state or has no permit) will get a temporary permit. The person who makes the final sale (retailer) to the consumer collects and pays the tax. At art fairs usually you collect and pay, but at art exhibitions probably the sponsor pays. A person going to an art fair or other sale in another state should check to see if nonresidents have to collect sales taxes.

Some business people like to engage in mail-order business to avoid sales taxes. In that case, postal receipts regarding mail transactions should be kept. Some states, such as Arizona, require payment of a 5 percent use tax if the out-of-state vendor sales tax is not paid.

Alice's Allegory #21 or Beware of Mellow Fellows

Alice was at the Third Annual Bread and Butter Crafts Fair in Marshmallow Beach, Nevada, when she discovered that she was the only craftmaker who had applied for and received a license to collect and remit sales tax by non-residents. Barabella the Batikist, Lulu the Lithographer, and Qunito the Quilter all laughed at her, for they were charging the sales tax but had not applied for the license,

*An individual not in business does not have to pay this. In California, the determination of whether or not you are in business depends on the number of sales you make. For example if you make fewer than five sales a year, then you probably are not in business.

**If you have a resale number, then you do not have to pay taxes on your supplies (such as canvas, paint, fibers) for those goods are taxed as part of the final work you sell. Looms, easels, potter's wheels, etc., are not exempt, for they are not contained in the final product.

had no intentions of remitting the sales tax, and were pocketing it instead. At the Fourth Annual Bread and Butter Crafts Fair she discovered that they had all had hassles with the state of Nevada. Some were assessed fines and penalties. Alice just smiled her quiet smile.

STATE AND LOCAL INCOME TAX

You should check with your state tax department, and county and city governments, to see what other taxes might be collected and to get copies of the necessary forms to pay these taxes. For instance, New York City, Chicago, and San Francisco have city taxes. A handful of states do not have a state income tax. Usually states imposing a state income tax have rules similar to the federal government, but some don't—so look carefully at your state tax package when you get it.

PROPERTY TAX

There are several kinds of property taxes—auto license tax, inventory tax, real property tax, and personal property tax. The imposition of these taxes as well as the rates vary from state to state. The latter two taxes, based on dollar values, are increased by a rise in the assessed value. Inventory taxes are locally imposed taxes on business inventory and equipment and are based on the market value of the property. If your state requires payment of an inventory tax, then reduce your inventory to the lowest workable minimum by the assessment date.

ESTATE AND GIFT TAX

Under the 1976 Tax Reform Act a person's estate (after 1987) would only pay an estate tax if the total of the taxable gifts and the taxable estate is greater than $600,000. It is beyond the scope of this primer to discuss this area in any detail.* You may need a will and an estate plan. See a competent lawyer for advice in this area.

*See *Legal Guide for the Visual Artist* by Tad Crawford (Madison Square Press, 1987) for an excellent discussion of this issue.

134

CHAPTER SEVEN

Especially for Writers

COPYING

COPYRIGHT
OTHER PROTECTION FROM COPYING

CONTRACTS

PUBLISHING CONTRACTS
CONTRACTS WITH LITERARY AGENTS
COLLABORATION CONTRACTS
AGENT AGREEMENT

BACK TO TAXES

RECORD KEEPING
BUSINESS DEDUCTIONS
HOBBY LOSS CHALLENGE
SOCIAL SECURITY
OTHER TAXES

MISCELLANEOUS

FREEDOM OF INFORMATION ACT AND SUNSHINE LAWS
CANADA'S ACCESS TO INFORMATION ACT
WILLS

LEGAL ADVICE? NOT ON YOUR LIFE.

INTRODUCTION

Many earlier sections of this book apply to writers. The discussions of libel, obscenity, and invasion of privacy in the content section of Chapter 2, "Legal Limitations on Content and Materials," are geared to writers as well as artists and craftmakers. This chapter supplements the others in this book and is best understood after reading them.

Legal matters arising from the writing business generally fall into three categories:

- protection of your work
  copyright
  sales contracts
  unfair competition
  misappropriation
- liability for the contents of your work
  libel
  obscenity
  invasion of privacy
  infringement
- governmental rights and obligations
  taxes
  freedom of information acts

COPYRIGHT

The basics of copyright law are discussed in Chapter 3, "Copying." Here, I cover the aspects of copyright law that especially concern writers.

HISTORY

Historically, copyright laws evolved to protect literary works. Just as ancient poets and dramatists refused to sing unless they were paid in food and lodging, writers wanted to control the use of their work and to share in its profits. In the United States, Noah Webster, eager to protect his *Blue-back Speller*, first published in 1783, journeyed to several Colonial state capitals to lobby successfully for the passage of state copyright acts. In 1790, the first federal copyright act passed and a few days later the first copyright issued for the *Philadelphia Spelling Book*. Nearly two hundred years later, in the year 1977, there were 122,080 registrations for books alone with the Copyright Office!

Writers frequently ask about the duration of copyright protection under the new law for their older, unpublished works. If an unpublished work was created before 1978 and was still protected by the old common law copyright on January 1, 1978 (that is, it had not been published), it automatically received copyright protection for the term common to all copyrighted works—the author's life plus fifty years. For anonymous or pseudonymous works or works for hire, the term is seventy-five years from the date of first publication or one hundred years from the date of the creation, whichever is less. However, in no event can the copyright term for these unpublished works expire before December 31, 2002. For example if the author of an unpublished work entitled *The Colorado River Early Inhabitants* died in 1950, the copyright would not expire in 2000 (author's life plus fifty years) but 2002.

POST-JANUARY 1, 1978 UNPUBLISHED WORKS

Under the new law unpublished works can now be registered. This has some disadvantages. When an unpublished work is infringed before registration, then you can win actual damages but no attorney fees or costs, if the owner of the unpublished work wins the suit. Also, if you register the unpublished work, the copy that you deposit with the Copyright Office is a public record that anyone can inspect.

Not copyright in 1942
Again not copyright in 1952
Anybody is welcome to help himself to any of it in any way.

Some people may not wish to copyright their work. J. Frank Dobie declined to copyright his work *Guide to Life and Literature of the Southwest* with the delightful non-notice that appears in the margin.

CONTENTS OF COPYRIGHT NOTICE

If you *do* want to copyright your work, the same requirements concerning the copyright notice apply here. The regulations describe what constitutes acceptable placement for the copyright notice and reasonable notice of the claim of copyright:

- title page
- page following title page
- either side of the front cover, and if none, either side of front pages (same for back)
- first page of work's main body
- last page of work's main body
- between the front page and first page of main body as long as the pages between don't exceed ten and the notice is prominent and separated from other material (same for back)

LOCATION OF COPYRIGHT NOTICE

In a collective work such as a magazine, the notice should additionally be placed by the masthead or near the front of the issue alongside the issue number, date, and title. In order for a separate contribution to a collective work to bear its own notice of copyright, the notice must be positioned in one of the following ways:

POSITION OF AN INDIVIDUAL NOTICE IN A COLLECTIVE WORK

- for contribution of one page or less, the notice must appear under the title, adjacent to the contribution, or somewhere else on the page as long as clear.
- for a contribution of more than one page, the notice must appear under the title or near the beginning of the contribution, on the first page of the main body, or at the immediate end of the contribution.
- or the notice could appear in a separate list of contributions by full titles and authors on a page, table of contents, or acknowledgments appearing in the front or back of the whole collective work.

Even if your contribution to a periodical does not have its own notice, you receive copyright protection based upon the magazine's copyright. However, you cannot use the registration form for group registrations unless each contribution bears your own notice.

GROUP REGISTRATION

Use Form TX (for registering nondramatic literary works) if you are making a single registration for a group of contributions to various periodicals. This way you can register all your contributions printed in a twelve-month period together and at once for a single fee of $10. At the same time, deposit two complete copies of each magazine, anthology, or periodical containing the works in question. Better yet, register these contributions quarterly so that no more than three months pass between publication and registration—the copyright annual fees would total $40 rather than $10, but you would not lose your statutory damages and attorneys' fees in the event of infringement. If it happens that your contributions are covered by a single copyright notice in the name of the publisher, then the publisher is the one to register the work and should register the work (make sure it is done in three months). It is better that you have the copyright in your name and you register it. Otherwise the publisher must assign it back to you.

REGISTER QUARTERLY

PUBLISHER REGISTRATION OF COLLECTIVE WORK

Since the new Copyright Act allows divisibility, a magazine notice of copyright covers all the works but does not mean ownership, so the writer should confirm his/her ownership of the copyright in the piece even though notice was in the name of the magazine publisher.

CONFIRMATION

We, _____ *(magazine)* _____ , of the State of _____ ,
_____ *(address)* _____ , confirm that *(writer)* is the true owner of copyright in the work(s) entitled _____
which appeared in the _____ issue of
_____ , which was registered in the U.S. Copyright office under the registration number TX _____ .

Date: _____   Signed: _____
                         Capacity: _____
                         For: _____
                              (Name of magazine)

(Notary—always have this notarized)

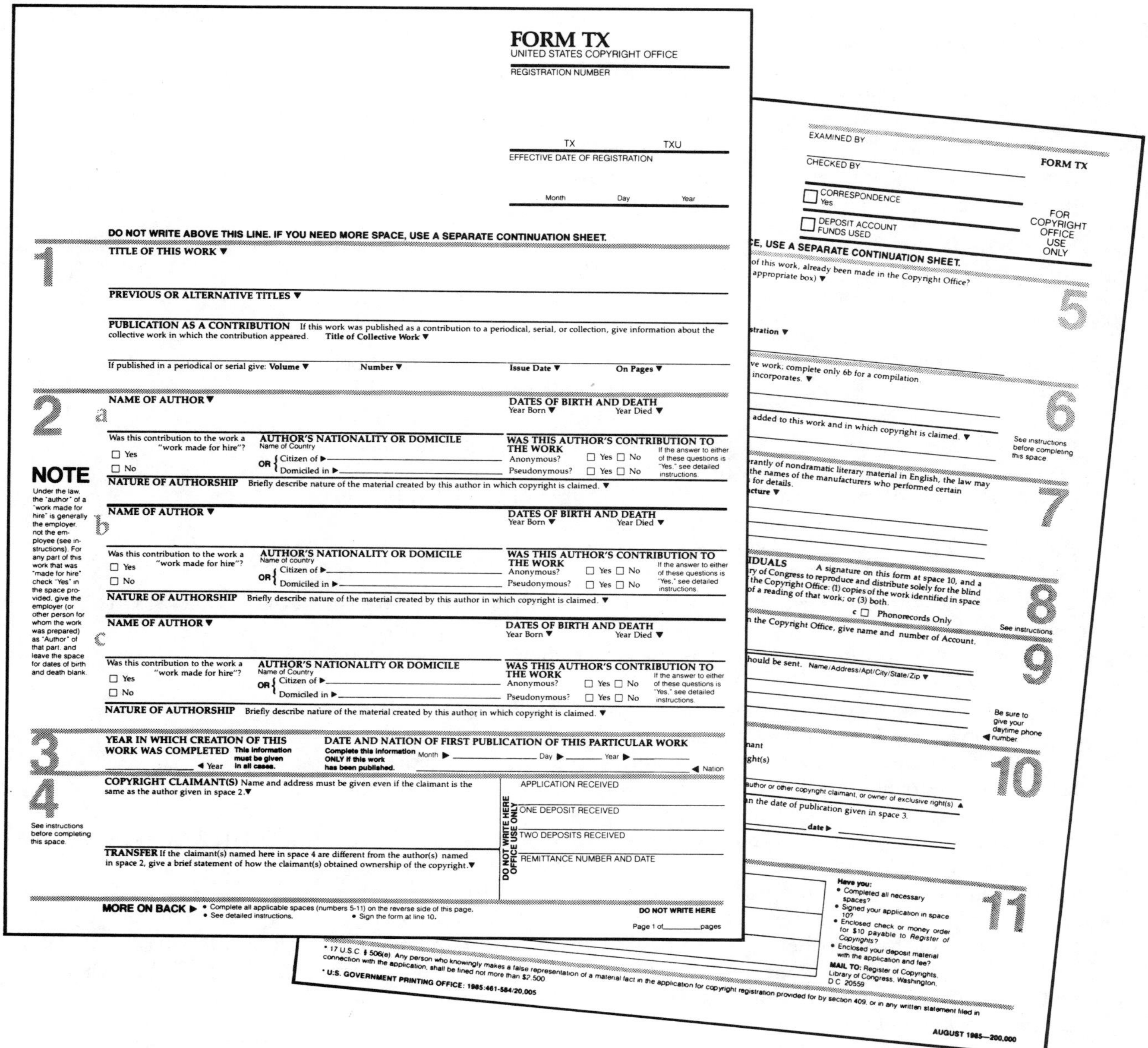

FORM TX
UNITED STATES COPYRIGHT OFFICE
REGISTRATION NUMBER

TX TXU
EFFECTIVE DATE OF REGISTRATION
Month Day Year

DO NOT WRITE ABOVE THIS LINE. IF YOU NEED MORE SPACE, USE A SEPARATE CONTINUATION SHEET.

1 TITLE OF THIS WORK ▼

PREVIOUS OR ALTERNATIVE TITLES ▼

PUBLICATION AS A CONTRIBUTION If this work was published as a contribution to a periodical, serial, or collection, give information about the collective work in which the contribution appeared. Title of Collective Work ▼

If published in a periodical or serial give: Volume ▼ Number ▼ Issue Date ▼ On Pages ▼

2 a NAME OF AUTHOR ▼ DATES OF BIRTH AND DEATH Year Born ▼ Year Died ▼

Was this contribution to the work a "work made for hire"? ☐ Yes ☐ No
AUTHOR'S NATIONALITY OR DOMICILE Name of Country OR { Citizen of ▶ Domiciled in ▶
WAS THIS AUTHOR'S CONTRIBUTION TO THE WORK Anonymous? ☐ Yes ☐ No Pseudonymous? ☐ Yes ☐ No If the answer to either of these questions is "Yes," see detailed instructions.
NATURE OF AUTHORSHIP Briefly describe nature of the material created by this author in which copyright is claimed. ▼

NOTE
Under the law, the "author" of a "work made for hire" is generally the employer, not the employee (see instructions). For any part of this work that was "made for hire" check "Yes" in the space provided, give the employer (or other person for whom the work was prepared) as "Author" of that part, and leave the space for dates of birth and death blank.

b NAME OF AUTHOR ▼ DATES OF BIRTH AND DEATH Year Born ▼ Year Died ▼

Was this contribution to the work a "work made for hire"? ☐ Yes ☐ No
AUTHOR'S NATIONALITY OR DOMICILE Name of country OR { Citizen of ▶ Domiciled in ▶
WAS THIS AUTHOR'S CONTRIBUTION TO THE WORK Anonymous? ☐ Yes ☐ No Pseudonymous? ☐ Yes ☐ No If the answer to either of these questions is "Yes," see detailed instructions.
NATURE OF AUTHORSHIP Briefly describe nature of the material created by this author in which copyright is claimed. ▼

c NAME OF AUTHOR ▼ DATES OF BIRTH AND DEATH Year Born ▼ Year Died ▼

Was this contribution to the work a "work made for hire"? ☐ Yes ☐ No
AUTHOR'S NATIONALITY OR DOMICILE Name of Country OR { Citizen of ▶ Domiciled in ▶
WAS THIS AUTHOR'S CONTRIBUTION TO THE WORK Anonymous? ☐ Yes ☐ No Pseudonymous? ☐ Yes ☐ No If the answer to either of these questions is "Yes," see detailed instructions.
NATURE OF AUTHORSHIP Briefly describe nature of the material created by this author in which copyright is claimed. ▼

3 YEAR IN WHICH CREATION OF THIS WORK WAS COMPLETED This information must be given in all cases. ◀ Year
DATE AND NATION OF FIRST PUBLICATION OF THIS PARTICULAR WORK Complete this information ONLY if this work has been published. Month ▶ Day ▶ Year ▶ ◀ Nation

4 COPYRIGHT CLAIMANT(S) Name and address must be given even if the claimant is the same as the author given in space 2.▼
See instructions before completing this space.

APPLICATION RECEIVED
ONE DEPOSIT RECEIVED
TWO DEPOSITS RECEIVED
REMITTANCE NUMBER AND DATE
DO NOT WRITE HERE OFFICE USE ONLY

TRANSFER If the claimant(s) named here in space 4 are different from the author(s) named in space 2, give a brief statement of how the claimant(s) obtained ownership of the copyright.▼

MORE ON BACK ▶ • Complete all applicable spaces (numbers 5-11) on the reverse side of this page. • See detailed instructions. • Sign the form at line 10.
DO NOT WRITE HERE
Page 1 of ______ pages

Figure 7.1 Copyright Form TX for the registration of non-dramatic, literary works

ASSIGNMENT

Since the new copyright law requires that any conveyance of ownership of copyright be written and signed by the owner of rights conveyed, you might have your lawyer adopt the following form to your needs.

That ______________________ with its principal place of business at ______________________ and called Assignor, grants to ______________ his/her successors and assigns the following:

a. the sole and exclusive license under the copyright set forth below and to use or authorize the use of the following rights in the work described below:

(List whether magazine, reprint rights, etc.)

OR:

a. Under the copyrights set forth below, the Assignor assigns, transfers, sets over and conveys to _____ all the right, title and interest in the copyrights registered in the Copyright office in and to the following work created by _____ and (*name of magazine, list title of pieces, and issue*), which work titled _____ was registered for copyright under the following number _____ .

Date: _____   Signed: _____
                         Capacity: _____
                         For: _____
                                   (*Name of magazine*)

(Notary—*always have this notarized*)

Whoever transfers and licenses a copyright can terminate the transfer at a later date. So if you want to save this right for your heirs or yourself, then you should get the copyright in your name. In this way you would be the grantor, the person giving the transfer, and could later terminate it.

TERMINATION OF COPYRIGHT TRANSFERS

The new copyright law provides for special treatment for contributions to collective works. Absent an agreement to the contrary the copyright of each contribution remains with the author even though the only copyright notice appearing on the collective work is the publisher's. Further, unless otherwise agreed, the publisher receives not only the right to use the contribution in the collective work, but also receives the right to use the contribution as part of any revision of the collective work or as part of a later collective work in the same series. So if you do not want your article "How to Make Fried Bread," which was contributed to the *Ole Cooking* magazine, to be used again in their annual publication, *100 Best Recipes of Ole Cooking*, or to be run again three years later, then you need to state in your contract that you are giving one-time-use rights *only*, or the new copyright law sweeps rights discussed above into your contract of sale.

COPYRIGHT WITH CONTRIBUTOR TO COLLECTIVE WORK

PUBLISHER'S RIGHTS TO USE OF CONTRIBUTION TO COLLECTIVE WORK

Old copyrights (pre-1978) are renewed on or before December 31 of the year the term ended for copyrights you originally registered between January 1, 1950,* and December 31, 1977, to obtain protection for a second term of forty-seven years. For example, a 1952 copyright must have been registered for renewal during the 1980 calendar year. (Use Form RE.) The same form renews a group of works first published as contributions to periodicals in the same year—for example, in 1980 a renewal registration could have been made for all the writer's contributions to collective works first published in 1952. If you are missing information that you need to complete the renewal form, the Copyright Office will do research for you.

RENEWAL OF FIRST-TERM COPYRIGHTS

RENEWAL OF PRE-1978 PERIODICAL CONTRIBUTIONS

For those pre-1978 situations where the publisher copyrighted the contribution, have the publisher assign the copyright back to you in writing and record the assignment.

There are provisions in the new copyright act which permit authors and certain of their heirs to terminate contracts before the end of their book's copyright term. One is the popularly termed "Widows and Orphans Exemption" and applies to all published works in which grants were made through the end of 1977. For grants made after that date, termination is allowed by the author and certain heirs thirty-five years after a book has been published or forty years after a contract has been signed, whichever comes first. These provisions address the unequal bargaining position of authors and publishers. If you plan to utilize these provisions, please consult a knowledgeable lawyer.

"WIDOWS AND ORPHANS EXEMPTION"

These guidelines for the educational fair use of copyrighted works set limits on

FAIR USE

*Any copyrights before that date have expired or are already in their second term.

the length of works that can be copied, require that the copyright notice be placed on each copied work, and limit the number of times works can be copied. Since many writers also teach, these guidelines for educational fair use are summarized. Acceptable fair uses for educational purposes include:

EDUCATIONAL PURPOSES

- use of a single copy in teaching a class or in scholarly research of:
  a book chapter.
  an article from a periodical.
  a short story, essay, poem.
  a cartoon, chart, diagram drawing, graph, or picture from a periodical.
- use of multiple classroom copies (one copy per student in class) of:
  a complete poem of less than 250 words and not longer than two pages.
  a poem excerpt of less than 250 words.
  a story, article, or essay of less than 2,500 words.
  an excerpt from a prose work of the lesser of 1,000 words or 10 percent of the work.
  one cartoon, chart, etc., per book or periodical.

A teacher *may not:*

- make multiple copies for classroom use if the work has been copied already for a class at the same institution.
- make multiple copies of a work from the same author more than once a term or more than three times a term from the same collective work or periodical.
- make multiple copies of works more than nine times in a term.
- make an overrun of copies for others.
- make a copy of works in place of an anthology.
- make a copy of materials such as workbooks that can be consumed.
- repeat copies from term to term.

LIBRARIES

For guidelines for fair use by libraries under the new law, obtain a copy of Circular R21, Reproduction of Copyrighted Works by Educators and Libraries, from the Copyright Office.

CRITICISM AND THE ADVANCE
OF SCIENCE AND ART

PARODY AND BURLESQUE

There are other areas of concern under the fair-use section of the copyright act. Under the fair-use doctrine, you can quote directly from a work in dramatic or literary criticism. Also, those working in the fields of sciences and art can use existing copyrighted works to write new works, including comments, discussions, and long quotes from the earlier works. Since old work is a jumping-off place for those new works, this is an important fair use, and is considered necessary to the advancement of science and art. Parody and burlesque necessarily involve the use of an original work, but the line between fair use and infringement is fine. Jack Benny performed a humorous sketch, "Autolight," which burlesqued a motion picture, *Gaslight,* and the court held that the use was unfair.

OBTAINING PERMISSION FOR THE
USE OF COPYRIGHTED MATERIAL

How long should quotations be before you get permission? Different publishers have different word limits depending on the nature of the work: for scholarly works—fifty to two hundred words; poetry—three to four lines. Possibly. If the use from poetry or musical lyrics is for *commercial purposes,* don't use a line or the author's name without permission. (See the sample permission form, page 50.) The notice printed in the front of some books stating that the "unauthorized use of [so many] words is forbidden" does not prevent the fair use of the work. A better practice is to authorize the use of up to a certain number of words without permission as long as it is not used for advertising or publicity, except for use in reviews. The Association of American Publishers (AAP) has designed a rapid and efficient permission system, and you should contact them to get a copy of their permission request form: AAP, 220 E. 23rd St., New York, NY 10010. A Copyright Clearance Center (CCC) 27 Congress St., Salem, MA 01970, establishes a central royalty-paying clearinghouse where payment terms for photocopying magazine articles are set in advance and coded on each contribution's title page. An extra copy of the title page, indicating the number of copies made and the payment, would be sent to CCC, who would forward it to the publisher, who would then forward it to the author.

Be sure to keep a record of permissions. Follow up if you don't hear from the company or person. Request full rights, which include translation rights, world-wide distribution, future editions, and subsidiary rights; otherwise you will have to omit the material or get another permission later. Negotiate to reduce any permission fees that might be quoted. See if the publisher can pay or share in those expenses. While some say that a safe rule of thumb sets the limit of their use at 300 words, it depends on the circumstances. For a long scholarly work *yes*, but use in an advertisement, *no*.

The new law grants another fair-use right for the performance or display of certain copyrighted works. This exception to the general rule of "no use without permission" is fairly specific. In summary, this fair-use exception applies to:

CERTAIN PERFORMING AND DISPLAY RIGHTS

- works displayed in face-to-face teaching at a nonprofit educational institution
- performance or display of works at a religious function, assembly, or church
- performance of nondramatic literary works if there is no admission, no commercial advantage, and no one (promoter, organizer, or performer) receives a fee

Under the third exception, if an admission fee is charged, then all proceeds must go to an educational, religious, or charitable purpose. In this case, the copyright owner can prevent the performance under most circumstances. Otherwise copyright owners would be supporting causes that they may personally oppose.

Remember, the copyright act protects the right of a subsequent author to use material from a prior author's works to serve the fundamental constitutional purpose of encouraging contributions to understanding and knowledge. Too, the original author is entitled to protection against others who borrow too much. When a person's work is a history manuscript that uses much factual material, it will be harder to prove copyright infringement. This is true in instances involving *scene a faire*, an obligatory scene, which would be included in writing a standard treatment of a topic, such as a writer's coming of age. *Scenes a faire* include the writer's first time published, the first time paid, and the first literary awards.

Facts, that is historical and biographical facts, are not protected.

Several fair-use cases preclude biographer's use of protected material even when it is paraphrased. In *Harper & Row v. Nation Enterprises* the court determined that the *Nations'* use of 13 percent of President Ford's memoirs was unfair; in *Salinger v. Random House* a court granted a preliminary injunction to stop publication of an unauthorized biography when the biographer used Salinger's unpublished copyrighted letters; and in *Craft v. Kobler* the court granted a preliminary injunction against a biographer of Stravinsky because of unfair use of protected material, even though the direct quotes and close paraphrasing constituted only 3 percent of the biography.

Writers or publishers bring the majority of legal actions for infringement. The following are examples of successful infringement cases:

LAWSUITS FOR INFRINGEMENT

- *Adventures in Good Eating*, a guidebook for restaurants and hotels infringed another guide where there was similarity of expression and organization.
- Classified Geographic, Inc.'s, compilation of cut-up copies of *National Geographic* magazine was an infringement.
- a fictional biography of Clara Barton in the form of a screenplay was found infringed by a so-called factual biographical book that used some of the fictionalized episodes.

The use of the same fundamental plot is not an infringement if there are differences in the leading characters, action, dialogue, episodes, and locale. In a case involving a movie entitled *The Seven Per Cent Solution*, the court failed to find that a scholarly piece concerning cocaine addiction at the turn of the century was infringed upon by the movie. Even though plaintiff speculated in his scholarly work that Holmes' fear of Professor Moriarity was a drug-induced paranoid delusion cured by Freud— the basic plot of the movie *The Seven Per Cent Solution*—no infringement was found.

On the other hand, the successful play *White Cargo* infringed Ida Vera Simington's novel *Hell's Playground,* for the infringing work repeated incidents and episodes from *Hell's Playground,* such as a setting in the African tropics, and a male central character who lived with a female native.

You must prove copying, as copyright protection does not extend to the expression of an idea. In a copyright infringement case involving *Abie's Irish Rose* and *The Cohens and The Kellys,* the court compared similar plots to Romeo and Juliet, for Jewish and Catholic young adults fell in love. The court concluded no author could step on another's toes vis-a-vis copyright infringement just from developing the Romeo-Juliet concept unless the *expression* was *identical.*

The Authors League 1982 Symposium on copyright gave infringement-avoidance tips to a second author doing research on a subject dealt with in a prior work:

- do your own independent research from many sources, including public domain sources and older works (never competing, recent works)
- don't paraphrase or quote
- credit the other's work
- don't appropriate expression
- if you request permission, state that you think the use you propose is fair use and the request is merely a courtesy
- avoid tracking the arrangement of the other material (order, arrangement, and reference)

Some publishers may require that your manuscript go through a legal manuscript review. A knowledgeable lawyer checks the work for libel, invasion of privacy, plagiarism, and so forth. A novelist I know was required to change the age, physical description, and residence of a law enforcement officer in a piece of fiction when the reviewer's concerns regarding possible libel exposure could not be satisfied.

Recalls of books are common. Random House recalled 58,000 copies of a biography titled *Poor Little Rich Girl: The Life and Legend of Barbara Hutton* because of erroneous statements about a doctor who purportedly treated Hutton at a time when he was fourteen. Closer to home, our law firm stopped publication of a book and required its revision when a graduate student wrote about a family she lived with one summer. We alleged that the work invaded the family's privacy.

As advised previously, consult a knowlegeable lawyer if you have a copyright infringement situation on your hands.

OTHER PROTECTION FROM COPYING

Chapter 3, "Copying," listed several subjects that could not be protected under the copyright law, some of which are especially important to writers. Titles cannot be copyrighted but sometimes have protection through the theory of unfair competition,* fraud, or misappropriation. Hemingway prevented the use of one of his titles, *The Fifth Column,* from utilization as the title for a motion picture called the *The Fifth Column Squad* using those legal theories. Other titles that have been protected are:

TITLES

- *Sex and the Single Girl,* against *Sex and the Single Man*
- *Sesame Street,* against use on commercial goods unless a disclaimer indicated that the product was not connected with the television show
- the name *Frank Merribell,* which appeared in the title of a thousand stories
- *The Story of O,* against the *Journey of O*

There is no part of the law which is more plastic than unfair competition.
—JUDGE LEARNED HAND

But *Alice in Wonderland,* (the title) of an expensive Walt Disney motion picture, was not protected from another movie with the same name, for the original work by Lewis Carroll was in the public domain. Also, the title *Test Pilot* was not given pro-

*See discussion of unfair competition in Chapter 3, "Copying."

142

tection because it was purely descriptive and had not acquired a secondary meaning. In order for unfair competition to protect titles, the title must have acquired a secondary meaning, that is, use of the title for a sufficient length of time so the title becomes connected to the work in the public's mind.

Characters are not usually protected under copyright laws. In one case a character was protected against misappropriation. Unfair competition protected the exclusive right of the cartoonists who created Mutt and Jeff to use the characters. Dashiell Hammett ultimately succeeded in arguing that his rights to the character Sam Spade of the famous *The Maltese Falcon* were not lost with the sale of a right to publish a copyrighted story. Since the sale did not specifically include the character Sam Spade, which was his property, the character could be reused by him.

CHARACTERS

UNFAIR COMPETITION

While Sam Spade was really given protection as a matter of contract, the court mentioned that copyright protection extends to the character when the character "constitutes the story being told" or when it is so developed that it leaves the realm of idea to become the expression. Hopalong Cassidy and Tarzan were also protected under this theory.

The Canadian courts have been pressed to determine whether copyright is assigned under a particular book contract, or if the author merely gives a license to publish to the publisher. Therefore, the contract terms should very explicitly indicate that the copyright remains with the author. If the author assigns the copyright to the publisher, then the publisher has the right to make successive editions of the work subject to the *droit morale* provision of the Canadian Copyright Act (discussed previously).

COPYRIGHT IN CANADIAN BOOK CONTRACTS

Writers make many contracts in the course of their business—with agents, magazines, book companies, newspapers, motion-picture studios, book clubs, record companies, and so on. In order to explore many of the basic issues found in most writers' contracts, this section will discuss three of the most common agreements made by writers—book publishing, collaboration, and literary agency contracts. Still, special issues arise from the peculiarities of each industry. Before dealing with a record company, for instance, consult a competent professional for advice and assistance as well as read any literature on the subject. After all, even such luminaries in the book world as the publishers of the *Guinness Book of World Records* have been involved in contract disputes.

CONTRACTS

INTRODUCTION

The Authors Guild (234 W. 44th St., New York, NY 10036) not only supplies their members with a model publishing contract and commentary but also takes important positions on various issues involving authors' rights. Membership in the Authors Guild is only available to authors of published works or works in process. Dues skyrocketed to $75 in 1988, but active membership in the guild confers a multitude of benefits, such as receipt of the quarterly Guild Bulletin which includes surveys on advances and royalties, and a "legal watch" column. Recently, the guild released revisions to its Recommended Trade Book Contract; these revisions included limiting the grant of rights to terms of twenty years rather than the full term of copyright (life plus fifty years). This is the ideal contract, from the author's perspective.

PUBLISHING CONTRACTS

AUTHORS GUILD

Publishers would disagree with the guild's statement that its recommended clauses "are fair and equitable to both the publisher and author."

If you don't qualify for membership in the Authors Guild or if you want a different perspective on negotiation, order "Negotiating Your Rights—A Key to Freelancing," sold for $4.50 by Council of Writers Organizations, CWO, 1501 Broadway, Suite 1907, New York, NY 10036. This pamphlet reports presentations at the 1984 First National Authors Rights conference. It includes software transactions; syndication; movie, television, and stage negotiation; and book club deals, as well as other topics.

Another reference that I like for readability and practicality on book publishing and contracts is literary agent Richard Curtis's work *How to be Your Own Literary Agent* (Houghton-Mifflin, 1984, $7.95); of particular interest is his appendix where he outlines a good, so-so, and poor deal for author for royalties on hardcover, trade, and paperback books. Two other good references on this subject are the previously mentioned *Author Law and Strategies*, by Brad Bunnin and Peter Beren (Nolo Press) and *The Writer's Legal Guide*, by Tad Crawford (Hawthorn), both currently out of print.

The current edition of *How to Get Happily Published*, by Judith Appelbaum and Nancy Evans (New York: Harper and Row, 1988), is a "must read" for all authors. It details the publishing process from the perspective of both parties from beginning to end and should contribute to a better working relationship between you and your publisher. As an adjunct to the book, Appelbaum, one of the coauthors, has started a book marketing consulting firm called Sensible Solutions (14 East 75th St., Suite 5C, New York, NY 10021) to promote the sale and distribution of books.

After fifteen rejection slips, who is going to quibble over the terms of an interested publisher's contract offer? After reading this section perhaps *you* will. Since the contract basically determines the final form of your book, as well as how much you will receive for it, it does not make sense to close your eyes, cross your fingers, and sign.

Even before you read the proposed agreement, consider the company with whom you are contemplating a contract. The discussion that follows is based upon a typical, large, commercial publisher's contract. You may decide that the advantages of smaller regional presses, university presses, alternative presses, et cetera, may better suit your needs and temperament. Richard Balkin has a chapter on alternatives to publishing with the large houses in his book, *A Writer's Guide to Book Publishing*, (Hawthorn Books, 1978) now out of print. If you do decide to choose a small press, check your prospective publisher very carefully to make sure that the press can and will handle your work the way you desire. Beware of deals where you have to pay a substantial sum of money to get your work published. Many times these arrangements result in losses to the writer.

Sit down, open your eyes, and read the proposed contract from top to bottom. Mark any terms that you don't understand. Read the unclear sections over one by one. Do anything to dispel the confusion—read sections aloud, type them up, sing them in the shower. Go back and read the entire contract again until the basic terms are pretty clear. Most writers are good readers and most contracts are less than ten pages.

Next, put the contract down and list *all* the plans for your work, real and imaginary—magazine serialization, special format, emphasis on West Coast distribution, photographs, paperback version, whatever. Note any terms in the contract that affect these plans and how you would wish to resolve any conflict. Decide which revisions you consider minimally necessary, what your ultimate goals are, and what your fallback positions are BEFORE you begin negotiations.

If your agent or lawyer is negotiating your contract, meet with him or her and discuss the contract, point by point, clarifying any puzzling terms. At each objectionable term, tell your representative *what* your objection is, *why* you object to the clause, and what your *alternative* term would be. Give your representative a memorandum clearly stating your thoughts. Your representative is not clairvoyant and cannot possibly know all the quirks of your particular work and your big plans for it. On the other hand, a good agent or attorney should know important items like the current percentage rates for royalties, the range for average advances, and when a publisher just won't budge. But in the final analysis, it is *your* work on sale, and who but you knows more of its needs and wants.

If a clause is not printed in the publisher's printed form, the author should negotiate to insert it as a rider. If the publisher's printed contract is changed, put a single non-obliterating line through the printed word(s) (so you can see what has been changed) and have all the parties initial each change. Changes may have domino-effects, so check other contract provisions to see if the change creates an internal conflict; you may very well need to change other provisions as well. Here is part of a negotiated contract which illustrates how this is done:

16. ~~Option. The Author gives to the Publisher the right to publish the Author's next full-length book, manuscript of which he will submit to the Publisher. In no case shall the Publisher be required to exercise this option before publication or within three months following publication of the Work which is the subject of this agreement.~~ *B.B.*

LD

17. *Notices.* Any written notice required under any of the provisions of this agreement shall be deemed to have been properly served by delivery in person or by mailing the same to the parties hereto at the addresses set forth above, except as the addresses may be changed by notice in writing.

18. Publisher shall pay to Author his share from book club, reprint and other licensing, less any unearned advances, within 60 days after Publisher receives such payments, accompanied by a copy of the statement of account provided by such licensee to Publisher.

19. Advertisements may not be inserted or printed in the work without Author's written consent. Such consent may be withheld at Author's sole discretion, and he may require that a share of the advertising proceeds be paid to him, as a condition of his consent, if he so desires.

Any license granted by the Publisher to reprint the Work in book club, cheap paperback or hardcover editions, or in any other medium except newspapers and periodicals, may explicitly prohibit the licensee from inserting advertisements in its edition of the Work without the written consent of the Author as provided above.

RIDERS

Be realistic about the terms you want changed. If you are negotiating about publication of an abstract scientific work, it will not be worthwhile to worry about the movie rights.

If you don't like the final contract, don't sign it simply because your editor says that this or that can be taken care of later. Your editor may not be there in six months, and you will be stuck with the terms of the contract.

In the first edition of this book, a standard contract was used for illustrative purposes from its beginning to end. Here, since standard contracts vary so much from publishing house to publishing house, I opted for a potpourri of contract provisions from my book contract collection. I collect these contracts like some people do stamps. This should give you a better idea of the various contract provisions you may encounter.

At the beginning of the contract, after the parties are named, there is a provision which identifies the work by a tentative title and may describe the writing project. Be sure the description coincides with your expectations about the project.

PREAMBLE

You had better trust your agent, because it is his or her address that usually will appear in the recital section of the contract. It is through your agent that you will receive important notifications from your publisher as well as advance and royalty payments. If you have an agent, your contract probably will contain an agency clause which authorizes the publisher to make all your payments to your agent. (See figure 7.2.)

AGENTS

AGENT
The Author hereby authorizes as agent:

of:

(1) to collect and receive all sums payable to the Author under this Agreement, the receipt of such sums by the agent being a full and valid discharge of the Publisher's obligation for the payment made, and (2) to act on behalf of the Author in all matters in any way arising out of this Agreement.

Figure 7.2 Agency Clause

RIGHTS CONVEYED TO PUBLISHER AND PAYMENTS TO AUTHOR

a. Rights and Royalties. The Author grants and assigns exclusively to the Publisher the following rights, for which the Publisher shall pay to the Author the royalties indicated:

(1) *Sale by Publisher of the Work in the United States, Philippines, and Canada.* The right to reproduce and distribute the Work in the English language, and all revisions and future editions of it, in the United States of America and its territories and dependencies, the Philippines, and Canada.

(2) *Sale of the Work by the Publisher in the exclusive territory.* The right to reproduce and distribute copies of the Work in the English language, and all revisions and future editions of it, for use in the United Kingdom, the Republic of Ireland, the Republic of South Africa, Australia, and/or New Zealand (all such countries constituting the exclusive territory) through the Publisher's subsidiaries.

Royalty. On all copies sold, one-half the applicable royalty payable on sales of the Work in the United States.

(3) *Sale of the Work by the Publisher in the open market.* The right to reproduce and distribute copies of the Work in all parts of the world other than the United States of America, its territories and dependencies, the exclusive territory, Canada, and the Philippines.

Royalty. On all copies sold, one-half the applicable royalty payable on sales of the Work in the United States.

(4) *License to others to sell the Work in the exclusive territory.* The right to license others to reproduce and distribute the Work in book form either through separate manufacture and publication abroad or through exportation of sheets or bound books of the Publisher's edition.

Royalty. On all copies sold by such licensee: if sold from an edition separately manufactured and published abroad, 75 percent of the Publisher's receipts; if sold from exported Publisher's sheets or bound books, 10 percent of the Publisher's receipts.

(5) *Translations.* The right to translate, reproduce, and distribute and to license others to translate, reproduce, and distribute the Work in all foreign languages.

Royalty. On all copies sold: if sold by the Publisher or its subsidiaries, 5 percent of the translation's list price; if under license to others, 75 percent of the Publisher's receipts.

(6) *Reprint editions.* The right to license a reprint publisher to reprint and distribute the Work in a paperback edition and/or a hardbound edition.

Royalty. 50 percent of the Publisher's receipts.

(7) *License to book clubs.* The right to license recognized book clubs to reproduce and distribute the Work, either in whole or as a condensation.

Royalty. If from an edition manufactured by the book club through lease of the Publisher's reproductive materials, 50 percent of the Publisher's receipts, less one-half the cost of any additional reproductive materials ordered by the book club and furnished by the Publisher; if from a condensation of the Work manufactured by the book club, 50 percent of the Publisher's receipts; if from an edition supplied by the Publisher, one-half the royalty paid by the book club to the Publisher.

(8) *First serialization.* The right to license others to publish first serializations of the Work (which shall comprise all serializations published before publication of the Work).

Royalty. 90 percent of the Publisher's receipts.

(9) *Second serialization.* The right to license others to publish digests, abridgments, selections, and second serializations of the Work (which shall comprise all serializations published after publication of the Work).

Royalty. 50 percent of the Publisher's receipts.

(10) *Dramatization.* The right to license others to exercise dramatic, motion picture, television, and radio rights to the Work.

Royalty. 90 percent of the Publisher's receipts.

(11) *Audiovisual rights.* The right to exercise and to license others to exercise any or all of the other mechanical, visual, audiovisual, sound-reproducing, and recording rights to the Work.

Royalty. If such rights are exercised by the Publisher, 10 percent of the Publisher's net receipts; if such rights are licensed, 50 percent of the Publisher's receipts.

(12) *Commercial rights.* The right to exercise and to license others to exercise all commercial rights to the Work which shall mean the exploitation of the Work itself, all material contained in it, and all rights in connection with merchandise and/or use of the Author's name in connection with the merchandise.

Royalty. If such rights are exercised by the Publisher, 10 percent of the Publisher's net receipts; if such rights are licensed, 50 percent of the Publisher's receipts.

Figure 7.3 Grant of Rights Clause

RIGHTS CONVEYED

PRIMARY RIGHTS

SUBSIDIARY RIGHTS

The grant-of-rights clause, figure 7.2, spells out what rights you grant your publisher and concerns rights to publish and distribute, translate, and otherwise use your work in commercial ventures. These rights are usually divided into two areas—primary rights (to publish and sell the work in the United States, the Philippines, and Canada) and subsidiary rights (all other rights including paperback, book club, movie, record, commercial, foreign language version, issuance in the British Commonwealth, serialization, abridgement, etc.). Usually, if you have an agent, the publishing rights in the British Commonwealth and the first serialization (prepublication in a magazine) rights are retained by the author and marketed separately by the agent. Authors' advocate groups suggest that you do not grant performing rights to your publisher. Further, the sale of any subsidiary rights should require your consent. Request that the right to receive copies of any of these subsidiary sales agreements be included in your contract. Some contracts provide for a cut-off date before which the publisher has to exercise these subsidiary rights or they revert to the author.

The Authors Guild suggests only a few months during which time the publisher must exercise subsidiary rights. If possible, limit the grant-of-rights clause only to those expressly discussed in the contract and retain any other rights not granted to the publisher by the contract.

Be careful what term you grant for rights, as the "whole term of copyright" now means life plus fifty years.

Keep the copyright in your name. In a case our firm handled, the publisher went bankrupt, the work was sold in bankruptcy and reached another publisher's hands. The head of a new publishing house wrote our client that the new house would publish her manuscript at its leisure, and ignored our client's letter demanding a reversion of rights. In the publishing contract, our client had negotiated the copyright in her name rather than that of the publisher, and this contributed to the successful resolution of her case.

This grant of rights from a university press, while short, picks up from other parts of its standard contract these additional rights: regular editions, cheap editions, permissions to reprint selections from the work; second serial, syndication, anthology and digest rights; bookclubs, foreign, and translation rights; as well as non-book rights such as dramatic, motion picture, radio and television rights.

The Author grants to the Press and its successors, representatives, and assigns full, sole, and exclusive license to print, publish, and sell the Work in book form, throughout the world, and to sell or lease such other rights as are enumerated in Article V hereunder, during the full term of the copyright of the Work, and any renewals thereof. Rights not specifically granted to the Press are reserved to the Author.

The author's warranty is an author's nightmare. First of all, you swear to the publisher that in no way is your work unlawful; it is neither libelous nor obscene; nor does it infringe on another's copyright; nor does it violate any other statutory or proprietary right. Yikes! Then, if that is not enough, you agree to pay any costs that your publisher may incur from any claims covered by the warranty term. Never mind that your publisher has a seventy-story office building and that you live in a teepee. The publisher wants a guarantee that all material in your book is lawful. If it's not, the entire financial burden is placed squarely on your shoulders. Furthermore, many publishing contracts allow the publisher to withhold all royalties in the event of a claim or lawsuit in this area. For obvious reasons, this particular term is the target of a major campaign of the Authors Guild, which feels that the indemnity clause is so onerous that it effectively denies the author important free-speech rights.

You can lighten the impact of the author's warranty and indemnity clause. First, make sure that you do not agree to pay the publisher's costs arising from controversies caused by the publisher's changes or inserts. Further, publishers may agree to author indemnification only in the situation where a claim against the publisher is reduced to judgment. Otherwise the indemnity clause requires the author to pay the publisher's costs no matter how frivolous the claim.

Since it is your money that will pay any settlement or judgment and other costs, include a term granting you the right to opt to participate in any proceedings through a lawyer of your choice. Also try to exclude the publisher's lawyer's fees from the author's indemnity coverage if you use your own attorney. You also might try to get your publisher to split any of these costs with you. Since, as indicated above, the indemnity clause gives the publisher the right to withhold royalties in the event of a controversy in this area, try to get this right deleted entirely from your contract, or at least limited to only a percentage of your royalties.

Guarantee of Proprietorship. The Author guarantees that the Work has not heretofore been published in book form, and that he is the Author and, for the purpose of making this agreement, the sole proprietor of the Work.

RESERVATION OF ALL RIGHTS NOT SPECIFICALLY TRANSFERRED

UNIVERSITY PRESS GRANT OF RIGHTS CLAUSE

WARRANTY AND INDEMNITY CLAUSE

AUTHOR'S WARRANTIES AND INDEMNITIES

Guarantee Against Violation of Property Rights, Libel, or Unlawful Matter. The Author guarantees that the Work is in no way whatever a violation of any existing copyright or other property right, and contains nothing libelous or otherwise unlawful; and that he will hold harmless and defend the Press from all manner of claims on the ground that the Work contains such violation, or anything libelous or otherwise unlawful; and that he will compensate the Press for any sums, including its attorney's fees, which it may find it necessary to pay in settlement of any claim or judgment against it, by reason of any violation of copyright or other property right or publication of libel or unlawful matter.

a. The Author warrants that he is the sole author of the work; that he is the sole owner of all the rights granted to the Publisher; that he has not previously assigned, pledged or otherwise encumbered the same; that he has full power to enter into this agreement; that except for the material obtained pursuant to Paragraph 3 the work is original, has not been published before, and is not in the public domain; that it does not violate any right of privacy; that it is not libelous or obscene; that it does not infringe upon any statutory or common law copyright; and that any recipe, formula or instruction contained in the work is not injurious to the user.

b. In the event of any claim, action or proceeding based upon an alleged violation of any of these warranties (i) the Publisher shall have the right to defend the same through counsel of its own choosing, and (ii) no settlement shall be effected without the prior written consent of the Author, which consent shall not unreasonably be withheld, and (iii) the Author shall hold harmless the Publisher, any seller of the work, and any licensee of a subsidiary right in the work, against any damages finally sustained. If such claim, action or proceeding is successfully defended or settled, the Author's indemnity hereunder shall be limited to fifty per cent (50%) of the expense (including reasonable counsel fees) attributable to such defense or settlement; however, such limitation of liability shall not apply if the claim, action or proceeding is based on copyright infringement.

c. If any such claim, action or proceeding is instituted, the Publisher shall promptly notify the Author, who shall fully cooperate in the defense thereof, and the Publisher may withhold payments of reasonable amounts due him under this or any other agreement between the parties.

d. These warranties and indemnities shall survive the termination of this agreement.

If your publisher has insurance against claims and suits for libel, invasions of privacy, and so forth, request that the publisher extend that coverage to you. Alternatively, the Authors Guild has the names of companies that will provide that insurance for authors.

NONCOMPETITION CLAUSE

Most publishing contracts include a noncompetition clause for the author (the publisher could publish and distribute a competing work). Attempt to have this clause deleted from the final contract, or limit its application by narrowing the subject matter or time period as much as possible. Another provision on conflicting publication follows:

The Author agrees that during the life of this agreement he will not, without the consent of the press, furnish to any other publisher any work on the same subject of similar extent and character, which may conflict with the sale of the Work.

Many of the publishers' contract forms have not been revised since the enactment of the Copyright Revision Act of 1976, so many of these copyright terms are outdated. The copyright should be in the author's name, and the publisher should agree to properly register the copyright and to place the author's copyright notice on all versions of the author's work. For more information on copyright, see the section in the chapter on copyright as well as Chapter 3, "Copying."

COPYRIGHT

The clause below refers to changes made by the author on galley or page proofs sent by the publisher for correction that are not correction of errors made by the printer. In the clause the author agrees to pay the cost of any changes, other than the correction of printer's errors, that exceed a certain percentage of the printer's initial bill. The sample contract provides for any costs over 15 percent of the initial bill; many contracts provide for any costs over 10 percent.

AUTHOR'S ALTERATIONS

You might try to negotiate a dollar cap, or raise the percentage, or both. If your book is technical, you might want to make copyediting subject to your review. Recently, Jacques Barzun attacked the changes publishers have made in his manuscripts under the auspices of copyediting. On the other hand, one of the glaring weaknesses of self-published books, in my opinion, is the lack of copyediting and polishing that a good publishing house gives an author's manuscript as a matter of course.

> If requested by the Publisher, the Author shall correct proof of the Work and return it promptly to the Publisher. If the Author makes or causes to be made any alterations in the type, illustrations, or film which are not typographical, drafting, or Publisher's errors and which exceed 15 percent of the original cost of composition and artwork independent of the cost of these Author's alterations, the cost of the excess alterations shall be charged against any sums accruing to the Author under this Agreement.

The Author agrees to deliver two complete copies (original and clean copy) of the manuscript of the work in the English language of approximately _____ words in length, satisfactory to the Publisher, together with any permissions required pursuant to Paragraph 3, and all photographs, illustrations, drawings, charts, maps and indexes suitable for reproduction and necessary to the completion of the manuscript not later than _____ .

DELIVERY OF SATISFACTORY COPY

If he fails to do so the Publisher shall have the right to supply them and charge the cost against any sums accruing to the Author. The complete manuscript shall include the following additional items:

(list)

If the Author fails to deliver the manuscript within ninety (90) days after the above date, or if any manuscript that is delivered is not, in the Publisher's judgment, satisfactory, the Publisher may terminate this agreement by giving written notice, whereupon the author agrees to repay forthwith all amounts which may have been advanced hereunder.

If the Author incorporates in the work any copyrighted material, he shall procure, at his expense, written permission to reprint it.

PERMISSION FOR COPYRIGHTED MATERIAL

This clause spells out the general responsibility of the publisher to produce your work. If you want to make sure that the publisher will produce a paperback version of the work, for example, write in this requirement or other publisher production requirements here. Include deadlines as part of the added term.

PUBLICATION OF THE WORK

After giving written notice to the Author that it has accepted the Work for publication, the Publisher shall within 12 months of written acceptance of the manuscript publish the Work at its own expense and in such style and manner and with such trademarks, service marks, and imprints of Publisher, and sell the Work at such prices, as it shall deem suitable. The Publisher shall publish the Work with a copyright notice and register the Work in accordance with the United States copyright laws in the name of the Publisher or Author as the Author may elect.

THE MANUSCRIPT

This term sets the all-important delivery date, the grace period, and the penalties for late or unsatisfactory delivery of the work. The definition of a "satisfactory" or "acceptable" manuscript has posed problems to authors in the past. Apparently, publishers have found manuscripts unsatisfactory for reasons far afield of the manuscript itself—change in the political climate, simple marketing considerations, et cetera. A very informative article about an author who successfully represented himself after his publisher had both rejected his manuscript and demanded the return of his advance, was written by A. E. Hotchner and appeared in the April 1978 issue of *More* magazine. It is entitled "A Fool for a Client" and is well worth reading.

In an attempt to avoid wrongful rejection of your manuscript, request that the word *reasonably* be inserted before the word *satisfactory* to make the contract clear that the publisher cannot reject your manuscript on the basis of pure whim.

I've had cases in which the publishers tried to use the "satisfactory manuscript" provision to cancel publication when the more likely reasons involved the facts that the sponsoring editor had moved on, another house had come out with a competing publication first, the publisher wanted to allocate funds to a different project, or the publisher got edgy about the controversial nature of the manuscript. While the provision seems to relate only to the professional competence of the work, it is possible for the publishing house's wide and loose standards to come into play. So, objectify the standard; make it revolve around the work by changing the language so that the manuscript's style and content are the determining factors.

Add language that requires the publisher to notify you of the manuscript's unacceptability within "x" number of days of final submission of the material. For some writers it could be beneficial to explicitly require the publisher to supply editorial assistance and/or guidance. Limit or omit the repayment of advances; negotiate for a refund of advance only in the event of successful placement of the manuscript with another publisher. Our law firm successfully negotiated the retention by our client of a five-figure advance after the publisher notified the client that they were no longer interested in the manuscript. Interestingly, his editor left as his manuscript crossed in the mail with the publisher's notification that the author could keep the advance until the manuscript was placed with another publishing house.

Secondly, when negotiating this clause, tie down specifics concerning the form in which any artwork, photographs, or other materials must be delivered.

ADVANCES, ROYALTIES, AND OTHER PROCEEDS OF THE AUTHOR

A good agent or an experienced writer can tell you the going rates for advances and royalties in your area of concern. Also, the Authors Guild makes results of its surveys on royalty and advance rates available to its members. An advance should be as high as possible since it could be the *entire* return for your work. Advances are many times split into at least two payments—the first made upon the signing of the contract and second upon the delivery of the satisfactory work or upon publication. Since advances are made against royalties, your publisher will take the amount of your advance out of any royalty sums due you after the book is released. An advance is, in effect, a loan.

The Publisher shall pay to the Author a royalty on the retail price of every copy sold by the Publisher, less actual returns and a reasonable reserve for returns (except as set forth below):

a. _____ percent (_____ %) up to and including _____ copies; _____ _____ percent (_____ %) in excess of _____ copies up to and including _____ copies; and _____ percent (_____ %) in excess of _____ copies.

Where the discount in the United States is forty-eight percent (48%) or more from the retail price, the rate provided in this subdivision a. shall be reduced by one-half the difference between forty-four percent (44%) and the discount granted. In no event, however, shall such royalty be less than one-half of the rate provided herein. If the semi-annual sales aggregate is fewer than 400 copies, the royalty shall be two-thirds (⅔) of the rate provided in this subdivision a. If such copies are sold from a second or subsequent printing. Copies covered by any other subdivision of this Paragraph shall not be included in such computation.

b. Five percent (5%) of the amount received for copies sold directly to the consumer through the medium of mail-order or coupon advertising, or radio or television advertising.

c. Five percent (5%) of the amount received for copies sold by the Publisher's Premium or Subscription Books Wholesale Department.

d. Ten percent (10%) for hard-cover copies and five percent (5%) for soft-cover copies sold with a lower retail price as college textbooks.

e. For a School edition the royalty provided in subdivision a. of the Paragraph but not more than:

    i. Ten percent (10%) of the amount received for a Senior High School edition.

    ii. Eight percent (8%) of the amount received for a Junior High edition.

    iii. Six percent (6%) of the amount received for an Elementary School edition.

f. Five percent (5%) for an edition published at a lower retail price or for an edition in the Modern Library (regular or giant size) or in Vintage Books; and two percent (2%) or two cents (2¢) per copy, whichever is greater, for an edition in the Modern Library College Editions.

g. Ten percent (10%) of the amount received for the original edition and five percent (5%) of the amount received for any lower-price edition for copies sold for export.

h. For copies sold outside normal wholesale and retail trade channels, ten percent (10%) of the amount received for the original edition and five percent (5%) of the amount received for any lower-price edition for copies sold at a discount between fifty percent (50%) and sixty percent (60%) from the retail price and five percent (5%) of the amount received for copies sold at a discount of sixty percent (60%) or more from the retail price, or for the use of the plates by any governmental agency.

i. No royalty shall be paid on copies sold below or at cost including expenses incurred, or furnished gratis to the Author, or for review, advertising, sample or like purposes.

j. Fifty percent (50%) of the amount received from the disposition of licenses granted pursuant to Paragraph 1, subdivision a, ii, iii, iv, vi and vii. At the Author's request his share from book club and reprint licensing, less any unearned advances, shall be paid to him within two weeks after the receipt thereof by the Publisher. If the Publisher rebates to booksellers for unsold copies due to the publication of a lower-price or reprint edition, the royalty on such copies shall be the same as for such lower price edition.

FIRST SERIAL

k. Ninety percent (90%) of the amount received from the disposition of licenses in the United States and Canada granted pursuant to Paragraph 1, subdivision a., v.

BRITISH

l. Eighty percent (80%) of the amount received from the disposition of licenses granted pursuant to Paragraph 1, subdivision b.

TRANSLATION

m. Seventy-five percent (75%) of the amount received from the disposition of licenses granted pursuant to Paragraph 1, subdivision c.

COMMERCIAL

n. Fifty percent (50%) of the amount received from the disposition of licenses granted pursuant to Paragraph 1, subdivision d., provided that all expenses in connection therewith shall be borne by the Publisher.

SHARE TO OTHER AUTHORS

o. If any license granted by the Publisher pursuant to Paragraph 1 shall include material of others, the amount payable to the Author shall be inclusive of royalty to other authors.

The guild recommends that the amount of the advance reflect the royalties you could expect to earn on first-year sales. Some publishers, I have found, actually come up with the advance figure utilizing that formula. Many authors take the position that all he/she may ever see is the advance if the book is not a commercial success. Unfortunately, that may be very true.

For adult trade books some authorities state that a good deal for an author means the royalty should be 6 percent for 10,000 copies, then escalate at 1½ percent per 10,000 copies. Others say it should be 10 percent on the first 5,000 copies, with corresponding increases at 2½ percent.

After you discover the standard royalty for works like yours and reach a mutually satisfactory rate and escalator clause, make sure that your contract provides for royalties based upon the *retail* sale (list) price. (Royalty rates based upon the net price should be considerably higher.) Also read the list of exceptions to the standard royalty rates in your contract, which usually includes:

EXCEPTIONS

- mail-order sales
- large order (discounted more than 48 percent)
- export sales
- sale of overstock
- copies of a small reprinting (to keep the book in circulation)

The royalty rate on the exceptions listed above should not be less than 50 percent of the regular rate.

The author's portion of the publisher's sale of subsidiary rights is sometimes glossed over in the excitement of the contract negotiations, usually to the author's disadvantage. Here again, discover what authors are getting on the sale of each of the subsidiary rights that you contemplate selling to the publisher. Check to see that your percentage of the proceeds of the sale is not reduced by any of the publisher's sale costs, such as an agent's fee.

RETURN FOR SALE OF SUBSIDIARY RIGHTS

If the publisher places the first serial rights, the Authors Guild recommends that the publisher (acting as an agent) get 10 percent. If the publisher won't budge from a higher percentage then try to negotiate that percentage only for the first $10,000 paid, then slide downward in percentage on $10,000 increments, i. e., 50 percent at $10,000, 40 percent after the next $10,000 and so on.

Small presses may offer quarterly accounting, but most publishers offer semi-annual accounting. Negotiation here is tough because you are bucking the business procedure for the whole house. Most statements don't include information about the number of copies in print, donated, defective, sent at no charge for review, or the number left on hand. You might want to add a provision that you are allowed to examine the books and records every so often.

Many authors feel that waiting for six months for royalties is too long a time. Even more unfair, say authors' advocate groups, is the clause which allows the publisher to hang on to any proceeds from the sale of a subidiary license for a full two months before the author sees a penny of it. The publisher W. W. Norton broke ranks with fellow publishers and now issues the author's share of any book club advance within two weeks of receipt of the advance. If Norton can. . .

STATEMENTS AND PAYMENTS

Another problem in this area is the percentage of royalties that is withheld by the publisher for returned books. Most publishers allow booksellers to return unsold books. Many publishers will automatically withhold up to 25 percent of the royalties for returns. For some books, where the return rate is small, the figure is greatly out of line.

ROYALTIES WITHHELD
FOR BOOK RETURNS

Another area of dispute in this section of the contract is the form of the royalty statement. Many times statements will not contain such vital information as number of copies sold or a description of what subsidiary rights were sold to whom and for how much. Authors should check these statements as they can be incorrect, especially with the advent of the computer. Also request a separate account for each publication to simplify the deciphering process. If your royalty statement still looks like Greek, ask your agent to assist in deciphering it.

> Royalty accounts as herein provided shall be rendered and paid quarterly in February, May, August, November, as of December 31, March 31, June 30, September 30. The author agrees that any accounts, bills, and amonts of any nature that may be due the publisher by the author on the date when royalty accounts are rendered, may, at the discretion of the publisher, be deducted from the author's royalty account before payment.

Delete the option clause granting your publisher first refusal on your next book. Many publishers today are agreeable to this. If your publisher will not delete the option term, then attempt to limit the publisher's decision time. Thirty to sixty days is a reasonable time depending on the material. Also if the publisher insists on an option clause make sure you can submit a book proposal plus a sample chapter, rather than a complete manuscript, and that you can do this, before the publication of the work *under* contract.

OPTION

Authors frequently live from advance to advance, and an option could seriously impede that schedule. For example, assume that the client who kept the five-figure advance from the first publisher finds another publisher eighteen months later, got no advance on the second contract (some small presses give none), and it took the second publisher twelve months to get the book in print after the author spent four months revising it to the new publisher's specifications. The second publisher pays royalties annually as of August, which means that money is actually paid in October. His book comes out in September. The lapse of time from the advance he got from the first publisher till any royalties from the second publisher is over *four* years.

This clause allows the publisher to discontinue publication of the work at any time. The author has the right to be notified in such event, and many times to purchase any plates, sheets, or bound stock of the book that may be available.

DISCONTINUANCE OF
PUBLICATION AND REVERSION

The reversion right returns all rights to the author in the event the work is out of print. Many times an author and a publisher will disagree over when a book is out of print, so define *out of print* as being when copies of a hard- or soft-cover version of the work are not available through normal trade channels. Also make sure that your reversion clause governs the return of *all* rights granted by the contract, not just publication rights.

The author or publisher may want to terminate the publishing contract for a variety of reasons other than that work is out of print. Be sure to have a termination agreement which covers the handling of licenses, assignment of copyright to author (if in publisher's name), disposition of existing copies of the work, and whether the warranties and indemnities survive. If the publisher wants monies back from you or you feel you've been treated unfairly, see a knowledgeable lawyer.

> a. When in the judgment of the Publisher the demand for the Work is not longer sufficient to warrant its continued publication, the Publisher shall have the right to discontinue the publication and declare the Work out of print, in which event the Author shall be so advised in writing.
>
> b. If the Work is not for sale in at least one edition (including any revised edition or reprint edition) published by the Publisher or under license from the Publisher and, within eight months after written demand by the Author, the Publisher or its licensee fails to offer it again for sale, then this Agreement shall terminate and all rights granted to the Publisher in it shall revert to the Author (except for material prepared by or obtained at the expense of the Publisher which shall remain the property of the Publisher).
>
> c. The termination of the Agreement under this Section or otherwise shall be subject to (1) any license, contract, or option granted to third parties by the Publisher before the termination and the Publisher's right to its share of the proceeds from these agreements after the termination and (2) the Publisher's continuing right to sell all remaining bound copies and sheets of the Work and all derivative works which are on hand at the time of termination.

DUTY OF PUBLISHER TO PUBLISH

Nine out of ten contracts that I have reviewed for author-clients have no provision spelling out the duty of the publisher to publish the work in a specific time. Here is an exception to that situation:

> The Publisher agrees to publish and distribute the work at its own expense within nine (9) months of the receipt of the manuscript in satisfactory form.
>
> Failure of the Publisher to comply with this provision, except for conditions beyond his control, shall require the return of all rights to the Author.

AUTHOR'S CONTROL

Authors normally do not have control either over the form and content of the final product or over the style, format, cover, retail price, number of copies in the first printing, and marketing procedures. I was able to negotiate final approval over a manuscript because of the legal nature of my material. This is true with most technical books. I was also able to include a clause which requires the publisher to consult with me in advance concerning the format, graphics, and dust jacket. Decide which items in this area are critical to the proper presentation of your work and try to include the requirements that any textual changes be made by mutual consent and that you at least be consulted on format, style, graphics, and dust jacket.

Among other terms that you might consider including is one which bans the insertion of all advertisements in any version of your work, including those licensed by your publisher, unless you consent to such insertion. Also request the return of all original materials and the right both to receive six to twelve free copies (or more) and to purchase an unlimited number of copies at least at a 40 percent discount, but better yet at the usual discount rates plus receive a royalty on sales to yourself. A sale is a sale.

COLLABORATION CONTRACTS

If you decide to work with someone on a book project, that is to collaborate, be sure to write down your agreement so that the two (or more) of you can work together smoothly and iron out your differences. Remember my earlier *caveat* about contracts: as long as matters are honky-dory the parties never refer to it, but let the going get a little rough and everyone starts looking around for something to help resolve the difficulties. That is the advantage of a written collaboration agreement, worked out in advance, in detail. It is a tool to resolve controversies. Although collaboration is a joint effort, it is pretty hard to cleave the work in half as you would a loaf of bread. Discuss how you plan to divide the work, what your working methods will be, and how you will make decisions. Avoid treating the collaboration as a partnership (remember my earlier warnings about partnerships); characterize the agreement as a joint venture or a tenancy in common (each treats the whole work as if he/she owns it). Specify how long the relationship will last (for instance, the term of copyright), how money will be handled (this includes income and expenses), what the credit lines will look like, and will you be willing to collaborate on another work on the same subject. Should there be a warranty and indemnity clause (if one is doing all or more research), knowing how you will resolve disputes, how you can get out of the arrangement, and who owns what are more specifics to be addressed.

I suggest that you both discuss all these issues, then write a letter outlining your conclusions (which you both should sign) or rough draft a collaboration agreement. Give either or both to a knowledgeable lawyer to review. These procedures will save you money. Get something in writing, though, between the two of you.

Basically, the Canadian author can refer to this discussion of contracts. Some old Canadian cases indicate that a literary agent must use reasonable care in carrying out the author's instructions, and if the agent doesn't obtain the proper contract in accordance with the author's instructions, then the agent can be liable for damages for the negligent performance of the agent's duties. Likewise, if the author breaches an agreement for sole agency, and disposes of the author's rights through another agent, then the first agent can recover from the author.

FOR CANADIAN AUTHORS

AGENT AGREEMENT

This will confirm the arrangement between us under which I appoint you my exclusive agent and you accept such appointment to handle the marketing throughout the world of all my literary rights including but not limited to publishing, motion picture, stage, radio and television rights and generally to advise me professionally, it being understood that:

- You will represent my interests to the best of your ability.
- You are to remit to me promptly monies due as collected.
- You will receive for me all monies due from my literary rights marketed in the United States, its possessions, and Canada; as your agency commission, you are to retain ten percent (10%) of monies so collected.
- Through your co-agent, you are to market my literary rights in the British Commonwealth of Nations, on which the total agency commission is fifteen percent (15%), divided between you and the co-agent.
- Through your co-agents in foreign language markets, you are to market my literary rights on which the total agency commission will be nineteen percent (19%), ten percent (10%) being retained by the co-agent, and ten percent (10%) of the net by your agency. You are to market my literary rights in all other foreign language markets direct and/or through co-agencies on which you are to retain ten percent (10%) of the monies received after payment of no more than ten percent (10%) commission to a co-agent.
- Whenever foreign taxes are deducted at the source of monies due me, your commission will be based on the balance after said tax deduction.
- In the event any monies due me as herein described are paid to me or to my assigns direct, the commission due you of such gross amounts will be remitted promptly to you by me or otherwise will be deductible

by you from other monies in my account with you; you are to reimburse yourself from such monies for advances from you to me and for expenses incurred on my behalf (such as copyright fees, manuscript retyping, telegraphs, cables, and long distance telephone calls to me or on my behalf, xerox or other photocopies of proposals or manuscripts, book galleys submitted to magazines, copies of books submitted overseas, and legal fees, the legal fees being chargeable only when I have agreed to them).

- Mail sent to me in care of you may be opened by you and dealt with, unless it is apparently of a personal nature which you shall forward to me promptly. When I am approached directly by any party interested in my material, I shall inform you immediately and refer the party to you.

This agreement is effective immediately and continues in effect until either you or I have cancelled it, which either may do by one giving the other thirty (30) days' notice in writing of such cancellation, providing that you will continue to function as agent and to receive your commission on all contracts theretofore negotiated and concluded during the life of this agreement, said commission being hereby assigned and transferred to you as an agency coupled with an interest. In the event within sixty (60) days after effective termination date hereof, I enter into a contract covering any of my aforementioned literary rights with a person or firm with whom you had, prior to such termination, been negotiating for the disposition of said rights, said contract shall be deemed to have been entered into during the term of the within agreement.

This letter, which is written in duplicate, will constitute an agreement between us when each of us has an executed copy.

BACK TO TAXES

This special section on taxes for writers will not cover the basics of federal income and other taxes. Please read Chapter 5, "Federal Income Tax," and Chapter 6, "Other Taxes," for the basic tax background. This section will only discuss the special tax problems of writers.

METHOD OF ACCOUNTING

Most writers use the calendar year as their tax year, and most use the cash-basis method of accounting. Record keeping for writers will vary depending on whether few or many works are sold each year.

If you sell numerous small works and/or do indexing, editing, et cetera, you probably will send bills for your work. Put the name of the job, the amount charged, and your name and address on the bill and address it to the publisher.

Some publishers may ask for your Social Security number, because the law requires one who pays another for services (payor) to fill out a Statement for Recipients of Miscellaneous Income, IRS Form 1099, when the recipient has done more than $400 worth of work during the year for the payor. Some payors do this regardless of the amount paid. You do not file Form 1099 with your return. Just remember that the IRS has a copy of it, and report this income.

A simple way of recording income and expenses is shown below:

INCOME

DATE BILLED/ OBLIGATED	TO WHOM/ FOR WHAT	AMOUNT	DATE RECEIVED
6-23-88	McGraw-Hill/Indexing "101..."	$ 105	7-31-88
6-30-88	*Smother Planet News*, article on chicken feed	50	7-28-88
	TOTAL FOR MONTH	155	
	TOTAL YEAR TO DATE	2,995	

ITEM	THIS MONTH	BASIS	YEAR TO DATE
Rent	$50	(1 room of 5: $250)	$350
Electricity	8	($40 1/5)	70
Telephone	15	(1/2 of total)	150
Office Supplies	22	PBSW	80
Promotion	32	(dinner 7/1/78)	
		for agent B.B.	150
Capital Expenses	0	Office furniture	200
(Depreciation)		Equipment	150

If you are a novelist, your record-keeping needs will differ from a contributor to periodicals. A job work card is more helpful to the writer who writes small pieces by giving the writer a bird's-eye view of his or her work, by totaling the amount of time required and respective amounts of earnings from specific assignments, and by providing information for copyright registration. Reproduced below is a sample job work card that could be adapted to your individual needs:

WORKS IN PROGRESS

IDEAS TO QUERY	OUT	IN RESEARCH	IN WRITING	MS OUT	ACCEPTED	PMT. DUE
Home Remedies of Indians	1-10-80 McCalls	2-80	3-80	6-80	11-80	1-5-81
Fairy Clothing	Sesame St. Magazine					
Homemade Puppets	Sesame St. Magazine	3-80	5-80			

Figure 7.4 Sample work card

If you are a free-lancer, you might want to keep a running tally of your works in progress. A sample format for a tally sheet is reproduced.

WORK CARD

Word length: _____

Subject: _____
Title: _____
Labor Hours (weeks, days, hours): _____
Queries _____
Date Begun _____ Date completed _____ Date Published _____
Copyright Reg. No. _____ Copyright Reg.: _____
Sold to: _____
Price: _____ Payments Due/Terms _____
Other Sales Information. _____
Rights Reserved: _____

Figure 7.5 Writer's tally sheet

Income levels for most writers vary greatly from year to year. Consequently, the methods of spreading income are of great importance here so that the lowest tax can be paid. See the discussion in Chapter 5, "Federal Income Tax," on cutting your taxes, and remember, if you are on the cash basis, to give special consideration to year-end transactions to manipulate year-end income levels, in order to show a three-out-of-five-year profit or to level out a particularly profitable year. Remember that even under the cash method of accounting, money received by your agent is taxable to you unless there are restrictions on how or when your agent makes payment. If you have hit the jackpot with a best seller, it would be worth your while to consult a tax attorney or accountant for some tax-planning assistance.

SPREADING INCOME

BUSINESS DEDUCTIONS

Some business-expense deductions that writers should not forget are:

- printing—letterheads, cards, etc.
- stationery
- postage—express, telegrams, messenger service
- commissions
- clipping-service charges
- courses in writing instruction
- typewriter repair and depreciation
- membership fees in writers' associations
- payments for publication
- insurance on manuscripts
- copyright registration and renewal fees or searches
- photocopying
- promotion

RESEARCH, TRAVEL, AND
SIMILAR EXPENSES

There is no clear or consistent answer as to whether research, travel, and similar expenses of professional authors can be deducted in the year incurred or whether those expenses must be capitalized. The current deduction of such expenses was allowed in a district court case, but the IRS would not follow that rule where publishers tried to deduct similar publication costs as current expenses. The Authors Guild has taken the position that *authors* engaged in the business of writing are entitled to currently deduct travel, research, and similar expenses. They argue that—although the taxpayer is required to capitalize the costs of producing books, records, and motion pictures and to deduct the costs over the life stream of income generated by the work—the legislative report on the Tax Reform Act implies that this capitalization requirement applies only where the work is acquired as a result of the taxpayer's *investment.* For this reason the Authors Guild takes the position that capitalization of travel and related expenses covers publisher and producer costs but not the author's expenses, since the author's income is earned by personal effort and not through investment of money.

The Authors Guild and its members, as well as others, lobbied successfully to exempt writers from some of the capitalization requirements of the new (1986) tax law, but the fight is still on.

COPYRIGHTS HELD BY CREATOR
ARE NOT A CAPITAL ASSET

A copyright held by the creator or the creator's heir or donee is not treated as a capital asset by the tax law. Thus the proceeds of a sale or exchange of a copyright by the author (donee or heir) is ordinary income to them. On the other hand, income from the sale or licensing of a copyright by persons not authors of a work is entitled to capital gains treatment if the copyright has been held the minimum required period of time.

HOBBY LOSS CHALLENGE

Writers may face a hobby loss challenge. You should keep records showing the profit motive in your writing including query letters, replies, rejection slips, sales, costs, manuscript mailing dates, proof of other submissions, contracts, deadline letters, and so forth. Refer to Chapter 5, "Federal Income Tax," for a discussion of the hobby loss challenges. One writer who was a full-time pilot had gross receipts from his writing of $2,500 in the fifties but nothing after that time. Although he wrote and submitted at least fourteen short stories and had two novels in process between 1958 and 1965, his deduction for expenses in 1964 and 1965 were disallowed because the court did not think he wrote for financial gain. Try to arrange sales so you show income from your writing in at least three years out of every five. This showing will beat most hobby loss challenges.

SOCIAL SECURITY

Since income tax returns will allow higher income amounts before income taxes owed, you may not owe taxes on the first $5,650 of income if you are single and 65 or older, and if married, $10,000. If you are under age 65, then the thresholds are $4,440 for single persons and $7,560 if married. Under the Social Security earnings limit, persons under 65 can earn $6,120 before a $1 drop in Social Security for each $2 earned. It changes to $8,400 for persons between the ages of 65 and 69, with no limit on earnings for persons over age 70; other special rules may apply to self-employed, retired writers.

OTHER TAXES

Some states or cities may have other taxes* such as an occupation license, which may affect a writer. An occupation license may require payment of a tax on your gross receipts but there may be certain nontaxable transactions such as out-of-state sales, which are excepted. Some states collect personal-property or intangible taxes on a writer's royalties.

FREEDOM OF INFORMATION ACT AND SUNSHINE LAWS

STATE LAWS

Facts are a basic stock-in-trade for many writers. The federal and state Freedom of Information Acts and Sunshine Acts are relatively new tools with which writers can pry information out of federal and some state governments. Not all states have enacted laws concerning the public's access to information. Check with your local chapter of the American Civil Liberties Union to see if your state has a Freedom of Information Act and a Sunshine Act.

The federal Freedom of Information Act (FOIA) was initially passed in 1966. The 1975 amendments closed some of the loopholes through which various federal agencies had previously denied citizens' requests for information.

The FOIA rules apply only to information held by administrative agencies of the federal government. It does not cover documents belonging to the legislative or judicial branches of government.** Also, the act exempts nine separate categories of documents to which agencies can deny public access:

DOCUMENTS NOT AVAILABLE UNDER FOIA

- classified documents concerning national defense and foreign policy
- internal personnel rules and practices
- information exempt from disclosure under other laws
- confidential business information
- internal communications
- protection of individual privacy
- investigatory files
- information concerning federal financial institutions
- information concerning wells

Your local congressman or senator's office may be helpful in determining whether your request for information falls within one of the nine categories above.

---

*See discussion in the *Law and the Writer*, edited by Keith Polking and Leonard S. Meranus (Writer's Digest, 1985), p. 120–122, for a discussion of one writer's local tax dilemmas.
**Much of this is public information.

The steps involved in obtaining government documents under the Freedom of Information Act are:

- locate the agency that has the records
- make a request for specific records
- send the requested search fee
- appeal to the head of the agency if the request is denied

LOCATE AGENCY   The first step in getting the information that you want is to determine which federal agency has the information that you are looking for. If you are not sure which agency has the information, call the U.S. Government Federal Information Center listed in your phone book or consult the *United States Government Organization Manual* for a list of all the federal agencies and their functions.

REQUEST LETTER   A sample FOIA request letter is reproduced in the illustration below. Be as specific as you can in your description of the documents. The better your description of the desired information, the smaller the search fee will be because of the savings in the search time.

Agency Head or FOIA Officer
Title
Name of Agency
Address of Agency
City, State, zip

Re: Freedom of Information Act
Request.

Dear ----------:
    Under the provisions of the Freedom of Information Act, 5 U.S.C. 552, I am requesting access to (identify the records as clearly and specifically as possible).
    If there are any fees for searching for, or copying, the records I have requested, please inform me before you fill the request. (Or: . . . please supply the records without informing me if the fees do not exceed $——.)

[Optional]   I am requesting this information (state the reason for your request if you think it will assist you in obtaining the information.)
[Optional]   As you know, the act permits you to reduce or waive fees when the release of the information is considered as "primarily benefiting the public". I believe that this request fits that category and I therefore ask that you waive any fees.
    If all or any part of this request is denied, please cite the specific exemption(s) which you think justifies your refusal to release the information, and inform me of the appeal procedures available to me under the law.
    I would appreciate your handling this request as quickly as possible, and I look forward to hearing from you within 10 days, as the law stipulates.

Sincerely,

Signature
Name
Address
City, State, zip

Figure 7.6 Sample FOIA request letter

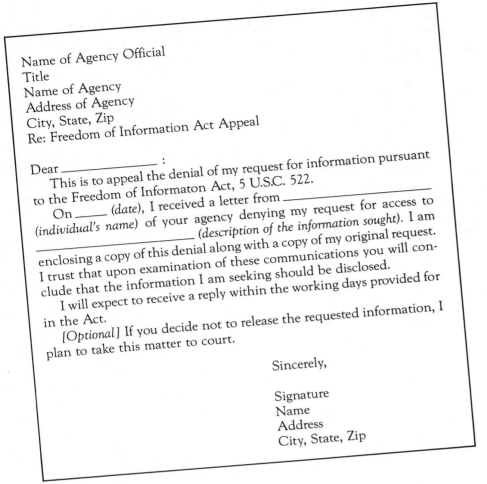

Name of Agency Official
Title
Name of Agency
Address of Agency
City, State, Zip
Re: Freedom of Information Act Appeal

Dear _____ :
    This is to appeal the denial of my request for information pursuant to the Freedom of Informaton Act, 5 U.S.C. 522.
    On ____ (date), I received a letter from _____ (individual's name) of your agency denying my request for access to _____ (description of the information sought). I am enclosing a copy of this denial along with a copy of my original request. I trust that upon examination of these communications you will conclude that the information I am seeking should be disclosed.
    I will expect to receive a reply within the working days provided for in the Act.
    [Optional] If you decide not to release the requested information, I plan to take this matter to court.

                                Sincerely,

                                Signature
                                Name
                                Address
                                City, State, Zip

Figure 7.7 Sample FOIA   appeal letter

Search fees are charged by the hour, and there is usually a nominal charge for the production of copies of standard-sized pages. The law provides that these fees can be waived if the agency determines that "furnishing the information can be considered as primarily benefiting the general public."

FEES

Federal agencies are supposed to reply to all requests for information within ten working days from the date of receipt of the request. If the agency denies your request for information, it must tell you the reason for the denial and to whom you can appeal within the agency. Most appeals must be filed within thirty days of your receipt of the denial. See figure 7.7 for a sample appeal letter.

DENIAL

The agency must act upon your appeal within thirty working days of the agency's receipt of your appeal. If this appeal is unsuccessful, you can take your case to court.

The federal government Sunshine Act became law on March 12, 1977. The policy behind the act was that "the public is entitled to the fullest practicable information regarding the decision-making processes of the Federal Government." To implement this policy, the act declares a presumption in favor of open meetings and requires publication of notices of meetings. Some states have also passed similar laws.

FEDERAL SUNSHINE LAW

There are two other federal acts you should be aware of: the Access to Information Act which gives the public a right to get government held information and the Privacy Act, which protects the privacy of personal nature information in government information.

OTHER FEDERAL REGULATIONS

CANADIAN LAW—ACCESS TO INFORMATION ACT

According to the Canadian Corporate Law Reporter (vol. 2, no. 9, July 1985), the Canadian Access to Information Act is a two-edged sword for businesses. It is estimated that about 80 percent of requests under FOIA are made by businesses seeking information about competitors' secrets (exclusive of FBI FOIA). To prevent this abuse, make the government aware that certain information is a trade secret, confidential, and/or commercially sensitive.

The Canadian Bar Foundation in Ottawa, Ontario, has a series of booklets, some of which could be of use to you. See, for instance, *Privacy Law and the Media in Canada* and *The Charter in the Media.*

WILLS FOR WRITERS

If a writer has a substantial body of work, then he/she should have a will which names a literary executor to handle copyrights, book contracts, agent relations, and so forth. The writer should incorporate instructions in the will regarding the disposition of unpublished or out-of-print manuscripts and works. The person named should be familiar with the testator's work and the business aspects of writing. A surviving spouse sometimes does not make the best literary executor.

CHAPTER EIGHT

Obtaining
Legal Assistance

WHAT DO I DO NOW?
WHAT CAN YOU DO YOURSELF?
SO WHEN DO I NEED A LAWYER?
FINDING A LAWYER
CHOOSING YOUR FAMILY LAWYER
WORKING WITH YOUR LAWYER
YOU AND YOUR LAWYER
QUESTIONS FOR YOUR LAWYER

LEGAL ADVICE? NOT ON YOUR LIFE.

Alice's Last Allegory

On Friday the thirteenth Alice was nearly swept away by a tide of unfortunate events.

Her new landlord sent her a special-delivery letter demanding a 300 percent rent increase. A Little Old Grandmother borrowed her grandson's souped-up, four-wheel-drive pickup to visit Rainbow Hill and purchase some of Alice's ceramic heart planters. She ran over one hundred heart planters and hit Alice's cat, Goldy. Goldy was rushed to Vera the Vet for treatment. Then Careless Contractor told Alice that he finished building her storage shed but instead of the plan's double doors he installed a single door. Romero called from jail. He had been picked up for driving while intoxicated and speeding when returning from his friend Big Boozer's bachelor party. That afternoon the Sheriff had come by Rainbow Hill to serve Romero with a paternity complaint.

At the end of the day Goldy died. Vera the Vet said they would bury the cat for a $25 charge, and Alice agreed; the Little Old Grandmother's insurance company, Not-Too-Fast Service, told Alice that a check was in the mail for $550 for the damage; Careless Contractor refused to put double doors on the shed; Romero was still in jail and the Sheriff served the paternity papers on him there. Alice called her family lawyer, Sam Violet, and told him all. He said for Alice to come in next week to discuss the other problems and he'd call the judge now to get Romero out. On her way to get Romero she went down the alley bordering Vera the Vet's and saw a pile of dead animals by the trash with Goldy on top. In tears she retrieved Goldy and picked up a grateful Romero at the jail. The check never came the following week from Not-Too-Fast Service, and the company refused to issue another check.

When Alice and Romero saw Sam Violet, he told her to write letters of compalint to the state regulatory agencies for contractors, insurance companies, and veterinarians. He agreed to handle the criminal charges against Romero, the paternity complaint (which Romero claimed was a case of mistaken identity), and the rent-increase problem.

Alice wrote the letters of complaint to the state regulatory boards. Sometime later she received a new check from the insurance company, a refund of the $25 cat-burial charge and a Siamese cat from Vera the Vet, and Careless Contractor sent his brother out to put a double door on the storage shed. Violet arranged to have the driving-while-intoxicated charges dropped in exchange for a plea of guilty to the speeding ticket because the arresting officer lost the blood-alcohol test. The paternity action mistakenly named Romero as a defendant instead of his brother Romeo, and the complaint was dismissed. Violet got a copy of Alice's lease from the old owner's lawyer and told the new owners that no increase was allowed, for the lease was still in effect. To top it all off, Alice's bachelor lawyer accepted in trade for his fee several ceramic valentine planters as gifts for his ladies and a ceramic sculptured fountain for his office.

Some of these situations Alice handled herself, and others were handled by her lawyer. This chapter will explore those two alternatives to solving legal problems. Besides suggesting what problems you might handle yourself and recommending when you should see a lawyer, I will also discuss the range and variety of available legal services, advise you on how to work with a lawyer, and outline steps for you to properly document potential legal problems.

In your business and personal life, you should make a habit of record keeping. Keep track of important documents and papers such as loans, mortgages, marriage licenses, juried-show brochures, leases, canceled checks and deposit slips, birth certificates, diplomas, court papers, copies of wills, disputed bills, tax returns, and warranties and guarantees on goods purchased. Keep those documents and papers which concern business and personal matters that could develop into legal difficulties. For example, save a letter from your ex-husband which says that he has been busted

SAVE IMPORTANT PAPERS

Remember the Chinese Proverb: "The best memory is not so firm as faded ink"

again but wants custody of his kids when he gets out. Keep them in a drawer, file cabinet, or metal box. At the beginning of any possible legal problem, keep notes of conversations and telephone calls, and write up a description of the events while your memory is fresh.

If you have been wronged, try a telephone call first and then a polite complaint letter to the wrongdoer.* If after contacting the wrongdoer there is still no relief, consider a complaint letter to the appropriate agency or filing in a small claims court.** Since states regulate many professions and occupations, a state could deny, suspend, or limit the use of a license of a wrongdoer. Those whose occupations are regulated in some states are (check with your Consumer Fraud Department):

- collection agents
- attorneys
- veterinarians
- insurance agencies
- contractors
- architects
- accountants
- cosmetologists
- doctors
- dentists
- real estate salesmen
- undertakers
- photographers

There are also Consumer Fraud Departments in most State Attorney General's Offices. If the wrongdoer lives in your state, write to the Attorney General's Office in your state's capital and mark your correspondence "Attention Consumer Fraud Division." Otherwise, contact the Attorney General in the state in which the company is located, because that investigating office may have jurisdiction over the offender. Be sure to include copies of your correspondence with the offending company as well as any proofs of purchase and payment in your letter to the Consumer Fraud Department.

STATE CONSUMER FRAUD DIVISION

Some cities have a Better Business Bureau to handle complaints against businesses. The BBB has established arbitration systems to handle complaints in most areas. Check your phone book.

BETTER BUSINESS BUREAUS

Keep these points in mind when writing a complaint letter:

- use correct address.
- direct letter to specific person (keep copies).
- state complaint clearly.
- state your demand.
- give an action deadline (if letter to wrongdoer).
- indicate where copies were sent.
- attach copies of documents (keep originals).

For a sample complaint letter see the section on enforcing your contracts in Chapter 4, "Making Contracts."

At the federal level there is the Federal Trade Commission (FTC), which deals with a variety of unfair business practices.*** The Post Office Department† handles mail fraud or mail-order problems. The Equal Employment Opportunities Commission (EEOC), 1800 G Street, NW, Washington, D.C. 20506 handles complaints on job discrimination by reason of age, sex, color, religion, and national origin. Write

FEDERAL AGENCIES

---

*You may want to have a lawyer review a rough draft of your complaint letter if it concerns a lot of money or a complex problem, such as copyright infringement.
**See the section on enforcing your contracts in Chapter 4, "Making Contracts," for more information on filing complaint letters and using small claims court.
***Bureau of Consumer Protection, FTC, Washington, D.C. 20580. Usually the FTC does not get involved in individual cases but looks for a pattern of wrongdoing.
†Contact the U.S. Postal Service, Washington, D.C. 20260 or the postal inspector in the city nearest the area in which the wrongdoer is located. Your local post office will supply the address.

the EEOC for a discrimination charge form. Remember, some states have non-discrimination laws. Check with the Attorney General's Office of your state for this information. The Department of Labor will investigate charges involving minimum wages, equal pay, and age discrimination. You also can complain to the Wage and Hour Division, Employment Standards Administration, U.S. Department of Labor, Washington, D.C. 20210. Besides the local federal information number for your state, there is a network of toll-free hotlines. Some of these are:

HOTLINES

Consumer Product Safety Commission Hotline (800/638-2772): Handles complaints or questions about safety of toys and other products. See Chapter 2: "Legal Restrictions on Content and Materials."

Housing Discrimination Hotline (800/424-8590): Call if you think you've been denied accommodation because of sex, race, religion, age, or national origin. Also advice on renting or buying a home.

National Highway Traffic Safety Administration Hotline (800/424-9393): Answers questions on automobile safety and gives advice about car recalls and where to complain about auto defects.

LEGAL MATTERS YOU DO YOURSELF

Other legal matters you may already handle include arranging small loans from credit institutions, negotiating routine small contracts with galleries and publishers, registering your copyright, registering your business name with the state, obtaining business licenses and permits, handling minor traffic complaints, and handling small insurance claims. In more serious or complicated matters, remember the old saying: The person who is his/her own lawyer has a fool for a client.

SO WHEN DO I NEED A LAWYER

Sometimes a lawyer just gives advice (consultation); other times a lawyer will do more work for you. You need a lawyer, and sometimes a specialist, in at least the following situations:

- before signing an agreement or legal document that you do not understand; for example, a waiver of appearance in court on a domestic matter.
- in adoptions, regardless of whether you are the adopting party or the natural parent of the child.
- in matters involving juvenile delinquency as well as temporary custody of your children and guardianships.
- in preparing a will and in estate planning.
- in a divorce, annulment, or separation involving property and/or children.
- when you purchase real estate, if the transaction involves a large sum of money.
- when you have a dispute with someone represented by a lawyer.
- in criminal cases when you are accused of a crime that involves jail time, heavy fines, or penalties (loss of driver's license).
- if a claim for money damages is made against you or if you have a claim for money damages against someone which involves a serious amount of money.
- if you form a business organization.
- if you want to obtain a patent or sue for patent infringement.
- if you are involved in a legal transaction that is important to your business, profession, or personal life, e.g., a long-term business lease, an exclusive gallery contract, a book contract.
- if you are considering bankruptcy or other debtors' remedies.
- if you want to register your trade name or trademark with the patent office.
- if you want to pursue a copyright infringement.
- if you have landlord-tenant problems.
- if you have received personal injuries, lost income, or had property destroyed.

- if you are denied benefits to which you believe you are entitled, e.g., Social Security, unemployment benefits, or workers' compensation.
- if you cannot resolve a consumer complaint, and the money involved is significant.
- if you have discriminatory employment problems.
- if you are being audited by IRS for a large amount of money or if the audit may show fraud.
- if a government agency takes or proposes to take action against you that you don't agree with, such as a zoning change, eminent domain, construction of a government nuclear installation.
- other problems or situations of a legal nature that are complex or very important to you.

WHO ARE LAWYERS

Lawyers in the United States represent their clients on legal problems by providing information, giving advice, writing letters, preparing legal documents, making telephone calls, doing legal research, and appearing in court. You need to locate the right lawyer for your problem. There are many kinds of lawyers. A general practitioner is just that—one who practices law in most areas. Some lawyers specialize in one area—domestic relations, estate planning, corporate, patent work, trials, tax work, and criminal law. The state or local bar association or your family lawyer should be able to refer you to a specialist if the need arises. Some lawyers are allowed to advertise their specialty.

FINDING A LAWYER

Studies show that 70 percent of people with legal problems do *without* legal advice because they don't know how to locate the right lawyer. This section will assist you in finding a helpful lawyer, whether free or paid.

CRIMINAL MATTERS

Free legal services usually are divided into two categories, civil and criminal. In criminal matters where you may go to jail, you have a right to a free lawyer if you are too poor to hire one. If you cannot afford a private lawyer, insist that a lawyer be appointed to represent you without charge or request to see the public defender. The public defender program handles criminal cases for poor persons in some courts.

CIVIL MATTERS

For free legal assistance in noncriminal areas there are two kinds of programs— government-supported legal aid and privately funded organizations. Several hundred Legal Aid programs operate in this country, servicing eligible people with civil legal problems. Eligibility for these services is limited by income level, residence, and type of problem. Organizations like State Education Associations, the American Civil Liberties Union, the National Association for the Advancement of Colored People, and the National Organization for Women Legal Defense Fund may help with problems that relate to their special interest.

LEGAL AID PROGRAMS

VOLUNTEER LAWYERS FOR THE ARTS (VLA)

Volunteer Lawyers for the Arts, a legal assistance program for the creative person, has been organized the past few years and has offices in some major cities. Write to VLA in New York* for information on where to contact a VLA group in your state. California's group used to be called Bay Area Lawyers for the Arts, but is now California Lawyers for the Arts. Publication lists are available under both names. Also, your State Bar Association may have an Art Law Committee that will refer you to lawyers interested in representing creative persons. If you can't find any of the legal assistance programs described by checking with an attorney's office, the courthouse, or the phone book, then contact the State Bar Association, which would be located in your state's capital.

LAWYER ADVERTISING

Between free legal services and traditional law firms are law firms and clinics that provide routine legal services for a set, advertised fee. Of course, your problem may not fall within the category of a simple, routine problem, so the prices quoted may be misleading. The standardization of their service may mean less personal attention on your problem, and perhaps there will not be expertise in other areas of in-

*Volunteer Lawyers for the Arts, 1285 Avenue of the Americas, Third Floor, New York, NY 10019.

terest to you—for instance, a name change might be easily handled by them but not a gallery contract.

PREPAID LEGAL SERVICES

There are also prepaid legal services available to people affiliated with special groups such as credit unions, teachers, labor unions, and so forth. For a set premium, you gain access to legal assistance that is covered by the plan. Sometimes consultations are free. Usually the fees for routine work are set in advance.

CHOOSING A LAWYER

If your choice, for whatever reason, is to use a private lawyer, then the search begins with talking to people you trust for suggestions. Be sure to find out why the lawyer is recommended—were your friends satisfied with the work, what sort of work was done, and was the bill reasonable. There are lawyer referral panels sponsored by local county bar associations which have lists of attorneys interested in receiving referrals who have agreed to charge a flat rate for a consultation. The disadvantage is that the luck of the draw applies: Ms. X may be the next lawyer on the list and she has never done a will, which may be the service you want. For the address of the nearest Lawyers Referral Service, write to the Standing Committee on Lawyers Referral Service, American Bar Association, 750 Lake Shore Dr., Chicago, IL 60611, or check your phone directory.

LAWYER REFERRAL SERVICES

Another aid in your search for a lawyer is a directory known as the *Martindale-Hubble Legal Directory*, which can be found in any law and other libraries. This "establishment" directory lists lawyers in most communities, sometimes their specialty, and often rates the lawyers on the basis of number of years of practice and other factors.

CHOOSING YOUR FAMILY LAWYER

At this point you should know what lawyers or legal services are available in your community, and you are ready to make a choice. As you can see, the selection process may be lengthy, so don't wait until the eleventh hour to choose your lawyer.

In my opinion, it makes sense for many in the art, craft, or writing fields (as well as others) to have their own lawyers. Most lawyers will not give legal advice to a stranger over the phone, because often the advice must be based on an examination of papers and documents, a personal interview, and of course the establishment of a paying relationship. If you are evicted, involved in an accident, land in jail, or have some other legal emergency, you can call your lawyer immediately for assistance. Aside from the benefits of an immediate telephone or personal consultation, the lawyer has knowledge about your particular circumstances, and you have, hopefully, established credit with the lawyer by paying your bill. In your search for a family lawyer, shop around.

ADVANTAGES OF HAVING A FAMILY LAWYER

A consultation with a prospective lawyer will be helpful in making a selection. Most offices have an initial fee for consultation on a legal problem. Sometimes a consultation may be all you need to help you with your problem. If the lawyer is lukewarm about your problem, then try another lawyer.

After a consultation with a lawyer, you might consider these additional factors in selecting your lawyer:

SELECTION FACTORS

- ability to explain things simply to you
- attention and interest in your problem
- kinds of clients represented by the lawyer
- the size of the firm
- specialization within the firm
- experience of the lawyer
- level of comfort you experience in the office (remember, all that glitters is not gold)
- specialization in your problem area
- fees charged for services
- age of lawyer

Keep in mind that the selection of an attorney is quite personal. Some people say you should like your attorney in order to confide in and trust him or her. Others say they would not want to pay someone they didn't like. All these considerations are valid, for a comfortable attorney-client relationship is quite valuable to you.

Prepare yourself before seeing your lawyer. Go over your papers and be sure *to bring them* with you. Read up on your problem if you have access to any information about it. Prepare a list of questions.

Discuss fees before you hire the lawyer for anything more than a consultation. Often a lawyer won't be able to give you an exact fee for handling your case, because the cost of the case will be dictated by which of the several solutions to your legal problem is chosen. There are several basic fee arrangements:

- hourly rate: tax experts may charge $150 or more an hour but have the information at their fingertips. The average charge for a lawyer's time in my community is $85 an hour.
- flat rates for routine cases: such cases include wills, adoptions, or divorces.
- contingent fee: under this arrangement the lawyer takes a percentage of the amount won in a lawsuit, and gets nothing if the case is lost. The contingent fee is used in cases involving personal injuries, property damage, bill collections, Social Security, etc. Nevertheless, you have to pay the out-of-pocket costs of such cases, i.e., phone, photocopying, filing fees, depositions, and court costs.
- percentage of an estate can serve as the fee.
- statutory attorneys' fees: examples would be discrimination complaints, certain consumer actions, and in some states complaints based on writings, for these laws permit the recovery of attorneys' fees.

Try to get the best deal and consider other possible fee arrangements. Bargain a little bit, suggest a lower percentage on a contingent-fee case, or discuss payment of the hourly rate if you have a simple, routine case. Offer to trade for your work or services. For example, jewelry, repairs, prints, rugs, pottery, tables, carpentry work, and typing services have all been traded for legal services. Lawyers seem to be more amenable to half-cash, half-trade proposals.

Sometimes the lawyer will expect a down payment (a retainer) on the case. The amount depends on the type of legal problem, the amount of work that may be involved, and whether you are an old or new client. If it is your family lawyer, then you may just be billed for the work.

After these discussions, you and your lawyer will make a contract concerning the specifics of his or her representation of you. Make sure that you are clear concerning the terms of the contract and that you sign and keep a copy of it. For more information on contracts, see Chapter 4, "Making Contracts."

There are many ways to save on fees:

- Drop off your papers before your appointment so your lawyer can review them.
- Completely fill out any forms or interview sheets your lawyer may use and read carefully any information papers your lawyer may give you.
- Write up a detailed narrative of the facts of your problem.
- Have names, addresses, and telephone numbers of witnesses and opponents.
- Don't repeat yourself.
- Keep brief notes on a calendar of the sequence of events.

One client who had been harassed by creditors had noted on his calendar the frequency and times a collection agent had called over one week. This was helpful in settling the case. Another client kept an extensive journal concerning incidents involving his children, who were in his ex-wife's custody. This helped in preparing the case for trial.

WORKING WITH YOUR LAWYER

A lawyer's time and advice are his stock in trade.
—ABRAHAM LINCOLN

FEE ARRANGEMENTS

TRADES

RETAINER

SAVING FEES

YOU AND YOUR LAWYER

FEE DISAGREEMENTS

Even after you get your bill, if you believe the fee is wrong or too much, discuss it first with your lawyer, as soon as you get the bill. The lawyer should be able to show the amount of work done on the problem. Usually, time is kept by the tenths of an hour. The lawyer may have spent a lot on time that you don't realize on research or investigation. Don't forget that in a fee dispute, the unpaid lawyer may exert a lien on the client's papers, documents, and file until the dispute is settled. If you are still not satisfied, some Bar Associations have a special committee to arbitrate fee disagreements.

Before you leave the lawyer's office, determine if the lawyer needs more documents or facts, whom you should or should not talk to, what work the lawyer will do on the case, when he or she will contact you, and how you will be kept informed of developments. Be sure the lawyer explains all the alternative solutions available to you on your particular problem. Listen to the lawyer's recommendation on what solution you should use *but* remember that some options may be too expensive for you. Paying a lawyer to file a suit for an unpaid account of $50 just doesn't make sense.

BE INFORMED

Your lawyer should inform you of developments as they occur on your case. If the lawyer doesn't, then request copies of correspondence, most court papers, and information on developments on your case. If you are involved in a lawsuit, you must be told of offers of settlement.

RIGHT TO CONFIDENTIALITY

You have a right to confidentiality. The law regards your conversations with your lawyer as confidential. Even if you reveal your involvement with a past crime or misconduct, your lawyer cannot release this information. Remember that your lawyer cannot give you advice unless he or she has all the facts. Do not lie or hide the facts. Lawyers are pretty hard to shock. Despite warnings about this, it is not uncommon for clients to hide or not admit certain facts that make them look bad and then decide in court to tell those facts. *Disastrous.*

MONEY AND YOUR LAWYER

A lawyer must keep clients' funds (cost deposit money and recoveries for clients) in a separate account. If you win money, then you should receive a statement from your lawyer indicating the costs involved, your share of the recovery, and the lawyer's share of the recovery. The lawyer may not mix clients' moneys with his or her business account (this is called "commingling"). If your lawyer has misspent your funds, report this immediately to the State Bar.

DISSATISFACTION WITH YOUR LAWYER

Sometimes clients have problems with their lawyer. Maybe the lawyer is too slow to work on your case, misses a deadline on your problem, gives you inaccurate advice, or represents your poorly. Discuss with your lawyer openly and frankly your dissatisfaction and try to resolve the matter.

If you are still dissatisfied after talking to your lawyer, then consult with another. Be sure to tell the consulting lawyer about your legal problem first, then relate your complaint about your lawyer and ask the consulting lawyer's advice.

DISCHARGING YOUR ATTORNEY

Discharge your attorney if necessary. In a court case you may need the judge's permission to do that (as would the lawyer if he or she did not want to represent you further). Sometimes attorneys are reluctant to take over a case in progress from another lawyer.

You should complain to your State Bar Association if you think your attorney has engaged in wrongdoing. As a last and final resort, consider making a malpractice claim if the lawyer made some serious mistake. Of course you should see a lawyer for assistance with this.

QUESTIONS FOR YOUR LAWYER / ACCOUNTANT

To recap, here is a list of the questions the creative person should ask the lawyer, or sometimes the accountant, he or she retains to handle legal problems. Perhaps an initial consultation would give you the answer to most. For the others, you could ask the lawyer to do only brief research and copy the statutes for you. See previous discussion on how to work out fees. In Canada, the word "provinces" should be substituted for state.

- What are the state exceptions and limits on garnishment?
- What business organization is best for you considering your business purpose, activities and funds?

- Do you need to file a certificate of doing business under a fictitious name?
- Do you have to pay state or city sales tax (accountant)?
- If someone could classify your work as obscene, what state and federal laws are there that could affect you, and have the Supreme Court rules changed?
- What are your state's (or any state you plan to sell in) laws on flag art, if you do such?
- If you are a writer, what specific laws does your state have on invasion of privacy (artists too) and defamation?
- Does your state have laws on commercial appropriation of likeness?
- If you are an artist/craftsperson who uses fibers, flammable fabrics, or parts of wildlife, be sure to send for the free government literature and if it requires explanation, ask your lawyer.
- After you order the copyright information circulars and the copyright forms, ask a knowledgeable lawyer to answer any questions you may have.
- Ask your lawyer if your state has any process to register trademarks and trade-names and, if so and if applicable to you, obtain the forms.
- Get the name of the department and the address where consumer fraud complaints are filed at the state level.
- If you do Indian arts and crafts, find out your state's laws on same.
- If you are an artist or craftmaker, find out if there are any specific state laws on consignment, resale profits, art in public places, gallery sales, prints, and related matters for visual artists.
- Find out when you should use a financing statement, and ask for a sample.
- Ask if the lawyer knows a reference book that uses lay terms and discusses your state's laws and particularly any forms for Small Claims Court.
- Ask for referral to a Certified Public Account, and go over with the CPA your business activities so that he or she can advise you about what forms and filings you need to do.
- Determine from your lawyer if your state has a Freedom of Information Act and Sunshine Laws, and obtain copies of same.
- Ask your lawyer if there are any state laws on authenticity of work, alteration, etc., relative to arts and crafts.

Dear Chatty Lawyer Syndicated Column:

I am so happy. After tripping through the Yellow Pages, seeing my friends' lawyers, trying the hectic legal clinics, I have finally found me a lawyer. It's actually two lawyers, Saphronia Green and Sam Violet, who consult together. I am a sculptress, and my work is rather controversial because I sculpt phallic symbols. My business is small and I've just started out on my own. My new lawyer's office is in a house and not a stuffy, tall office building. It is full of artworks. The waiting room has unusual reading material, such as *Sunset, Mother Earth News,* and *Art and the Law.* Best of all they are interested in me and my problems. They have told me things I can do myself if I want to save on my fee. I understand my papers after they explain them. I called them on the phone last week when my brother was in jail, and they got him out. Sure sometimes they're pretty busy and aren't there when I call, but they get back to me.

They have also accepted a half-cash, half-trade fee arrangement. Last year I deducted what I paid them as a business expense, but their services saved me more money than the fees! They renegotiated my studio lease for a longer term with a fixed rent, got a refund on some defective merchandise, made the Annual City Art Festival accept my work in a recent show even though it shocked the city council, and negotiated my exclusive gallery contract with terms more favorable to me.

So tell your readers to keep looking for their lawyer, for somewhere out there is the right lawyer for them.

Love ya,
The Sensuella Sculptress

Index

NOTES

NOTES

NOTES

NOTES

IMPORTANT
TAX INFORMATION UPDATE

Under the 1986 tax-law revision, the rules regarding uniform capitalization burdened creative persons, as certain expenses now require capitalization (rather than expensing) to conform to what my accountant describes as the longest set of regulations implementing a tax-code provision. The Author's Guild and other groups representing writers, photographers, and artists worked assiduously to ameliorate the effects of these rules, and a full exemption from the uniform capitalization regulations was included in a recent technical tax-correction bill that left the House Ways and Means Committee in mid-July 1988, on its way through the legislative process.

The Author's Guild was successful in obtaining some dilution of the effect of the new law for writers by the limited exemptions called "safe harbor" rules, which allow the writer to capitalize promotional expenses, agent commissions, and the like over a period of three years. It is hoped that by year's end, 1988, Congress will fully exempt creative persons from the uniform capitalization rules. There may still be time upon this book's release for you to contact any professional organizations that you may belong to and find out what you personally can do to assist in the resolution of this problem.

If you will send the coupon at the bottom of this page and a proof of purchase (sales receipt, etc.) to Northland Publishing Co., P. O. Box N, Flagstaff, AZ 86002, you will receive supplemental information on capitalization of expenses for creative persons by March 15, 1989.

- -

Yes, I want to know the status of the technical tax-correction bill as it relates to uniform capitalization for creative persons. I have enclosed a proof of purchase for MAKING IT LEGAL, Revised and Expanded. I understand that I will receive this information by March 15, 1989.

SEND TO:

Name _____

Street / P. O. Box _____

City _____ State _____ Zip _____

Return coupon to Northland Publishing Co., P. O. Box N, Flagstaff, AZ 86002.

ECONOMIC COMMISSION FOR EUROPE, GENEVA

ANNUAL BULLETIN OF

TRANSPORT STATISTICS
FOR EUROPE AND NORTH AMERICA

COMMISSION ÉCONOMIQUE POUR L'EUROPE, GENÈVE

BULLETIN ANNUEL DE

STATISTIQUES DES TRANSPORTS
POUR L'EUROPE ET L'AMÉRIQUE DU NORD

ЕВРОПЕЙСКАЯ ЭКОНОМИЧЕСКАЯ КОМИССИЯ, ЖЕНЕВА

ЕЖЕГОДНЫЙ БЮЛЛЕТЕНЬ

СТАТИСТИКИ ТРАНСПОРТА
ДЛЯ ЕВРОПЫ И СЕВЕРНОЙ АМЕРИКИ

Vol. LI - Том LI

2001

UNITED NATIONS
New York and Geneva

NATIONS UNIES
New York et Genève

ОРГАНИЗАЦИЯ ОБЪЕДИНЕННЫХ НАЦИЙ
Нью-Йорк и Женева

2001

PER
UNI
E/ECE
T6 S7

UNITED NATIONS PUBLICATION
PUBLICATION DES NATIONS UNIES
ИЗДАНИЕ ОБЪЕДИНЕННЫХ НАЦИЙ

Sales number Numéro de vente Номер для заказов	} E/F/R.02.II.E.4

ISBN 92-1-016353-2
ISSN 0250-9911

TABLE OF CONTENTS

	Page

TABLE DES MATIERES